Microsoft® Money For Dummies

M000011410

Recording a Transaction in an Account Register

1. Open the register of the account in which you want to record a transaction.

2. Click the tab — Withdrawal, Deposit, or Transfer — that describes the transaction you intend to record.

3. In the transaction form at the bottom of the register, click the Number tab to move to the Number text box.

   You can move from box to box in a transaction form by clicking an individual box or by pressing Tab or Shift+Tab.

4. Enter a number in the Number text box, if necessary.

5. Enter the date in the Date text box.

   You can quickly enter dates by clicking the down arrow to the right of the Date text box, opening the minicalendar, and clicking a date.

6. Enter whom you paid the money to in the Pay To text box or received the money from in the From text box.

   If you've previously entered this name in the text box, simply type the first few letters to make the entire name appear.

7. Enter the transaction amount in the Amount text box.

8. In the Category text box, enter a category or subcategory.

9. If you care to, write a few words in the Memo text box to describe the transaction.

10. Click the Enter button or press the Enter key.

What to Do If You Can't Reconcile an Account

✔ Look for a transaction on the bank statement that isn't in the register. For example, if there is a difference of $25.17 between your records and the bank's, chances are you forgot to record a $25.17 transaction.

✔ Look for amounts that were entered incorrectly in the register. Transposed numbers (entering $32.41 instead of $34.21, for example) are often the culprit.

✔ Look for duplicate transactions in the register that were accidentally entered twice.

✔ See whether you entered a deposit where you meant to enter a withdrawal — or vice versa. Entering transactions on the wrong tab causes problems when you reconcile.

✔ See whether the Ending (Statement) balance is incorrect. You can't reconcile an account if you entered the ending statement balance incorrectly. Double-check the interest and service charges as well to see whether you entered them correctly.

For Dummies: Bestselling Book Series for Beginners

Microsoft® Money 2005 For Dummies®

Cheat Sheet

Tab Buttons and Where They Take You

Clicking This Tab	Takes You to . . .
Home	The Home Page, your starting point for doing any number of tasks.
Banking	The Account List window, where you see a list of your accounts and account balances.
Bills	The Bills Summary window, where you can record the bills you pay regularly and enlist the Money program's help in paying bills on time.
Reports	The Reports window, where you can generate reports and charts that show right away where you stand financially.
Budget	The Budget window, where you can formulate a budget and find out whether you're meeting your budget goals. (See Chapter 12.)
Investing	The Investing window, where you can monitor stocks, bonds, mutual funds, and other investment holdings.
Planning	The Planning window, where you can plan for retirement, make a plan to get out of debt, and project your future cash flow.
Taxes	The Taxes window, where you can estimate your income taxes, estimate capital gains taxes, and locate your tax-deductible expenses.

Five Things That Every Money User Should Do

- ✔ Keep your checking account, savings account, and credit card account registers up-to-date.
- ✔ Balance your bank accounts each month.
- ✔ Create categories and subcategories so that you can track your spending, income, and tax deductions.
- ✔ Back up your data file to a floppy disk or Zip drive.
- ✔ Generate a Spending by Category chart.

For Dummies: Bestselling Book Series for Beginners

Microsoft® Money 2005 FOR DUMMIES®

by Peter Weverka

WILEY

Wiley Publishing, Inc.

Microsoft® Money 2005 For Dummies®

Published by
Wiley Publishing, Inc.
111 River Street
Hoboken, NJ 07030-5774
www.wiley.com

WILEY

About the Author

Peter Weverka is the bestselling author of several *For Dummies* books, including *Office 2003 All-in-One Desk Reference For Dummies* and 22 other computer books about various topics. Peter's books have been translated into 16 languages and sold three-quarter of a million copies. His humorous articles and stories — none related to computers, thankfully — have appeared in Harper's, SPY, and other magazines for grown-ups.

Dedication

For my pals in the South End Rowing Club.

Author's Acknowledgments

This book owes a lot to many hard-working people at the offices of John Wiley & Sons in Indiana. I would foremost like to thank Tiffany Franklin for giving me the opportunity to write it, and Beth Taylor for being such a devoted project editor.

Thanks go as well to copy editors Jean Rogers and John Edwards for their excellent work, and technical editor Allen Wyatt for dogging my every step to make sure this book is indeed accurate. I would also like to thank TECHBOOKS Production Services for writing the index and Rich Tennant for the witty cartoons you will find on the pages of this book.

These people at Wiley & Sons gave their all to this book, and I want to thank all of them:

I would be remiss if I didn't thank the talented editors who worked on earlier editions of this book, so thank you Susan Christophersen, Bob Woerner, Steve Hayes, Jim McCarter, Kyle Looper, Tammy Castleman, Kathleen Dobie, Stephanie Koutek, Brian Kramer, Patricia Pan, Rev Mengle, Diane Smith, and Gareth Hancock.

Finally, thanks go to my family — Sofia, Henry, and Addie — for indulging my vampire-like work schedule and my eerie demeanor at daybreak.

Peter Weverka
San Francisco
August 2004

Publisher's Acknowledgments

We're proud of this book; please send us your comments through our online registration form located at www.dummies.com/register/.

Some of the people who helped bring this book to market include the following:

Acquisitions, Editorial, and Media Development

Project Editor: Beth Taylor

(Previous Edition: Susan Christophersen)

Acquisitions Editor: Tiffany Franklin

Copy Editor: John Edwards

Technical Editor: Allen Wyatt

Editorial Manager: Leah Cameron

Editorial Assistant: Amanda Foxworth

Cartoons: Rich Tennant, www.the5thwave.com

Composition

Project Coordinator: Erin Smith

Layout and Graphics: Stephanie D. Jumper, Michael Kruzil, Melanee Prendergast, Heather Ryan

Proofreaders: John Greenough, Brian Walls, TECHBOOKS Production Services

Indexer: TECHBOOKS Production Services

Publishing and Editorial for Technology Dummies

Richard Swadley, Vice President and Executive Group Publisher

Andy Cummings, Vice President and Publisher

Mary Bednarek, Executive Acquisitions Director

Mary C. Corder, Editorial Director

Publishing for Consumer Dummies

Diane Graves Steele, Vice President and Publisher

Joyce Pepple, Acquisitions Director

Composition Services

Gerry Fahey, Vice President of Production Services

Debbie Stailey, Director of Composition Services

Contents at a Glance

Table of Contents

Part V: Improving Your Financial Picture *243*

Introduction

T his book is for users of these editions of Money 2005: Standard, Deluxe, and Premium. It is for Microsoft Money 2005 users who want to get to the heart of the program without wasting time. Don't look in this book to find out how Money works. Look in this book to find out how *you* can manage *your finances* with Money.

I show you everything you need to know to stay on top of your finances — from recording checks and deposits to tracking investments. On the way, you have a laugh or two. And you can shed light on parts of your finances that have never seen the light of day before. After you read this book, you can start admiring what a financial wizard you have become.

This book doesn't cover Microsoft Money 2005 Small Business edition.

About This Book

This book is jam-packed with instructions, advice, shortcuts, and tips for getting the most out of Money. Here's a bare outline of the seven parts of this book:

- ✔ **Part I: Setting Up and Starting Out:** Part I spells out everything you need to know to use Money wisely. It explains how to find your way around the Money windows, set up accounts, and record transactions.

- ✔ **Part II: Banking with Money:** Part II explains how to get the banking done with Money's help. It explains categorizing your spending and income, reconciling an account, and printing checks.

- ✔ **Part III: Money for Investors:** Part III is for investors. It shows how to track your investments with Money, enlist Money's help in researching investments, and update the prices of securities from the Internet.

- ✔ **Part IV: Getting Your Money's Worth:** In Part IV, you discover how to budget with Money, schedule bill payments so that you make them on time, estimate your income tax bill, plan for retirement, and do the mundane chores, such as backing up your financial data, that make Money run more smoothly.

- ✔ **Part V: Improving Your Financial Picture:** Part V explains how to generate reports and charts so that you can see exactly where you stand financially, and analyze investments and loans.

✔ **Part VI: Going Online with Money:** If your computer is connected to the Internet, you are invited to go online and take advantage of Money's online features. Among other high-tech tasks, Part VI explains how to download bank statements over the Internet and pay bills online.

✔ **Part VII: The Part of Tens:** Each of the four chapters in Part VII offers ten tidbits of advice — advice for staying on top of your finances, improving your financial health, using Money if you are self-employed, and converting from Quicken to Money.

But wait — there's more! Turn to the glossary to look up the financial terms that appear in this book.

Foolish Assumptions

Please forgive me, but I made one or two foolish assumptions about you, the reader of this book. I assumed these things:

✔ You use one of these Windows operating systems — Windows 98, Windows NT, Windows XP, or higher.

✔ You own a copy of Microsoft Money 2005 Standard edition, Deluxe edition, or Premium edition. This book does not cover Microsoft Money 2005 Small Business edition.

✔ You are kind to foreign tourists and small animals.

Conventions Used in This Book

I want you to understand all the instructions in this book, and in that spirit, I've adopted a few conventions.

To show you how to give commands on menus, I use the ⇨ symbol. For example, you can choose File⇨Back Up to make a backup copy of the data you store in Money. The ⇨ is just a shorthand method of saying "Choose Back Up from the File menu."

Where you see boldface letters in this book, it means to type the letters. For example, "Type **Where Did the Money Go?** in the Report name text box" means to do exactly that: Type the words **Where Did the Money Go?**.

Icons Used in This Book

To help you get the most out of this book, I've placed icons here and there. Here's what the icons mean:

Next to the Tip icon, you can find shortcuts and tricks of the trade to make your visit to Moneyland more enjoyable.

Where you see the Warning icon, tread softly and carefully. It means that you could be about to do something that you may regret later.

When I explain a juicy little fact that bears remembering, I mark it with a Remember icon. When you see this icon, prick up your ears. You will discover something that you need to remember throughout your adventures with Money.

When I am forced to describe high-tech stuff, a Technical Stuff icon appears in the margin. Good news: Only two Technical Stuff icons appear in this entire book (I don't like reading about technical stuff any more than you do). The first reader who finds both Technical Stuff icons wins a free trip to the Happyland Desert Park in Blythe, California (just kidding!). You don't have to read what's beside the Technical Stuff icons if you don't want to.

Part I
Setting Up and Starting Out

The 5th Wave   By Rich Tennant

"Can't I just give you riches or something?"

In this part . . .

*H*ello, this is your captain speaking. Thank you for flying Money. In the next four chapters, you can take off, soar above the clouds, and discover the basics of tracking your finances with Microsoft Money 2005.

Please observe the "Fasten your seat belt" sign. And if I ask you to hold your breath and flap your arms to help the plane stay aloft, please do so promptly.

Chapter 1

Introducing Money

In This Chapter

▶ Getting the program started

▶ Using Money for the first time

▶ Understanding how Money handles your finances

▶ Shutting down Money

Microsoft Money 2005 makes managing your personal finances very easy. Well, not "very easy," but close to it. With Money 2005, you don't need a bookkeeper to track your finances. You don't need an accountant or financial counselor, either. And you don't need to be a computer expert. All you need to know is how to use Money 2005.

After you start using the techniques I describe in this book, you will know how to record financial transactions, how much you spend in different areas, and what your net worth is. You will know what any investments you may have are worth and roughly how much you owe in taxes. You will know how to print checks, generate reports and charts that show in clear terms what your spending habits are, plan for retirement, and analyze different kinds of investments.

Most important, you will be able to make wise financial decisions by taking advantage of the program's numerous financial analysis tools, all of which I explain in this book. And you will also make wise decisions, because you will have the raw data on hand. After you record transactions in Money, the raw data is right there inside your computer. I show you how to analyze it, scrutinize it, dissect it, investigate it, and contemplate it. I show you how to admire it, too.

Chapter 1 is where you get your feet wet. Don't be shy. Walk right to the shore and sink your toes in the water. Don't worry; I won't push you from behind. Not so bad, is it? In this chapter, you discover the various ways that Money 2005 can help you stay on top of your finances. You also discover how to start and shut down the program.

Starting Money

Starting Money is as easy as falling off a log. You can start the program from the menus or by means of the Microsoft Money shortcut icon on the desktop. Start Money with one of these methods:

- **Microsoft Money shortcut icon:** Double-click the Microsoft Money 2005 shortcut icon on the desktop.

- **From the Program menu:** Click the Start button, choose Programs (or All Programs), and choose Microsoft Money 2005.

- **From the Start menu:** Click the Start button and choose Microsoft Money 2005 on the Start menu.

Creating a shortcut icon for Money

When you installed Money, the installation program should have put a Money shortcut icon on the desktop, but if it didn't, you can still create a shortcut icon for starting Money. To do so, follow the standard Windows procedure for creating shortcut icons:

1. **Click the Start button and choose Programs (or All Programs).**

2. **Locate the Microsoft Money 2005 menu command on the Programs menu and right-click it.**

   A shortcut menu appears.

3. **Choose Send To⇨Desktop (Create Shortcut).**

   The shortcut icon appears on the Windows desktop.

Pinning Money to the Start menu

Short of double-clicking a shortcut icon on the desktop, the fastest way to start a program is to pin its name to the Start menu. This menu appears right away when you click the Start button. By clicking a program name on the Start menu, you can start a program, as shown in Figure 1-1.

Follow these steps to pin Microsoft Money 2005 to the Start menu:

1. **Click the Start button.**

2. **Choose All Programs.**

3. **Locate Microsoft Money 2005 on the All Programs menu.**

4. **Right-click Microsoft Money 2005 and, on the shortcut menu, choose Pin to Start Menu.**

Now, when you click the Start button, you see the command for starting Microsoft Money 2005. If you want to remove this command from the Start menu, right-click it and choose Unpin from Start Menu.

Figure 1-1:
Starting
Money on
the Start
menu.

Starting Money for the First Time

The first time you start Money, the program grasps you by the hand and attempts to help you do a number of things that I respectfully suggest you should wait until later to do. First, Money creates a data file called My Money for storing your financial data. So far, so good. Then, as shown in Figure 1-2, Money asks you to do these things:

- ✔ Choose a sign-in name and password. You can secure your financial data by requiring anyone who opens your My Money file to enter a password or a .NET passport, as Chapter 11 explains.

- ✔ Create a bank account for recording transactions in your savings or checking account. Money stores financial transactions in accounts, as Chapter 3 explains.

Rather than dealing with passwords or setting up a bank account now, I think you are better off waiting until you know your way around Money. All you have to do is turn to Chapter 3 when you want to set up an account and turn to Chapter 11 when you have entered enough financial data in Money to warrant locking the data with a password.

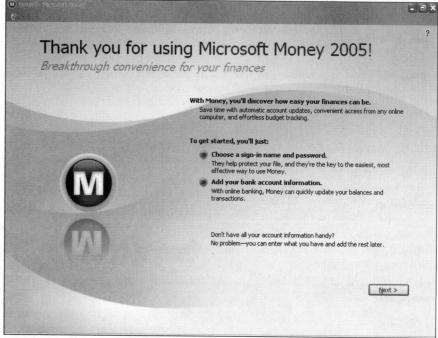

Figure 1-2:
You see
this screen
when you
start Money
for the
first time.

Follow these steps to cruise through the initial screens that Money presents when you start the program for the first time:

1. **Click the Next button in the Thank You for Using Money window (refer to Figure 1-2).**

   The next window, Help Protect Your Online Privacy and Security, appears.

2. **Click the Decline button.**

   By clicking the Decline button, you tell Money that you don't want to create a .NET passport just yet. Remember: You can turn to Chapter 11 to find out about .NET passports and passwords.

3. **Click the Yes button in the message box that asks whether you want to continue without setting up a .NET passport.**

   The Add a Password to Your File window appears. Do you get the impression that Money wants you to have a password? Don't worry about it. As I've already informed you three times, you can find out how to create a password in Chapter 11, if you decide you need one.

4. **Select the I Don't Want to Use a Password for My Money File check box, and click the Next button.**

   You see the Add Your Accounts window. I don't know why Money is in such a hurry to make you set up an account and create a password. It's not as though you can't do these tasks whenever you want to. I re-repeat: Turn to Chapter 3 when you want to create an account for tracking your checking and savings account activities.

5. **Click the Skip Account Setup link.**

   You come to the Congratulations! window.

6. **Click the Finish button.**

   Finished at last! Not a moment too soon, the Home Page window appears. This is the window you see each time you start Money.

Chapter 2 explains what the Home Page is, how to find your way around Money, and what the various Money windows are for. Go to Chapter 2 if you are the kind of person who likes to plunge right in. If you like to take your time, consult the rest of this chapter. It describes the many ways that Money can help you track your finances and be a smarter, wiser person — financially speaking, of course. Oh, and the end of this chapter explains how to shut down Money.

How Money Can Help You with Your Finances

This is your tour guide speaking. What follows is a quick tour of Money. Read on to discover the many ways that the Money program can help you. Money is much, much more than an electronic checkbook. It is a research tool and a means of gazing into the future. It's a way to track your investments and be a better saver. You can bank online and even estimate your income taxes with Money.

Keeping accurate records of your spending and income

All the personal finance advisors agree that keeping good, accurate records is the first step toward financial security. Before you can start saving for a down payment on a house, you have to know how much you are capable of saving. Before you can tell whether your investments are doing well, you have to track them carefully. If you want to make sound financial decisions, you need to know what your spending habits are and how much income you really have.

Microsoft Money makes keeping accurate financial records very, very easy. All financial transactions you make — writing a check, making a deposit, transferring money between accounts, charging an item on your credit card, buying and selling stocks and mutual funds, and so on — are recorded in account registers like the one shown in Figure 1-3. You create one account (and one account register) for each bank account you have and each account you have with a brokerage house. The account register shown in Figure 1-3 is for tracking activity in a checking account. Chapter 3 explains how to create accounts, and Chapter 4 explains how to enter transactions in account registers.

Entering data correctly in Money is essential. Money can't do its job well unless you carefully and conscientiously enter financial data. If all you want to do is balance your savings and checking accounts, you've got it made, because Money offers lots of opportunities for double-checking the accuracy of transactions in savings and checking accounts. However, to track investments and loans, draw up a budget, or do a handful of other sophisticated things, you need to take care when you enter the data.

Figure 1-3:
A typical account register.

Account Register

B of A Check

Change register view

All Transactions covering All Dates, Sorted by Date (Increasing)

!	Num	Date ▲	Payee	C	Payment	Deposit	Balance
	ATM	4/29/2004	Withdrawal	R	200.00		7,394.57
	2415	4/30/2004	Dept. Of Parking And Traffic	R	35.00		7,359.57
	DEP	4/30/2004	Franchise Tax Board	R		705.00	8,064.57
	2416	5/1/2004	Susan Thack	R	250.00		7,814.57
	DEP	5/3/2004	SFUSD - Addie's Pay	R		2,742.50	10,557.07
	2417	5/4/2004	Capitol One	R	1,637.80		8,919.27
	ATM	5/4/2004	Withdrawal	R	200.00		8,719.27
		5/10/2004	Billingfee - BillPay	R	5.95		8,713.32
	ATM	5/10/2004	Withdrawal	R	200.00		8,513.32
		5/12/2004	Bank Of America Credit Card	R	328.62		8,184.70
		5/12/2004	Bank Of America	R	1,908.90		6,275.80
	2418	5/12/2004	Cal State Auto Insurance	R	196.00		6,079.80
	2419	5/12/2004	California Casualty	R	1,212.00		4,867.80
	2420	5/12/2004	Homecomings Financial	R	331.34		4,536.46
	ATM	5/12/2004	Withdrawal	R	200.00		4,336.46
	DEP	5/12/2004	Micro Corp.	R		6,000.00	10,336.46
	ATM	5/13/2004	Withdrawal	R	200.00		10,136.46
	ATM	5/15/2004	Withdrawal	R	100.00		10,036.46

☐ Show transaction forms

New   Edit   Delete   Ending Balance: **$12,361.16**

Categorizing your spending and income

Each time you record a transaction in an account register, you categorize it. A check you write to a clothing store, for example, is assigned the Clothing category. A credit-card charge you make after stuffing yourself in a restaurant is assigned the Dining category. A paycheck deposit is assigned the Salary category. After you have recorded transactions for a few months, a picture of how you spend your hard-earned cash will start to come into focus. You can generate reports or charts that show precisely what your expenses are. The guy who generated the chart shown in Figure 1-4 spends the majority of his money on mortgage payments. Chapter 5 explains how to set up categories; Chapter 15 describes how to generate reports and charts.

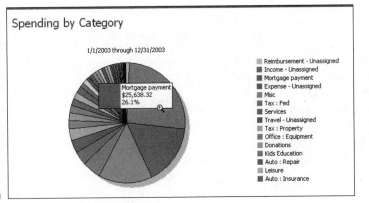

Figure 1-4:
By carefully
entering
your
financial
data, you
can create
meaningful
charts like
this one.

Estimating your income taxes

Another advantage of categorizing expenses and income is being able to estimate your income tax bill. Rather than pay an accountant to search for tax-deductible expenses or determine what your income sources were, you can generate tax reports that do the job in lieu of an accountant. By totaling the amount you spent in categories that describe tax-deductible expenses, you can find out what your tax-deductible expenses are. You can see exactly how much you received in income from different clients. Money also offers tools for estimating capital gains taxes and exporting Money data to a tax-preparation program such as TaxCut Deluxe. Chapter 14 explains tax tracking with Money.

Handling your investments

In the late 1990s, all you had to do to be a successful investor was to plop down money on stocks or mutual funds, but bears have overrun the bull markets of the 1990s. These days, you have to be shrewd and insightful to be an investor.

Money makes it possible to find out — literally in seconds — how well your investments are doing. You can find out how much they have grown (or shrunk) and compare the performance of your investments against stocks, mutual funds, and bonds you don't own, as well as compare your investments to indexes such as NASDAQ or the S&P 500. You can download security prices from the Internet and find out right away what the stocks and mutual funds you own are worth. As long as your computer is connected to the Internet, you can also research stocks, mutual funds, and bonds without leaving the Money program. You will find links throughout Money that you can click to go on the Internet and research investments. Chapters 8, 9, and 10 describe how to handle and research investments with Money.

Turning off the ads

As I explain in Chapter 2, Money is modeled after a Web site. Rather than choosing options in dialog boxes and opening menus, most of your activity in Money is done by clicking links. I like this computer-program-as-a-Web-site concept very much. I like everything about it except for one thing: Like most Web sites, Money is full of advertisements. Some of the links are thinly disguised advertisements that take you to Web sites that tout different financial services.

Fortunately, you can turn off the ads if they bother you. Follow these steps to turn off advertisements in the Money program:

1. **Choose Tools⇨Settings to open the Settings window.**

2. **Click the Program Settings link.**

3. **On the General tab of the Options dialog box, select the Turn Off Sponsorship and Shopping Links check box.**

4. **Click OK.**

Pinching your pennies

As I already explained, you categorize your income and spending when you record transactions in Money. Categorizing this way makes it easy to formulate a budget. Because you know precisely how much you spend in the different categories, you can set realistic budget goals by limiting your spending on a category-by-category basis. You can tell Money to alert you when you have exceeded your budget goals and in this way tame your spending. Money can also tell you when bills fall due so that you can pay your bills on time. The program can even track your frequent flyer miles. These and other techniques for pinching your pennies are described in Chapter 12.

Planning ahead

Planning for your retirement isn't easy. It's hard to tell what the future will hold. Money, however, can help you peer into the future and plan for your retirement. If you track your investments with Money, you use the Retirement Planner to project how your investments will grow and see whether your investments will cover your living expenses in retirement. Money allows you to realistically find out whether you are saving enough. The program can also show you how to plan better for your retirement and do the things you need to do now to ensure that your retirement years are golden ones. Planning ahead with Money is the subject of Chapter 13.

Banking online

Money was the first computer program to offer online banking services. Over the years, Money has refined these services such that online banking is easier than it has ever been. You can pay bills online, download bank and credit-card statements, and balance your account online. Online banking is covered in Chapters 17 and 18.

Shutting Down Money

When the time comes to close the Money program and get on with your real life, do one of the following:

✔ Click the Close button (the X in the upper-right corner of the program window).

✔ Choose File⇨Close.

✔ Press Alt+F4.

Veteran computer users are accustomed to saving files before exiting a program, but that isn't necessary with Money because the program saves data as soon as you enter it. If you look for a Save command or button in Money, you will look in vain — there isn't one.

When you shut down Money, the last thing you see is the Back Up to Floppy dialog box, as shown in Figure 1-5. This dialog box makes backing up the data you just entered in Money very easy, and I strongly recommend taking advantage of it. Chapter 11 explains everything you need to know about backing up a data file, including how to tell Money where to back up a data file. For now, click the Back Up Now button to be done with it.

Figure 1-5:
The Back Up to Floppy dialog box is your cue to make a backup copy of the Money file.

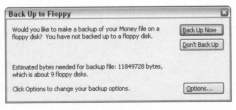

Chapter 2

The Basics

*N*ow that you know how Money can help track your finances, it's time to take your first baby steps into the program. This chapter gives you the lay of the land. It explains how to get from place to place in Money by clicking links, clicking tabs, and clicking toolbar buttons. You also find out how to customize the Home Page, which is easy to do and worth knowing how to do, because the Home Page is the window you see each time you start Money. You also find directions in this chapter for surfing the Internet without leaving Money and for customizing the toolbar.

Getting Around in Money

Money is a little different from most computer programs in that it is modeled after a Web site. Rather than negotiate dialog boxes to get things done, you visit different windows. Rather than open menus and choose commands, you click links. This is not to say that there aren't dialog boxes and file menus in Money — there are. But for the most part, you spend your time clicking links and going to different windows to get things done.

Links for going from window to window

Figure 2-1 shows the Home Page window that you see when you start Money. This window is the starting point for all your excursions in Money. Don't worry — the Home Page window is not as complicated as it looks. It offers a peek at different aspects of your finances, links that you can click to go to different Money windows, and links to sites on the Internet.

Tabs   Toolbar

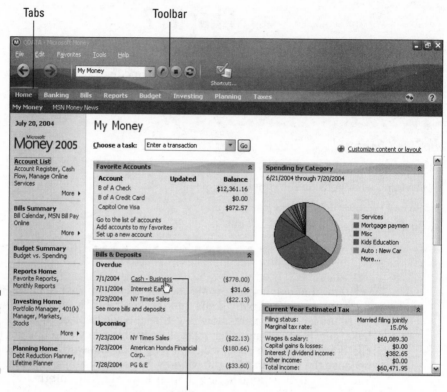

Link

Figure 2-1:
The Home
Page
window.

 You find many links in this and all other Money windows. To see where the links are, try moving the mouse pointer around the screen. When the mouse pointer changes into a hand and text is underlined, you have encountered a link. These links look and work exactly like links on a Web page. Click a link to go to a different window and undertake a new task.

Toolbar buttons for getting around

No matter where you go in Money, you see the toolbar along the top of the screen, right below the main menu. Does this toolbar look familiar? It looks much like the standard toolbar found in Web browsers such as Internet Explorer and Netscape Navigator — and it works like a Web browser toolbar, too. It includes a Back button and a Forward button so that you can revisit Money windows you saw earlier (the other buttons on the toolbar are for surfing the Internet and are explained in the section "Browsing the Web in Money," later in this chapter):

✔ **Back button:** Takes you to the window you looked at previously

✔ **Forward button:** Takes you to the window you most recently backed away from

Move the mouse pointer over the Back or the Forward button and you see a little downward-pointing arrow. Click the little arrow, and you see a shortcut menu that lists the windows you visited. I recommend clicking the little arrows beside the Back and Forward buttons early and often. Clicking the arrows and choosing window names is the fastest way to get from place to place in Money.

Tabs for going to different windows

Yet another way to get from place to place is to click a tab — Home, Banking, Bills, Reports, Budget, Investing, Planning, or Taxes. Figure 2-2 shows what you see when you click the Banking tab. You go to the Account List window, the starting point for handling banking account transactions. Click a tab when you want to undertake a certain kind of task. Click the Budget tab, for example, when you want to formulate a budget in the Budget window; click the Taxes tab to estimate how much tax you owe in the Taxes window. Table 2-1 describes the different tabs.

Table 2-1	Tab Buttons and Where They Take You
Clicking This Tab	*Takes You to . . .*
Home	The Home Page, where you can see summaries of your financial activity and click links to quickly go to other windows in Money. (See the section "Customizing the Home Page Window," later in this chapter.)
Banking	The Account List window, which lists the name of each account you set up. You can click an account name to go to its account register. Open the Bank Account window when you want to set up an account, enter account transactions, balance an account, or bank online. (See Chapters 3 through 6.)
Bills	The Bills Summary window, where you can record the bills you pay regularly and enlist the Money program's help in paying those bills on time. (See Chapter 12.)
Reports	The Reports window, where you can generate reports and charts that show right away where you stand financially. (See Chapter 15.)

(continued)

Table 2-1 *(continued)*

Clicking This Tab	Takes You to ...
Budget	The Budget Window, where you can formulate a budget and find out whether you're meeting your budget goals. (See Chapter 12.)
Investing	The Investing window, where you can track stocks, bonds, mutual funds, and other investment holdings. Start here when you want to download security prices from the Internet. (See Chapters 8, 9, and 10.)
Planning	The Planning window, where you can plan for retirement, make a plan to get out of debt, and project your cash flow. (See Chapter 13.)
Taxes	The Taxes window, where you can estimate your income taxes, estimate capital gains taxes, and locate your tax-deductible expenses. (See Chapter 14.)

Task links   Tabs   Buttons

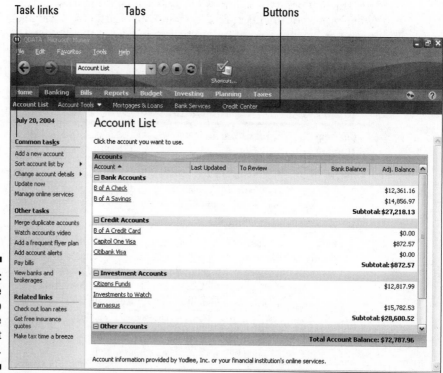

Figure 2-2:
Click the
Banking tab
to go to the
Account List
window.

When you click a tab and go to a new window, you are presented with a whole new set of task links on the left side of the window. You can click these links to undertake tasks pertaining to the window you are in. The Account List window, for example, offers links for creating new accounts and listing accounts in different ways. Each window offers its own set of buttons as well. The Account List window offers the Account Tools, Mortgages & Loans, Banks Services, and Credit Center buttons (refer to Figure 2-2). Click one of these buttons to investigate an area of interest.

Customizing the Home Page Window

When you start Money, you see the Home Page window (refer to Figure 2-1). The Home Page is supposed to give you a quick look at your finances, and if you play your cards right, it can do that. Instead of letting Money decide what goes on your Home Page, you can decide for yourself.

Choosing which window appears at startup

Suppose that you don't care to see the Home Page when you start Money. Maybe you prefer another window, an account register, or the last account register you were looking at when you closed the program. Follow these steps to choose which window you see when you start the program:

1. **Choose Tools⇨Settings to go to the Settings window.**

2. **Click the Program Settings link.**

You see the General tab of the Options dialog box.

3. **Under Display, open the Start Money with This Page Open drop-down list and choose the window you would like to see. The Last Account Register Used option opens Money to whichever account register was showing last when you closed the program.**

4. **Click OK.**

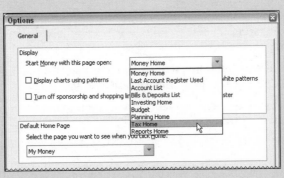

Notice that the Home Page is divided into two columns. In each column are links, reports, and alerts pertaining to different aspects of your finances. It's up to you to decide what goes in those two columns of the Home Page. Money makes it very easy to customize the Home Page.

Follow these steps to decorate the Home Page after your own fashion:

Home

1. **Click the Home tab to go to the Home Page.**

2. **Click the Customize Content or Layout link.**

   This link is found on the right side of the Home Page. After you click it, you see the Customize Content or Layout window, as shown in Figure 2-3. You can also get to this window by choosing Tools⇨Settings and clicking the Home Page Display Options link in the Settings window.

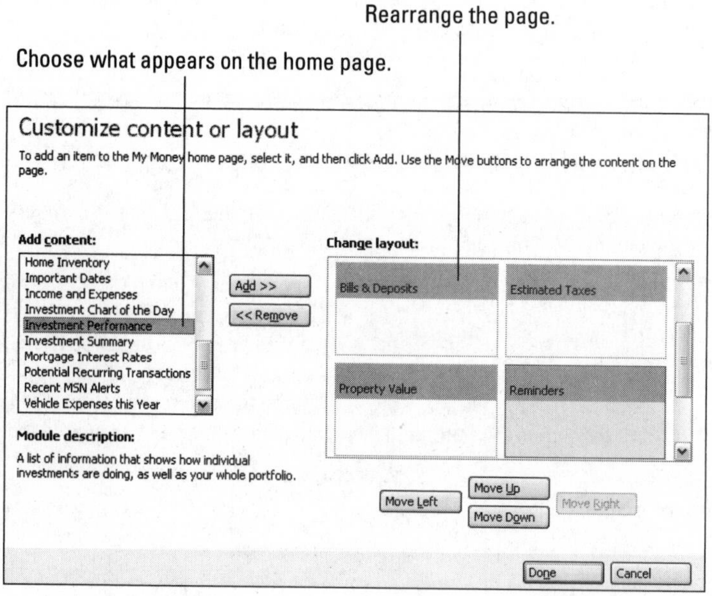

Rearrange the page.

Choose what appears on the home page.

Figure 2-3:
Choosing
the items
that you
want to see
on the
Home Page
when you
start Money.

3. **To select which items will be in view, select them one at a time in the Add Content box and click the Add button.**

4. **To remove an item, select it in the Change Layout box and click the Remove button.**

5. To set the order and column in which items appear on the Home Page, select an item in the Change Layout box and click the Move Up, Move Down, Move Left, or Move Right button.

6. Click the Done button when your customized Home Page is just right.

Browsing the Web in Money

Money has a split personality. Besides being a program for tracking your finances, Money is a Web browser. The makers of Money want you to be able to go straight from Money to the Internet and back again as you research investment opportunities, check the latest financial news, see how your stocks are doing, or, on a less serious but certainly more fun note, check the latest baseball scores.

Do you notice anything peculiar about Figure 2-4? How did Dummies.com get in the Money window? It got there because I typed the address of the Dummies.com Web site in the Address box on the toolbar and clicked the Go to Website button.

Figure 2-4: Money as a Web browser. Huh?

Cataloging your favorite Web sites

Suppose that you're tooling along in the Money browser and you come to a useful or fun Web site that you want to revisit later on. For occasions like that, Money offers you the opportunity to add the Web site to your Favorites list. Favorite Web sites are easy to revisit:

✔ To revisit the Web site in Money, choose Favorites⇨Favorite Web Sites and the name of the Web site on the submenu that appears.

✔ To revisit the Web site in Internet Explorer, choose Favorites⇨Financial Links and the name of the Web site. When you installed Money, the program put a new folder called Financial Links in the Internet Explorer Web browser.

With a Web site you want to revisit on-screen, choose Favorites⇨Add to Favorites. You see the Add Favorite dialog box. Enter a more descriptive name for the site, if necessary, and click OK.

If you intend to save more than a dozen Web sites, I suggest creating folders to keep track of them. Do that by clicking the New Folder button in the Add Favorite dialog box and entering a name in the Create New Folder dialog box that appears. Click the Create In button and choose a folder name to save a Web site in a particular folder.

Do the Web sites you added to the Favorites menu need reorganizing? Choose Favorites⇨Organize Favorites⇨Web Sites. You see the Organize Favorites dialog box. It offers buttons for deleting and renaming Web sites, as well as for moving them to different folders.

Here are thumbnail instructions for handling the Web browser side of Money's split personality:

✔ **Getting from Web page to Web page:** The Back and Forward buttons work just like buttons in a standard Web browser. Click Back or Forward to revisit Web pages or travel deeper into the Internet. By clicking the down arrow beside a button and choosing a Web page from the drop-down list, you can leap forward or backward several Web pages at a time.

✔ **Returning to the Money windows:** Click a tab or click the Back button as many times as necessary to return to a Money window.

Choose Tools⇨Settings, click the Program Settings link in the Settings window, and click the Browser button to dispense with Money and see a Web page in a real, live browser.

Customizing the Toolbar

Money makes it very easy to add a few buttons to the toolbar. Why not add a few buttons? Without them, you waste the screen space on the right side of the toolbar. Besides, if you decide you don't want them, removing buttons from the toolbar is as easy as putting them there in the first place.

Money offers buttons that take you to account registers, the Account List, all the different windows, and other places as well. Follow these steps to add buttons to the toolbar:

1. **Click the Shortcuts button on the toolbar.**

   You see the Customize Toolbar dialog box, as shown in Figure 2-5.

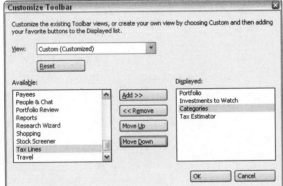

Figure 2-5:
Adding
buttons to
the toolbar.

2. **In the Available list, select a button and then click the Add button to add a button to the toolbar.**

   The button you chose appears in the Displayed list.

3. **To remove a button from the toolbar, select it in the Displayed list and click the Remove button.**

   You can change the order of toolbar buttons by clicking the Move Up or Move Down button.

4. **Click the OK button.**

If you regret tinkering with the toolbar, open the Customize Toolbar dialog box and click the Reset button.

Chapter 3

Setting Up Your Accounts

· ·

In This Chapter

▶ Understanding how accounts and registers record financial activity

▶ Identifying the 17 kinds of accounts

▶ Setting up checking and savings accounts

▶ Listing account numbers, contact persons, and the like

▶ Changing account names and types

▶ Setting up a credit card account

· ·

Chapters 1 and 2 get you going with Money. In this chapter, you get down to the nitty-gritty: how to set up accounts so that you can track financial activity.

In this chapter, you discover how to set up savings, checking, and credit card accounts. You also find out about Money files, how to put an account on the Favorites menu, and how to change account names and account types.

Accounts and Registers for Recording Financial Transactions

The first step in tracking your financial activity is to set up an account for each type of item you want to track — a checking account, a savings account, or an IRA, for example. When most people hear the word *account*, they think of savings accounts, checking accounts, and other kinds of bank accounts. However, accounts in Money are a little more than that. For example, you can create a home account for tracking the value of a house. You can also create a credit card account for tracking credit card charges.

When you set up an account, you need to name the kind of account you want. Money offers 17 kinds of accounts. Table 3-1 describes the different kinds of Money accounts and mentions where you can turn to read more about them.

Table 3-1	Microsoft Money's 17 Kinds of Accounts
Account	*What the Account Is For*
Asset	Tracking the value of items that you own — real estate, a truck, a baseball card collection. Asset accounts can be useful for finding out your net worth. (See Chapter 16.)
Bank	Recording transactions made to a bank account, but not a savings account, checking account, or line of credit.
Car or Other Vehicle	Recording the equity and market value of a car, boat, or other item for which you have taken out a loan. (See Chapter 16.)
Cash	Recording cash payments and tracking petty cash accounts.
Checking	Recording activity in a checking account. (See "The Basics: Setting Up Checking and Savings Accounts," later in this chapter. Chapter 4 explains how to record transactions in checking accounts.)
Credit Card	Recording credit card purchases, finance charges, and credit card payments. (See "Setting Up an Account to Track Credit Card and Line of Credit Transactions," later in this chapter. Turn to Chapter 4, as well.)
Employee Stock Option	Tracking stock options you receive from the company you work for. (See Chapter 8.)
Home	Tracking how much equity is in a house and determining a house's market value. (See Chapter 16.)
Home Equity Line of Credit	Tracking payments and transactions made against a home equity line of credit account. (See "Setting Up an Account to Track Credit Card and Line of Credit Transactions," later in this chapter.)
Investment	Tracking the value of something you own and intend to sell later for a profit — stocks, bonds, securities, annuities, treasury bills, precious metals, real estate investment trusts (REITs), and unit trusts. (See Chapter 8.)
Liability	Tracking debts for which you don't have to pay interest — income taxes that you owe and private loans, for example. (See Chapter 16.)
Line of Credit	Recording payments made with a *debit card* — a charge card that debits, or deducts money from, a bank account. (See "Setting Up an Account to Track Credit Card and Line of Credit Transactions," later in this chapter.)

Account	What the Account Is For
Loan	Tracking debts for which you have to pay interest, such as car loans. (See Chapter 16.)
Mortgage	Tracking mortgage payments for which you have to pay interest. (See Chapter 16.)
Other	Recording transactions that — you guessed it — don't fit neatly in the other 16 categories. Hmm. I've been racking my brain for an example of an account that doesn't fit into the other 16 categories, and for the life of me I can't think of one. Maybe this account is where someone would track laundered money.
Retirement	Tracking tax-deferred retirement plans, such as 401(k)s, Keoghs, SEPs (Simplified Employee Pensions), and IRAs. (See Chapter 8.)
Savings	Recording activity in a savings account. (See "The Basics: Setting Up Checking and Savings Accounts," later in this chapter. Chapter 4 explains how to record transactions in a savings account.)

Each time you set up an account, Money creates a new register for recording transactions. As all bookkeepers know, a *register* is a place for recording income and expenses, withdrawals, deposits, payments, and the like. Figure 3-1 shows a checking account register for recording checks, deposits, and withdrawals in a checking account.

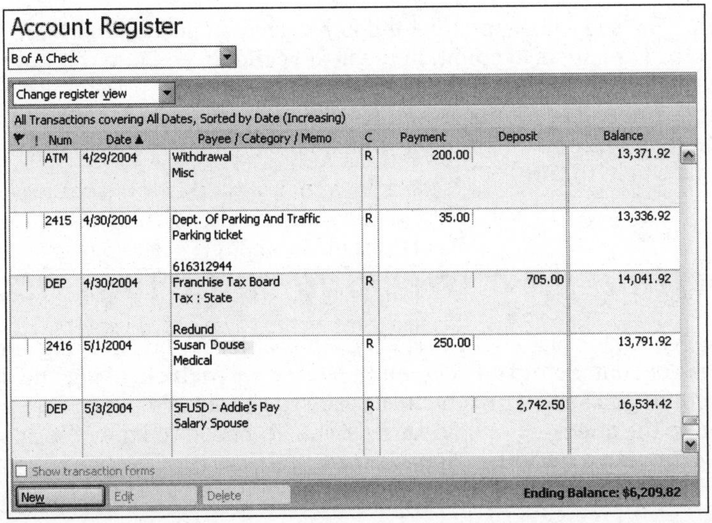

Figure 3-1: A checking account register.

A word about Money files

After you install Money, the program gives you the opportunity to create a file called My Money for storing your transactions. Chances are, that file is the only one you need, but some rare birds require a second file (Chapter 11 explains how to create one). Create more than one file if

✔ You intend to use Money to track both your personal finances and your business finances, and you want to keep the two separate. Self-employed people don't necessarily need a second file. I'm self-employed and

I use the same file to track my personal and business transactions. However, if you run a small business, you absolutely need a separate file. The general rule is this: If you submit a separate tax return for your business and yourself, you need two Money files.

✔ Someone other than you uses your computer to track his or her finances with Money.

✔ You track someone else's finances.

Registers look different, depending on the type of account you have set up, but all registers have places for recording transaction dates and transaction amounts. Registers also show balances. The *balance* is the amount of money in the account, or, in the case of an asset, liability, or investment account, the value of the thing that you're tracking.

The Basics: Setting Up Checking and Savings Accounts

After you see the big picture and know what an account and a register are, you can create an account. In the next sections, you find out how to set up a checking account, savings account, and credit card account. Setting up the other kinds of accounts is a bit more complicated, and I explain them elsewhere in this book. (Table 3-1, which appears earlier in this chapter, mentions where to turn.)

Setting up a checking or savings account

Everybody, or just about everybody, has at least one checking and one savings account. Set up an account in Money for each checking and savings account you keep with a bank. Be sure to get out the paperwork before you set up the checking or savings account. You need to know the account number and a few other details.

Follow these steps to set up the account:

Banking

1. **Click the Banking tab.**

   You land in the Account List window. This window is the starting point for managing accounts you have set up in Money.

2. **Click the Add a New Account link, the first one listed under Common Tasks.**

   The Choose an Account Type window, shown in Figure 3-2, appears. This window is somewhat misleading. The first option, Banking, appears to be the one for setting up a checking or savings account, but the Banking option is really for setting up online checking and savings accounts. If you select the Banking option, you may be asked for passwords and the like. Rather than setting up an online banking account at this time, I suggest setting up a conventional account by selecting the fourth option, Other Account Type. If you select that option, you will still be able to set up a checking or savings account. Online banking isn't for everybody. Later, if you so choose, you can make your conventional checking or savings account into an online banking account (see Chapter 17).

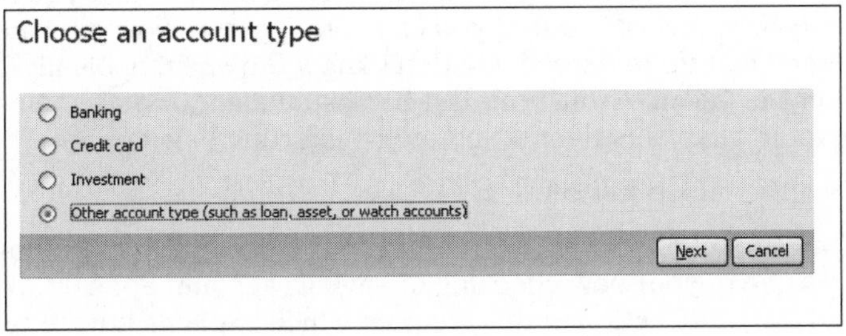

Figure 3-2:
Select the
fourth
option,
Other
Account
Type, to set
up your
account.

Choose an account type

- ○ Banking
- ○ Credit card
- ○ Investment
- ◉ Other account type (such as loan, asset, or watch accounts)

[Next] [Cancel]

3. **Select the Other Account Type option, and then click the Next button.**

   As Figure 3-3 shows, the next window, Choose an Account Type, permits you to set up checking and savings accounts.

4. **Choose Checking or Savings, and then click the Next button.**

   You see the New Account dialog box.

5. **Type a descriptive name for the account, and then click the Next button.**

   The name you type appears in the Accounts window. Type a descriptive name so that you can distinguish this account from the others you set up in Money.

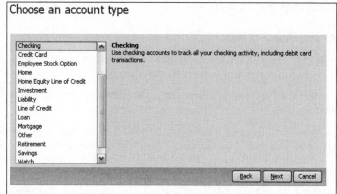

Choose an account type

Checking
Credit Card
Employee Stock Option
Home
Home Equity Line of Credit
Investment
Liability
Line of Credit
Loan
Mortgage
Other
Retirement
Savings
Watch

Checking
Use checking accounts to track all your checking activity, including debit card transactions.

Back   Next   Cancel

Figure 3-3:
Choose
Checking or
Savings to
set up your
account.

6. **Enter a figure for the account balance, choose a currency if need be, and click the Next button.**

Knowing the balance isn't as important as you may think — you can change the starting balance after you set up the account by changing the first entry in the account register.

More power to you if you know the starting balance and you have diligently kept records so that you can enter past transactions and bring the account up to date. If you don't know the opening balance, either enter the balance from your last bank statement or make an estimate. Chapter 4 explains the ins and outs of starting balances.

7. **Click the Finish button.**

At the end of the ordeal, you return to the Account List window, where the name of your new checking or savings account appears. Be sure to read the next section in this chapter, which explains how to record account numbers, phone numbers, and other useful information about accounts.

Listing contact names, phone numbers, and other information

Before you put away the paperwork and say good-bye to an account you set up, take a moment to record information about the account. The program has a special Change Account Settings window for entering a bank's telephone number, an account's minimum balance, and anything else you care to enter.

Selecting your "favorite" accounts

Checking accounts, credit card accounts, and other accounts that you have to dig into on a regular basis are good candidates for "favorite" status. The names of favorite accounts appear on the Favorites menu. All you have to do to open a favorite account is choose Favorites➪Favorite Accounts and the name of the account. As Chapter 2 explains, you can also make your "favorite" accounts appear on the Home Page so that account balances stare you in the face, for good or ill, whenever you start Money. By clicking an account name on the Home Page, you can view the account's register and enter transactions.

Follow any of these instructions to make an account a favorite account:

✔ Right-click an account name in the Accounts List window and choose Favorite (click the Account List button to open the Accounts window).

✔ Choose Favorites➪Organize Favorites➪Accounts and, in the Select Your Favorite Accounts window, check the names of accounts.

✔ Click the Add Accounts to My Favorites link on the Home Page and, in the Select Your Favorite Accounts window, check the names of accounts.

✔ Select the Favorite Account check box in the Change Account Settings window.

Favorite Accounts		☆
Account	**Updated**	**Balance**
B of A Check		$6,209.82
B of A Credit Card		($57.95)
B of A Savings		$6,856.97
CapitalOne Credit Card		$0.00
Parnassus		$1,946.05
Go to the list of accounts		
Add accounts to my favorites		
Set up a new account		

The Change Account Settings window is a handy place to store bank telephone numbers and other information. If you lose your passbook, ATM card, or credit card and need to call the bank, for example, you can get the number from this window. The window also has a check box for making an account appear on the Favorites menu.

Follow these steps to get to the Change Account Settings window and enter the pertinent information or view information about an account you already set up:

Banking

1. **Click the Banking tab to go to the Account List window.**

2. **Select the name of the account for which you will enter information.**

3. **Click the Change Account Settings link.**

   This link is located under Other Tasks. You see the Change Account Settings window.

   The fastest way to get to the Change Account Settings window is to right-click an account name in the Account List window and choose See Account Settings from the shortcut menu.

4. **Enter or view information about your account in the window.**

   In the Change Account Settings window, I entered a contact name and a telephone number, for example.

5. **Click the Done button if you entered information in the Change Account Settings window.**

   Where is the Done button? It's at the bottom of the window. You may have to scroll down to get there.

Changing an Account's Name or Type

Suppose that you got it wrong. Suppose that you gave the account the wrong name or told Money that a checking account was a savings account. All is not lost. You can fix these grievous errors by returning to the Account Details window and clicking the Change Account Details button.

If all you want to do is change the name of an account, here's the fastest way: Right-click the name of the account in the Account List window, choose Rename from the shortcut menu, enter a new name, and click OK.

Follow these steps to change the name and other information about an account:

Banking

1. **Click the Banking tab to go to the Account List window.**

2. **Click the name of the account that needs an overhaul.**

   Clicking opens the account register.

3. **Click the Change Account Settings link.**

   You land in the Change Account Settings window. From here, you can change the account number, the minimum balance, and more trivial things as well. You can also rename an account or change its type.

4. **Rename the account or change the account type:**

   • **Rename an account:** Enter a new name in the Account Name text box.

   • **Change an account type:** Open the Account Type drop-down list and choose a new account type.

If you want to change account types but can't find an option button on the list for the account type you want, you're out of luck. In its wisdom, Money lists only accounts to which your account can be changed. Camels can't fly, and credit card accounts can't, for example, be changed into investment accounts.

Setting Up an Account to Track Credit Card and Line of Credit Transactions

Except for filling out an extra dialog box or two, setting up a credit card or line of credit account works the same way as setting up a checking or savings account. Set up a credit card or line of credit account for each credit card you have. When you set up the account, Money asks how much you owe and whether you want a reminder when the credit card bill is due.

Get out your last credit card or line of credit statement and follow these steps to set up a credit card or line of credit account:

1. **Place a finger of your right hand on this page and, with your left hand, turn back several pages to the "Setting up a checking or savings account" section.**

2. **Follow Steps 1 through 3 of the instructions for setting up a checking or savings account.**

   In other words, go to the Account List window, click the Add a New Account link, select the Other Account Type option, and click the Next button. You come to the Choose an Account Type window (refer to Figure 3-3).

3. **Select the Credit Card, Line of Credit, or Home Equity Line of Credit option and click the Next button.**

   If you are setting up a line of credit account, you see the Choose Level of Detail window. Make sure that the Track Transactions and Other Details option is selected. Unless you select this option, you can't categorize charges you make against the line of credit.

4. **Enter a name for the account, and click the Next button.**

   You see the first of several New Account dialog boxes, as shown in Figure 3-4. The first dialog box asks how much you owe. I hope that you are all paid up and owe nothing, but if you resemble the average citizen, you owe the bank or credit card issuer some money.

5. **Type 0 if the credit card is paid in full; otherwise, type how much your last statement says that you owe, and then click the Next button.**

6. **Select the Credit Card or Charge Card option, and click the Next button.**

   This dialog box asks whether your account will track a credit card or charge card. As the dialog box explains, charge cards have to be paid in full each month, but you can carry debt from month to month with a credit card.

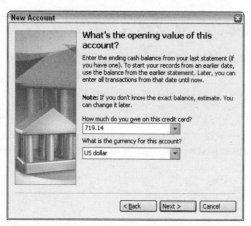

Figure 3-4:
In this dialog box, tell Money how much you owe the bank or credit card issuer.

Select the Credit Card option if the account tracks credit card spending. Otherwise, select Charge Card. If yours is a credit card that you don't need to pay in full but you intend to pay off each month, select the Always Pay Entire Balance Each Month check box.

What happens next depends on whether the account tracks a credit card or charge card.

If the account tracks a charge card, skip ahead to Step 8.

If the account tracks a credit card or line of credit, the dialog box that appears asks you to list the interest rate you get charged for carrying debt, as Figure 3-5 shows.

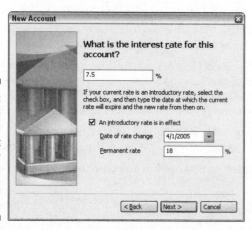

Figure 3-5:
Enter the interest rate you get charged for carrying debt on a credit card.

7. **Tell Money what rate of interest you are charged for using the credit card or line of credit, and then click the Next button.**

   List the interest rate in the first % box. If the rate is a temporary, introductory rate, select the An Introductory Rate Is in Effect check box and enter the permanent rate and the date that the temporary rate expires. Money needs this information for the Debt Reduction Planner and other features designed to help you manage debt.

8. **In the dialog box that follows, type the maximum amount that you can charge on your credit card or charge card; then click the Next button.**

   Your credit card statement lists the most you can borrow on your credit card. Get the figure from your statement.

9. **Make sure that the first option, No, Don't AutoBalance This Account, is selected, and then click the Next button.**

   This dialog box is kind of misleading. It seems to say that if you pay your credit card bill in full each month, you should select the second option, Yes, AutoBalance This Account. But you should do no such thing. Select the second option button only if you *don't* want to track the charges you run up on your credit card.

10. **If you want the bill to appear in the Bills Summary window, make sure that you select the Yes, Remind Me When the Bill Is Due check box. Enter an estimate of how much you owe in the Estimated Monthly Amount text box; also, enter a date in the Bill Is Due Next On text box. Then click the Next button.**

    As shown in Figure 3-6, the dialog box asks whether you want to put the monthly credit card payment on the Bill Calendar. If you click Yes, a reminder to pay the bill appears in the Bills Summary window. Chapter 12 explains how to schedule bills and deposits. For now, all you need to know is that the Bills Summary window reminds you when bills are due. If you want, the notice can also appear on the Home Page, where you can see it each time you start Money.

    I strongly recommend placing a check mark in the Yes, Remind Me When the Bill Is Due check box. Credit cards and lines of credit can get very, very expensive if you don't work to pay them off or if you forget to pay them on time. Banks charge outrageous interest rates on lines of credit and credit cards. A reminder to pay the bill can help keep you from being squeezed by creditors.

    Credit card and line of credit bills fall due on the same day each month. Each month, Money reminds you five days before each payment is due.

11. **Click the Next button in the following dialog box, which asks whether you can earn frequent flyer miles with your credit or charge card.**

    Chapter 12 explains how to track frequent flyer miles. Don't worry about it for now.

Figure 3-6:
You can add
the credit
card or line
of credit
payment to
the Bills
Summary
window
and maybe
pay the bill
on time.

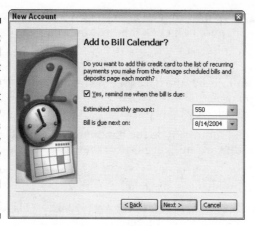

Figure 3-6

12. Click the Finish button.

You return to the Account List window.

After you set up your credit card account, go to the Change Account Settings window and enter the phone number of the credit card issuer or bank. You may need the number, for example, if you must report a lost credit card. The section "Listing contact names, phone numbers, and other information," earlier in this chapter, explains how the Change Account Settings window works.

Chapter 4

Recording Your Financial Activity

. . . .

. . . .

*T*his chapter tackles the four or five things you have to do each time you run the Money program. It explains how to open an account register and how to record deposits, withdrawals, payments, and charges in registers. You also find out how to record a transfer of money between accounts, how to move around in a register, and how to find transactions in large registers. This chapter describes how to delete and void transactions as well. Finally, for the person who likes to leave behind a wide paper trail, this chapter explains how to print a register.

Accomplish the tasks described in this chapter, and you are well on your way to becoming a Microsoft Money 2005 ace.

Opening an Account Register

After you set up an account (the subject of Chapter 3), you're ready to start recording transactions in the account's register. A *register* is the place where checks, payments, deposits, charges, and withdrawals are recorded. Figure 4-1 shows a checking account register. As with all registers, this one has places for numbering transactions, recording transaction dates, and viewing balances.

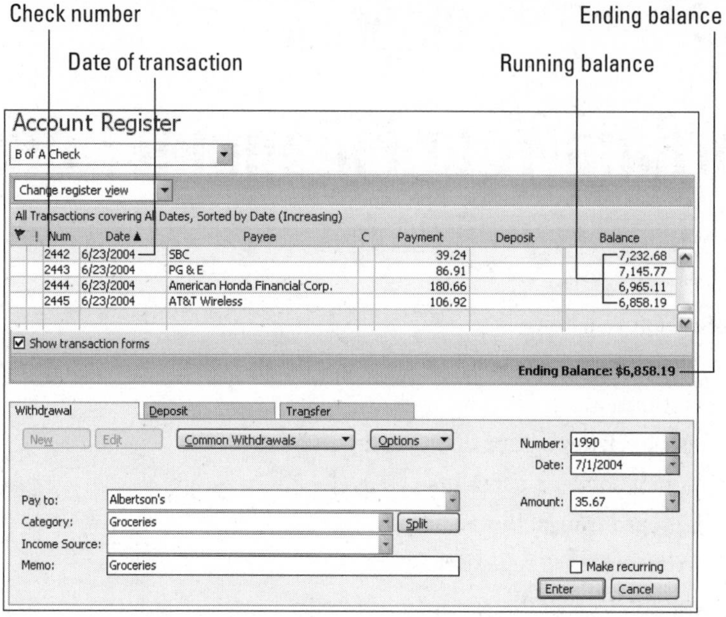

Check number

Ending balance

Date of transaction

Running balance

Account Register

B of A Check

Change register view

All Transactions covering All Dates, Sorted by Date (Increasing)

▼	!	Num	Date ▲	Payee	C	Payment	Deposit	Balance
		2442	6/23/2004	SBC		39.24		7,232.68
		2443	6/23/2004	PG & E		86.91		7,145.77
		2444	6/23/2004	American Honda Financial Corp.		180.66		6,965.11
		2445	6/23/2004	AT&T Wireless		106.92		6,858.19

☑ Show transaction forms

Ending Balance: $6,858.19

Withdrawal	Deposit	Transfer

New   Edit   Common Withdrawals ▼   Options ▼

Number: 1990
Date: 7/1/2004

Pay to: Albertson's
Category: Groceries   Split
Income Source:
Memo: Groceries

Amount: 35.67

☐ Make recurring

Enter   Cancel

Figure 4-1:
Financial
trans-
actions are
recorded
in account
registers
like this one.

The first step to opening an account register is to go to the Account List window, as shown in Figure 4-2. This window is Account Central as far as Money is concerned. By clicking an account name in the list, you can open the account's register. The Account List window shows each account you have and how much money is in each account. Negative balances — credit card balances are usually negative because they represent money that you owe — are shown in red and are surrounded by parentheses. At the bottom of the window is your total account balance, the sum of your savings, debts, assets, and liabilities, also known as your *net worth*.

Because so much of your time in Money is spent in account registers, Money offers no fewer than four ways to get to the Account List window:

Banking

✔ Click the Banking tab.

✔ On the Home Page, open the Choose a Task drop-down list, choose Enter a Transaction, and click the Go button.

✔ Press Ctrl+Shift+A.

✔ In a register window, open the Register drop-down list and choose View Account List.

Click an account name to open an account register.   Account balances

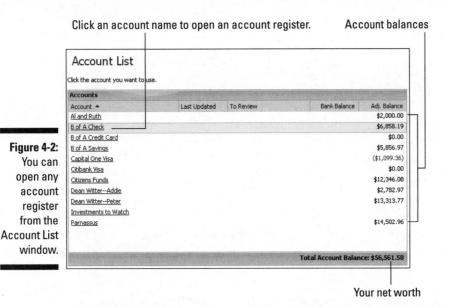

Figure 4-2:
You can
open any
account
register
from the
Account List
window.

Your net worth

As I explain earlier in this chapter, you can click an account name in the Account List window to open an account register. But suppose you're in a hurry? To bypass the Account List window and go straight to an account register, use one of these techniques:

✔ Choose Favorites➪Favorite Accounts, and then click the name of an account, assuming that you opted to make it a favorite. (Chapter 3 explains how to make an account a favorite account.)

✔ Click the account's name on the Home Page. (See Chapter 2 for information about placing favorite accounts on the Home Page.)

✔ In a register window, open the Register drop-down list, choose Other Open Accounts, and choose the name of an account, as shown in Figure 4-3. Use this technique to skip merrily from account register to account register.

To begin with, accounts in the Account List window are arranged by type, but you can change that. You can arrange accounts by name, bank, or brokerage firm. To do so, click the Sort Account List By hyperlink and select an option from the drop-down list.

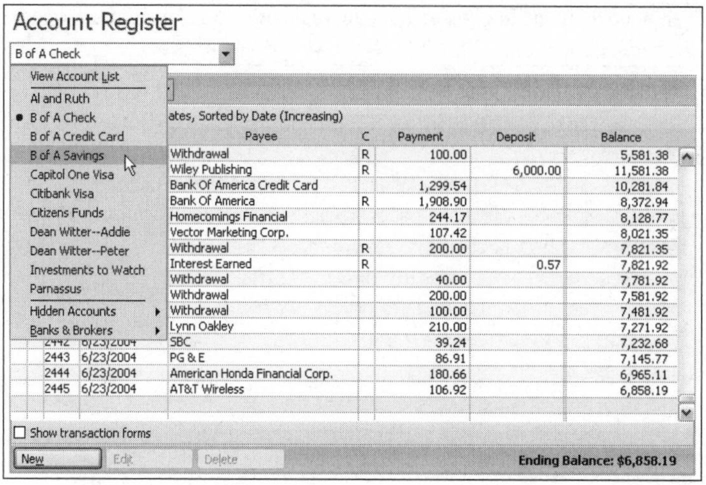

Figure 4-3:
Going from
one register
to the next.

Recording Transactions in Registers

At the bottom of the Account Register window is a form for entering transactions in the register, as shown in Figure 4-4. (If you don't see the form, select the Show Transaction Forms check box in the lower-left corner of the window; if that check box is grayed out, open the Change Register View menu and choose Top Line Only.) To enter a transaction, click a tab — Withdrawal, Deposit, or Transfer — and then fill in the transaction form.

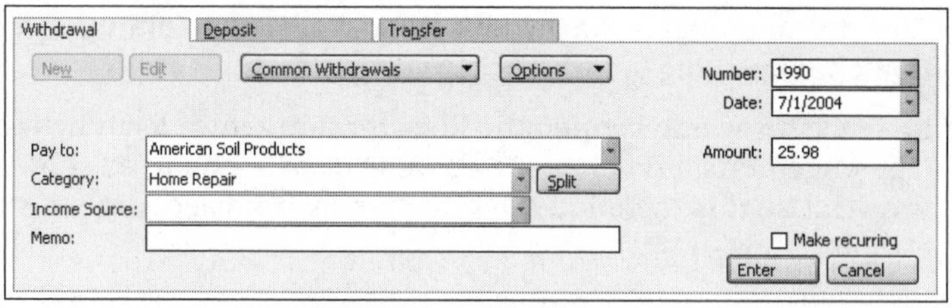

Figure 4-4:
Recording a
transaction
in an
account
register.

Which tab you click depends on which type of transaction you want to enter:

✔ **Withdrawal tab:** Taking money out of an account? Stealing from yourself isn't really stealing, but so that you don't feel guilty, let Money know how much you're taking out on this tab. Use this tab when you record check payments and cash withdrawals — any transaction in which money leaves an account.

✔ **Deposit tab:** When you put money into an account, record the transaction on this tab. Record all deposits to an account on this tab. That includes check deposits and deposits made at a cash machine.

✔ **Transfer tab:** Shifting money from one account to another? Click the Transfer tab.

Follow these steps to record a check, deposit, withdrawal, cash-machine withdrawal, or debit card purchase in a register:

1. **Open the register of the account in which you want to record a transaction (see the "Opening an Account Register" section, earlier in this chapter).**

2. **Click the Withdrawal or Deposit tab.**

   Is money going in or going out of the account? Outgoing money is recorded on the Withdrawal tab; incoming money is recorded on the Deposit tab.

3. **Tell Money what kind of transaction you want to record.**

   In some cases, you have to click the Common Withdrawals or Common Deposits button to describe a transaction.

   • **Cash withdrawal:** Do nothing. You're all set.

   • **ATM cash-machine withdrawal:** Click the Common Withdrawals button and choose ATM. If you have made cash withdrawals before, you can choose an amount on the submenu, but if you haven't withdrawn before or the amount you want to withdraw isn't listed, choose Other Amount. When you are done recording the transaction, the letters ATM (automated teller machine) will appear in the Number box of the register so that you know that the withdrawal was made at a cash machine.

   • **Check:** Click the Common Withdrawals button and choose Write a Check. Money enters the next available check number in the Number box. If this number is incorrect, enter the correct number.

   • **Check to pay a credit card bill:** Click the Common Withdrawals button, choose Credit Card Payment, and choose the name of the credit card issuer from the drop-down list. Later in this chapter, the section, "Recording a credit card payment," explains this kind of transaction in detail.

   • **Debit card purchase:** Click the Common Withdrawals button and choose Debit Card Purchase. (If you got cash back with your purchase, see "Recording a Deposit or Debit Card Purchase with Cash Back," later in this chapter.)

- **Cash deposit:** You're all set. Do nothing.

- **Deposit of a check or checks:** You're all set, unless you want to record a deposit of more than one check or you got cash back after the deposit. See "Splitting a Transaction" and "Recording a Deposit or Debit Card Purchase with Cash Back," later in this chapter.

4. Enter a number in the Number text box, if necessary.

To move from place to place on a transaction form, click elsewhere, or press Tab or Shift+Tab.

Only checks require a number, but you can enter deposit slip and withdrawal slip numbers if you want to track deposits and withdrawals carefully.

Money should have entered the next available check number, but if it didn't, click the down arrow to open the Number drop-down list and then choose Next Check Number. If the number that Money enters is incorrect, enter the correct number.

5. Enter the date in the Date text box, if necessary.

Money puts today's date in the Date text box, so you don't need to do anything if you are recording a transaction you completed today. See the sidebar, "Tips for entering transactions quickly," to discover fast ways to enter future and past dates and to fill in other parts of a transaction tab.

6. Enter whom you're paying the money to in the Pay To text box, or whom you received the money from in the From text box.

The Deposit form has a From text box rather than a Pay To text box. As the "Tips for entering transactions quickly" sidebar explains, you can simply type in the first few letters of a name (if you received or paid money to this person or party before) to scroll the list of names and go to the one you want.

For deposits, enter the name of the person or business who wrote you the check or checks you deposited. For withdrawals, enter **Cash** if you withdrew cash from the bank. For ATM withdrawals, Money enters the word *Cash* automatically.

If you've entered this name in the register before, the amount you last paid or received appears in the Amount text box. Not only that, but the category that you assigned to the last transaction with this person or company appears in the Category text box. You may not have to change the amount or category choices. If this transaction is identical to the one you recorded last time, your work is almost done and you can skip to Step 10.

Tips for entering transactions quickly

Money offers a bunch of techniques for entering transactions quickly on transaction forms:

✔ **Dates:** A fast way to enter the date is to click the down arrow to the right of the Date text box to make the minicalendar appear. If the calendar shows the right month, simply click a day. Otherwise, click the arrows on either side of the month name to go backward or forward month by month, and then click a day.

Press the + (plus sign) on the keyboard to advance the date by a day; press – (minus sign) to go back a day.

✔ **AutoComplete:** Money "remembers" all the people and businesses you pay and from whom you receive payments. If you have entered a name in the Pay To or From text box before, all you have to do to make the entire name appear is to type the first few letters — Money fills in the rest. Or you can click the down arrow next to the text box, scroll through the list of people or businesses you entered on past occasions, and click a name to enter it. This feature, which

Money calls AutoComplete, ensures that you don't have to keep entering the same names repeatedly.

> Church's Produce
> Citibank Visa
> Citizens Fund
> Citizen's Funds
> Clam Bucket Restaurant
> Clarendon Elementary
> Cliff's Hardware
> Cliff's Variety
> Coastal Kitchen
> Community Music Center
> CompUSA
> Copeland Sports
> Copeland's
> Cost Less Upholstery
> CostCo
>
> CompUSA

✔ **Doing the math:** Click the down arrow to the right of the Amount text box to see a minicalculator that you can use to do calculations — totaling the checks in a deposit, for example. Pressing the equals key (=) enters the total directly into the Amount text box. If you need a calculator that can handle advanced calculations, choose Tools⇨Calculator to bring up the Windows calculator. You can cut and paste calculations that you make there into the Amount text box.

7. **Enter the amount of the transaction in the Amount text box.**

   To enter a round number, you don't have to enter the decimal point or trailing zeroes. In other words, to enter "$21.00," all you have to type is **21**. Money adds the zeroes for you.

8. **In the Category text box, enter a category (or category and subcategory).**

   Creating and choosing the right categories and subcategories is so important that I devote most of Chapter 5 to the subject. By assigning categories and subcategories to income and expense transactions, you can discover where you spend your hard-earned money and where it comes from — critical information, especially if you itemize on tax forms.

   Expense categories are at the top of the drop-down list. Payments require an expense category. Deposits require an income category, which are found in the middle of the drop-down list.

9. **If you care to, write a few words in the Memo text box to describe the transaction.**

   Write a memo if for any reason you may come back to the account register in the future, see the transaction, and not know what it was for.

10. **Click the Enter button or press the Enter key.**

    Click the New button if you want to clear the entry form and record another transaction. By the way, if you start recording a transaction but then decide to finish it later or start all over, click the Cancel button. The Edit button is for altering a transaction you entered already.

Do you have to record past transactions?

I'm sorry to say it, but almost everyone has to record at least a few transactions from the past. When you set up an account, Money asks you to list or estimate a balance. If you follow Money's recommendation and enter the closing balance from your last bank statement, you have to enter all the transactions that don't appear on that statement because they haven't cleared the bank. In other words, if you wrote a check on June 30 and it didn't appear on the statement that you received on July 15, you have to enter that check in order to make your account balance.

To enter uncleared transactions, either use your own records or wait until next month's statement arrives and use it to record the absent transactions.

If you intend to use Money to help with tax returns, you'll need to record transactions back to the beginning of your tax year, usually January 1. If today is September 30 or December 2, you have a great deal of work to do — or you can wait until next year to use Money in earnest. By way of encouragement, I can tell you that Money makes entering transactions an easy task, as this chapter and Chapter 5 show.

You can always change the opening balance of an account by changing the amount of the initial deposit. The opening balance of a brand new account is easy to figure out, but tracking an account you've had for a while requires a little detective work. You have to find out how much money was in the account as of the starting date that you entered when you set it up in Money. That isn't easy. Rather than dig through old records, you may simply tinker with the initial deposit until the ending balance of the account matches the one on your last bank statement.

Don't be alarmed if the transaction you just entered doesn't appear on the register's last line. Transactions appear in date order.

If you have trouble finding a transaction, open the Change Register View drop-down list and choose an option to get a different view. The Sort By options determine the order in which transactions appear in the register. You can also sort transactions by date or see only transactions that haven't been reconciled.

If you entered a deposit where you should have entered a withdrawal, or entered a withdrawal where you should have entered a deposit, click the Options button on the transaction form, choose Change Transaction Type To, and choose Withdrawal or Deposit from the submenu.

Splitting a Transaction

Suppose that you try to record a transaction in a register but it doesn't fit in a single category. For example, suppose that you write a check to the Old Country Store to buy motor oil, a blouse, and a rocking chair. The transaction doesn't fall neatly in the Automotive, Clothing, or Household: Furnishings categories. And suppose that you deposit two checks at one time, one from your place of work and one from the New Jersey Lottery Commission. To record a transaction like that, you *split* it. Money offers the Split button on the transaction form for that very purpose, and you use it by following these steps:

1. **Record the transaction as you normally would.**

   To total the checks in a deposit, click the down arrow beside the Amount box and total the checks on the minicalculator. After you click the = (equals) button, the total is entered in the Amount box.

2. **Click the Split button or press Ctrl+S.**

   You see the Transaction with Multiple Categories dialog box shown in Figure 4-5. The Category list is already open so you can select the first category.

   By the way, if you are depositing several checks, you can also click the Common Deposits button and choose Deposit Multiple Items from the menu to open the Transaction with Multiple Categories dialog box.

3. **For the first item that you purchased or deposited, select a category on the first line of the dialog box.**

Choose a category · · · · · Enter an amount

Transaction with Multiple Categories

Itemize the amount spent in each category below. The amounts should add up to the total transaction amount.

Category	Description	Amount	
Auto : Fuel		12.95	Delete
Clothing		32.12	Delete All
Household		111.19	Help
			Done
			Cancel

Sum of splits:	$156.26
Unassigned:	$0.00
Total transaction:	**$156.26**

Figure 4-5:
Splitting a transaction that doesn't fit into a single category.

4. **If you care to, enter a description in the Description text box on the first line.**

5. **In the Amount text box on the first line, enter the cost of the first item or the amount of the first check you deposited.**

6. **Repeat Steps 4 and 5 for each item you purchased or for each check you deposited.**

   When you finish, the Sum of Splits figure should equal the Total Transaction figure, and the Unassigned figure should be 0.00. If the figures don't add up, tinker with the numbers in the Transaction with Multiple Categories dialog box until they do.

7. **Click the Done button to return to the transaction form.**

8. **Make sure that the transaction form is filled out properly; then click the Enter button.**

When a transaction has been split, the words "Split/Multiple Categories" appear in the Category text box, as shown in Figure 4-6. To see how a transaction in a register was divided across categories, click the transaction, click the transaction form, and then click the Split button to open the Transaction with Multiple Categories dialog box. You can also move the pointer over the transaction to see the categories in a pop-up box.

Suppose that you split a transaction but regret doing so. Click the transaction; then choose a single category in the Category box. That's all there is to it. Money removes the words "Split/Multiple Categories" and enters the name of the category you chose.

This transaction was divided across categories.

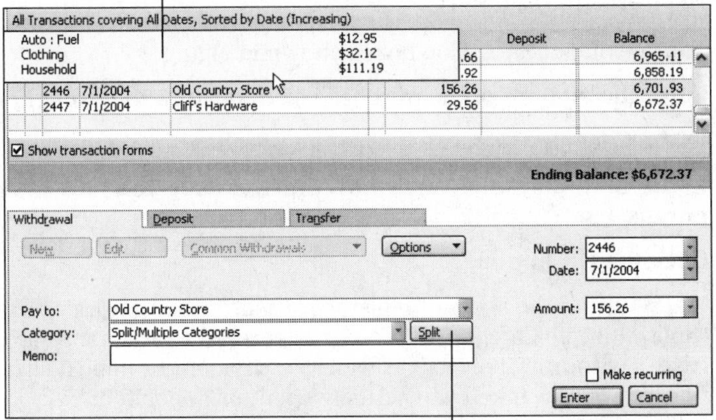

All Transactions covering All Dates, Sorted by Date (Increasing)					
Auto : Fuel		$12.95		Deposit	Balance
Clothing		$32.12	.66		6,965.11
Household		$111.19	.92		6,858.19
2446	7/1/2004	Old Country Store	156.26		6,701.93
2447	7/1/2004	Cliff's Hardware	29.56		6,672.37

☑ Show transaction forms

Ending Balance: $6,672.37

| Withdrawal | Deposit | Transfer |

New   Edit   Common Withdrawals ▼   Options ▼   Number: 2446
                                                   Date: 7/1/2004

Pay to: Old Country Store   ▼   Amount: 156.26
Category: Split/Multiple Categories   ▼ Split
Memo:

☐ Make recurring
Enter   Cancel

Figure 4-6:
When you split a transaction, the words "Split/Multiple Categories" appear in the register.

Click the Split button to see how a transaction was split.

Recording a Deposit or Debit Card Purchase with Cash Back

Suppose that you deposit a check or make a debit card purchase and ask for a little cash back. Who doesn't need a little cash now and then? The problem with recording a cash-back deposit or debit card purchase with extra cash is that the transaction is really two transactions in one. In the case of the debit card purchase, part of the transaction is a debit card purchase and part is a cash withdrawal from a bank account. Likewise with cash-back deposits — part of the transaction is a deposit and part is a cash withdrawal.

Fortunately for you, Money offers special commands for recording these kinds of transactions. Follow these steps to record a cash-back deposit or debit card purchase:

1. **Open the register of the account in which you want to record the deposit or debit card purchase.**

2. **Click the Withdrawal tab to record a cash-back debit card purchase; click the Deposit tab to record a cash-back deposit.**

3. **Click the Common Withdrawals or Common Deposits button.**

   A menu appears with commands for handling special kinds of transactions.

4. **To record a cash-back debit card purchase, select Debit Card Purchase with Cash Back; to record a cash-back deposit, select Deposit with Cash Back.**

   You see one of the dialog boxes shown in Figure 4-7.

5. **Enter the amount of the purchase or deposit in the Amount box.**

6. **In the Category box, categorize the purchase or deposit.**

7. **In the Cash Back box, enter how much money you took back with the purchase or deposit.**

8. **Click the OK button.**

   You return to the account register. Notice, in the Category box, the words "Split/Multiple Categories." You have entered a split transaction — in this case, a withdrawal of cash as well as a payment or deposit. The Amount box shows how much you actually spent or deposited.

   If you need to tinker with the figures, click the Split button to open the Transaction with Multiple Categories dialog box (refer to Figure 4-5). From here, you can review the figures one last time or adjust them if need be.

9. **Complete the transaction as you normally would and click the Enter button.**

To examine a split transaction in a register, select the transaction, click the transaction form, and click the Split button.

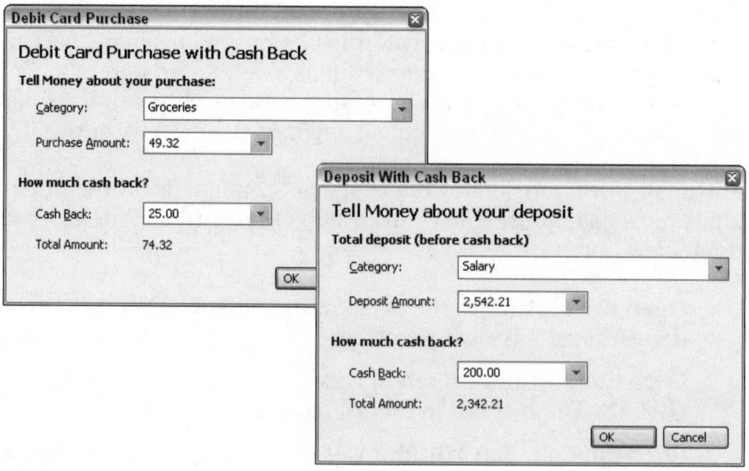

Figure 4-7:
In the Cash Back text box, enter how much you withdrew as part of your debit card purchase or deposit.

Transferring Money between Accounts

Sometimes, good luck comes your way; you earn a few extra dollars, so you transfer money from your checking account to a savings account or investment account. And sometimes, in a fit of panic, you have to transfer money from a savings account to a checking account to cover a couple of large checks. When you transfer money between real-life bank accounts, record the transfer in your Money account registers as well.

Follow these steps to record a transfer of money from one account to another:

1. **Open the register of the account from which you're transferring the money.**

   In other words, to transfer money from a checking to a savings account, open the checking account register.

2. **Click the Transfer tab.**

   You see the transaction form, as shown in Figure 4-8.

   The fastest way to record a transfer is to click the Common Transfers button and choose a transaction from the drop-down list. The menu lists the last five transfers you recorded. If the transfer you want to record is identical to a transfer on the menu, select it.

3. **Enter the date that the transfer was made in the Date text box.**

4. **In the Amount text box, enter the amount of the transfer.**

5. **Click the down arrow on the To drop-down list and choose the account receiving the transferred money.**

   All the accounts you set up in Money appear on the To drop-down list. The name of the account from which you are transferring the money should already appear in the From text box. Leave the Pay To text box empty when transferring money between bank accounts.

6. **Click the Enter button or press the Enter key.**

   The transfer is counted as a debit — the amount you transferred is deducted from one account and added to the other.

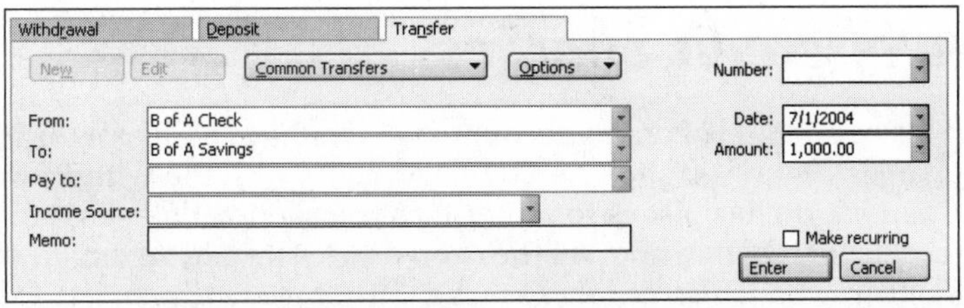

Figure 4-8:
Transferring
money
between
accounts.

Withdrawal	Deposit	Transfer		
New	Edit	Common Transfers ▾	Options ▾	Number:
From:	B of A Check		Date:	7/1/2004
To:	B of A Savings		Amount:	1,000.00
Pay to:				
Income Source:				
Memo:			☐ Make recurring	
			Enter	Cancel

Transferring is more than meets the eye

It seems odd at first, but Money requires you to transfer funds not only when you transfer funds between bank accounts but also when you contribute to IRAs or other kinds of investments. Think of it this way: If you open an IRA and you write a $1,000 check for a contribution to your IRA, that $1,000 still belongs to you. You haven't really spent it. All you have done is transfer it from one account (checking) to another account (the retirement account with which you track the value of your IRA). Therefore, when you open a new account, you record the initial deposit as a transfer from your checking account to the new account.

You also transfer money between accounts when you pay a credit card bill. Here's how it works: Each time you record a charge in a credit card account, the charge is added to the amount of money that you owe. Suppose that at the end of a month your account shows that you owe $200 because you charged $200 worth of items. To pay the $200 that you owe, you record a check for $200 to the credit card issuer, but in the register, the $200 is shown as a transfer from your checking account to your credit card account. After the transfer is complete, the $200 that you owed is brought to zero. The section, "Recording a credit card payment," later in this chapter, explains how to pay credit card bills.

Recording Transactions in Credit Card and Line of Credit Accounts

If you slogged through the previous few pages and discovered how to record checking and savings account transactions, you may experience *déjà vu* in the next few pages. Entering credit card and line of credit transactions is mighty similar to recording transactions made in savings and checking accounts.

Besides leaving credit cards at home, one way to keep credit card spending under control is to diligently record charges as you make them. Watching the amount that you owe grow larger and larger in the credit card register should discourage you from spending so much with your credit card.

Recording credit card and line of credit charges

Credit card and line of credit account registers have a Charge form for recording charges. Figure 4-9 shows a Charge form. As with the Withdrawal form, the Charge form has places for entering a transaction date, amount, payee name, category, and memo. All the drop-down lists and keyboard tricks work the same way on a Charge form as on a Withdrawal form.

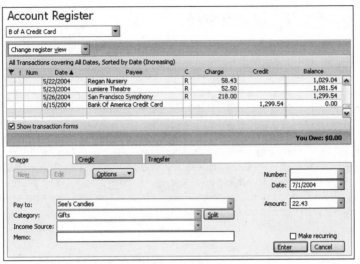

Figure 4-9:
Record
credit card
and line
of credit
transactions
exactly as
you would
record a
check.

To fill in the Charge form, follow these steps:

1. **Open the account register.**

2. **Click the Charge tab.**

3. **Enter a reference number (optional).**

4. **Enter the charge date.**

5. **Enter the business you purchased the item(s) from in the Pay To box.**

6. **Enter the amount of the charge.**

   Don't concern yourself with recording service charges and interest on
   your credit card. You can do that when you reconcile your account
   (a topic I explain in Chapter 6).

7. **Select a category.**

8. **Enter a description (optional).**

9. **Click the Enter button (or press Enter).**

Credit card and line of credit accounts track what you owe, not what you
have. Don't forget this all-important detail. In the credit card register shown
in Figure 4-9, you can clearly see the words *You Owe* where the words *Ending
Balance* appear in a savings or checking account register. In effect, the You
Owe number is a negative number. It represents an amount that you will have
to pay out of your checking account one of these days.

Recording a credit

If you receive a credit from a bank or credit card issuer, perhaps because you overpaid, disputed a bill, or returned an item you bought, record the credit in the credit card account register. To do so, click the Credit tab and fill in the blanks in the Credit form. The Credit form works exactly like the Charge form (see the preceding section, "Recording credit card and line of credit charges").

Be sure to record the credit in an expense category. Seems odd, doesn't it, to record credits as expenses? But when you recorded the purchase in the register, you assigned it to an expense category. Now that you're getting a refund, assign it to the same expense category so that the amount you spent in the category is accurate on your reports.

Recording a credit card payment

Before you make a credit card or line of credit payment, reconcile the credit card or line of credit account (Chapter 6 explains how). Then take note of how much of the debt you intend to pay, and follow these steps to make a payment to the bank or card issuer:

1. **Open the register of the account from which you intend to make the payment (see the section, "Opening an Account Register," earlier in this chapter).**

   You probably want to open your checking account register.

2. **Click the Withdrawal tab at the bottom of the register window.**

3. **Click the Common Withdrawals button, choose Credit Card Payment, and then choose the name of the credit card account where you track the credit card that you want to make a payment on, as shown in Figure 4-10.**

   The words "Credit Card Payment" and the name of the credit card account appear in the Category box on the transaction form, as shown at the bottom of Figure 4-10.

4. **Enter a check number in the Number text box if the number that appears there isn't correct.**

   Remember, you can click the down arrow and choose Next Check Number to enter the next available check number in the box.

5. **In the Date text box, enter the date that you wrote or will write on the check.**

Choose Credit Card Payment.

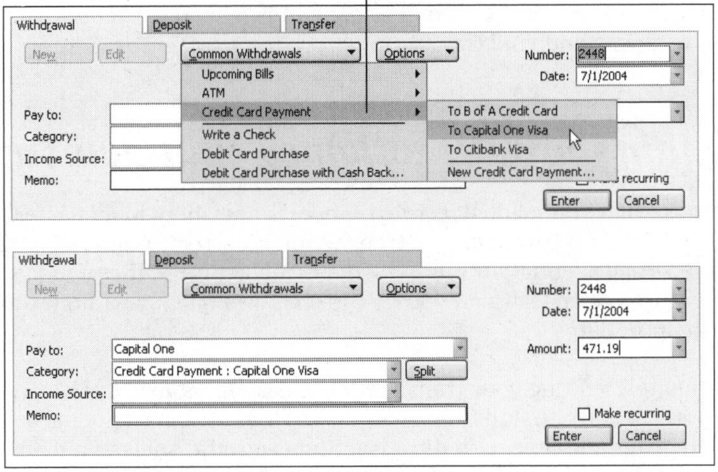

Figure 4-10:
Paying all or
part of a
credit card
bill.

6. **Enter the amount of the check in the Amount text box.**

   I hope that you can pay off the entire credit card or line of credit bill, but if you can't, Money doesn't care. Money continues to track what you owe from month to month.

7. **If you care to, write a few descriptive words in the Memo text box.**

8. **Click the Enter button or press Enter.**

   The amount you paid is deducted from the checking account. Meanwhile, the You Owe amount in the credit card or line of credit register decreases or is brought to zero. In effect, you have transferred money from your checking account to the account where you track credit card charges. Earlier in this chapter, the sidebar, "Transferring is more than meets the eye," explains the mystery of why you transfer money between accounts to satisfy a credit card debt.

Right-click a credit card payment in a register and choose Go To Account: *Credit Card Name* (or press Ctrl+X) to go to the account register where you track credit card charges.

Fixing Mistakes in Account Registers

Everybody makes mistakes, and absolutely everybody makes mistakes when entering transactions in account registers. Most people do not have an expert typist's nimble fingers or sureness of touch. Therefore, the following sections explain how to find and fix mistakes, how to get from place to place in large registers, how to move transactions from one account to another, and how to delete and void transactions.

Finding a transaction so that you can fix it

Suppose that you made a terrific blunder somewhere in a register but aren't sure where. You categorized a transaction incorrectly, entered a transaction in the wrong account, or misspelled a name. Suppose that you made the error many times over. How can you fix the mistakes quickly without wasting an entire morning?

Fortunately, editing your transactions is easy in Money. But before you can fix errors, you have to find them. Read on to find out how to get around quickly in a register and how to find transactions with the Tools⇨Find and Replace command.

It helps to see more transactions on-screen when you are looking for a specific transaction. To see more transactions, deselect the Show Transaction Forms check box. You can also open the Change Register View menu and choose Top Line Only.

Moving around in an account register

One way to find a transaction is to eyeball the account register. With this technique, you put the register on-screen, move around in it like mad, and hope you find the transaction you are looking for. Table 4-1 presents keyboard and scroll bar techniques for getting around quickly in an account register.

Table 4-1	Keyboard and Scroll Bar Techniques for Moving Around in Registers
Press/Click/Drag	**To Go**
Ctrl+Home	To the first transaction in the register.
Ctrl+End	To the last transaction in the register.
↑ or ↓	To the previous or next transaction in the register.
PgUp or PgDn	Up or down an entire screen of transactions.
Scroll bar arrows	To the preceding or next transaction. Click the arrow at the top of the scroll bar to go up, the one at the bottom to go down.

Press/Click/Drag	To Go
Scroll bar	Up or down an entire screen of transactions. With this technique, you click the scroll bar but not the arrows or the scroll box. Click above the scroll box to go up; click below to go down.
Scroll box	Willy-nilly through the register. Drag the scroll box, the elevator-like object in the middle of the scroll bar, to go up or down very quickly.

Searching with the Find and Replace command

The surest way to pinpoint a transaction or a bunch of similar transactions is to choose Tools⇨Find and Replace (or press Ctrl+F). This command looks for transactions in all the registers, not just the one that is open, so you don't have to be in a specific register to start looking for transactions.

Follow these steps to look for transactions in your account registers:

1. Choose Tools⇨Find and Replace.

You see the Find and Replace dialog box, shown in Figure 4-11. You can also press Ctrl+F to see this dialog box.

From here, you can conduct a simple search of all your accounts, or an advanced search in which you tell Money in great detail where to search and what to search for.

2. If you want to search only in investment or loan accounts, open the Search Across drop-down list and make a choice.

You may as well start with a simple search and hope for the best. If you don't find what you are looking for, you can try an advanced search.

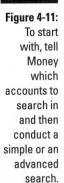

Figure 4-11:
To start with, tell Money which accounts to search in and then conduct a simple or an advanced search.

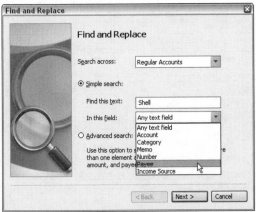

3. **Type what you are looking for in the Find This Text box, and if you know in which column of the register the thing is located, make a choice from the In This Field drop-down list; then click the Next button.**

Figure 4-11 shows the fields you can choose from — Category, Payee, and so on — when you search regular accounts. If you are searching in a particular field, choose it in the In This Field drop-down list *before* you type anything in the Find This Text box. That way, you can simply choose a field in the Find This Text drop-down list instead of typing one in. For example, if you choose Payee, a list of payees appears on the Find This Text drop-down list.

With a little luck, Money finds what you are looking for and you see search results like those shown in Figure 4-12. Examine the transactions and click the scroll bar, if necessary, to find the one you are looking for. A couple of pages hence, the "Changing or editing transactions" section explains how to fix transactions in the search results.

Try clicking the Num, Date, Account, Payee, Category, or Amount button at the top of the columns to arrange the transactions in a new way. For example, clicking the Date button arranges the transactions in date order. Clicking Payee arranges them in alphabetical order by payee. Click a button a second time to reverse the order (a little arrow on the button shows whether the column is arranged in ascending or descending order).

4. **If you found the transaction you want to change, double-click it to open the Edit Transaction window and change it there.**

What if Money can't find what you are looking for — or, as often happens, the Search Results list is too long and you need to pinpoint one or two transactions? I'm afraid you have to click the Back button to return to the Find and Replace dialog box (refer to Figure 4-11) and start your search over: It's time to conduct an advanced search.

Figure 4-12:
The results
of a search.
Click the
Back button
if you need
to start
all over.

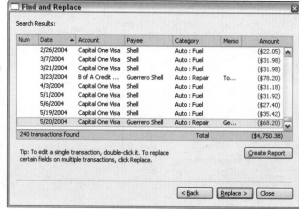

Conducting an advanced search

Sometimes you really have to beat the bushes to find the transaction you are looking for. To begin searching, click the Advanced Search option button in the Find and Replace dialog box (refer to Figure 4-11) and then click Next. The dialog box offers seven tabs (more if you classify as well as categorize transactions) for entering search criteria. Table 4-2 explains what the different tabs are. Fill out one tab or a combination of tabs. You needn't fill out all the tabs. Do your best to tell Money precisely where the thing you are looking for is located and what you know about it.

Click the Next button when you are done. You see a list of transactions that met your criteria (refer to Figure 4-12). Double-click a transaction to change it in any way. The next section explains how to edit transactions.

Table 4-2	Advanced Searching for Transactions in the Find and Replace Dialog Box
Tab	***What It Does***
Text	Searches for specific words. For example, if you are searching for a check on which you wrote "Damn the torpedoes" on the Memo line, type **Damn the torpedoes** in the Find Transactions with This Text box.
Account	Selects which accounts to search in. To search in specific accounts, click the Clear All button and then click the names of the accounts you want to search.
Date	Searches in specific date ranges. Either click the down arrow next to the Range text box and select a time period, or enter a From and To date in the text boxes.
Amount	Searches for transactions of a certain amount. Enter a specific amount or number range in the From and To box.
Category	Searches in specific categories. Click the Clear All button and then click a Select button to narrow the search to income, expense, or tax-related categories. You can also click next to individual categories to search for them. Select the Show Subcategories check box to narrow the search to subcategories. (Chapter 5 explains more about fixing categorization errors.)
Payee	Searches for specific payees. Click the Clear All button and then click the name of the payee or names of the payees for which you recorded transactions.

(continued)

Table 4-2 (continued)

Tab	What It Does
Details	Searches by transaction type (payments, deposits, unprinted checks, unsent online bill payments, transfers), reconciliation status (unreconciled and reconciled), and check number.
Classification	Searches for transactions that you classified a certain way, if you use classifications. (Chapter 5 explains classifications.)

Changing or editing transactions

All right, so you found the transaction that you entered incorrectly. What do you do now? If you are staring at the transaction in an account register, either double-click it or click it and then click the Edit button on the transaction form. Then go right into the transaction form, fix the mistake in whatever text box or drop-down list it is located in, and click the Enter button.

If you found the error by way of the Tools⇨Find and Replace command (see the "Searching with the Find and Replace command" section in this chapter), double-click the transaction in the Search Results list (refer to Figure 4-12). When the Edit Transaction dialog box appears, repair the transaction and click OK.

Suppose, however, that an error was made in numerous places. You misspelled a payee's name. You categorized several transactions incorrectly. In that case, follow the directions in the "Searching with the Find and Replace command" section of this chapter to display the errant transactions in the Find and Replace dialog box (refer to Figure 4-12). Then follow these steps to fix the transactions *en masse:*

1. **Click the Replace button in the Find and Replace dialog box.**

   You see the dialog box shown in Figure 4-13.

2. **On the Replace drop-down list, choose which part of the transactions needs repairing.**

   You can change payee names, category assignments, memo text, or transaction numbers.

3. **In the With box, either type a new entry or select one from the drop-down list.**

   If you chose Payee or Category on the Replace drop-down list, a list of payees or categories is made available on the With menu.

Select the transactions that need replacing.

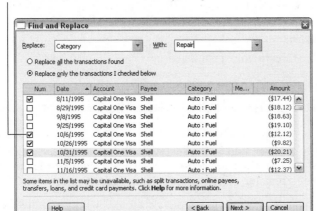

Figure 4-13:
Use the Find
and Replace
dialog box
to change
several
transactions
simul-
taneously.

4. **Select the check boxes next to transactions you want to edit, or select the Replace All the Transactions Found radio button to edit all the transactions in the list.**

5. **Click the Next button.**

   A "last chance" dialog box appears and lists all the transactions that will be altered. If you are prudent, look through the list one last time. If you are daring and reckless, click the Finish button right away. You can click the Back button if you get cold feet.

6. **Click the Finish button.**

Voiding and Deleting Transactions

To strike a transaction from an account register, either delete or void it. What's the difference? A deleted transaction is erased permanently from your financial records. It may as well have never happened. But a voided transaction stays in the account register, where `**VOID**` clearly shows that you entered the transaction but voided it later on. What's more, a voided transaction can be "unvoided."

Void a transaction when you want to keep a record of having made it. For example, if you start writing check number 511 but accidentally enter the wrong payee name, void the check instead of deleting it. That way, the account register records what happened to check number 511, and you know that the check wasn't lost or stolen. Likewise, if you stop payment on a check, void it (and explain on the Memo line why you stopped payment).

History records what happened to voided transactions, but deleted transactions are lost forever in the prehistoric murk.

Voiding a transaction

Follow these steps to void a transaction:

1. **Select the transaction in the register.**

2. **Right-click the transaction and choose Mark As⇨Void or press Ctrl+V.**

After a transaction has been voided, `**VOID**` appears in the balance column of the register, and R (for Reconciled) appears in the C (for Cleared) column to show that the transaction has cleared. Figure 4-14 shows a voided transaction in a register. (Chapter 6 explains what reconciling is.)

To unvoid a transaction, click it in the register and choose Edit⇨Mark As⇨ Void all over again (or right-click and choose Mark As⇨Void). Because voided transactions are reconciled automatically, a dialog box asks whether you're dead sure that you want to change this reconciled transaction. Normally, you click No in this dialog box, because changing a reconciled transaction throws your record and the bank's out of sync. In the case of voiding, however, click the Yes button to make the change. All you're trying to do here is reverse a mistake you made.

Deleting a transaction

Follow these steps to delete a transaction:

1. **Select the transaction in the register.**

2. **Right-click and choose Delete from the shortcut menu, or press Ctrl+D.**

   Sorry, you can't delete a transaction by pressing the Del key.

3. **Click Yes when Money asks whether you really want to go through with it.**

If you try to delete a transaction that is marked as cleared in the register (R appears in the C column), Money warns you that deleting the transaction could upset your account balance and put the account out of sync with bank records. I strongly suggest clicking No in the dialog box to keep the transaction from being deleted. Very likely, the transaction was cleared because it appeared on bank records, so it should appear on your records as well. Investigate the matter before deleting the transaction.

Figure 4-14:
A voided
transaction.

2447	7/1/2004	Cliff's Hardware Home Repair	R	29.56		**VOID**

Flagging transactions so that you can review them

It so happens now and then that a check you've written or charge you've made needs looking after. A charge on your credit card is under dispute. A check you wrote hasn't been cashed and you're not sure why. In cases like these, you can flag the transaction. Flagging makes it easier to follow up checks and credit card charges. A flag appears in account registers beside transactions that have been flagged. Move the pointer over the flag icon and a pop-up box tells you why the flag is there.

To flag a transaction, right-click it in the register and choose Flag for Follow-Up. You see the Flag for Follow-Up dialog box. In the Follow Up By text box, enter a date to tell Money how long to leave the flag icon in the register. In the Notes text box, enter the note that will appear when you move the pointer over the flag icon.

To remove the flag from a transaction, right-click it and choose Edit Flag for Follow-Up. Then in the Flag for Follow-Up dialog box, deselect the Flag This Transaction check box and click OK.

To find a transaction that you flagged, scroll through the account register or go to the Home Page. On that page is a list of flagged transactions. Click a transaction to see it in the Edit Transaction dialog box.

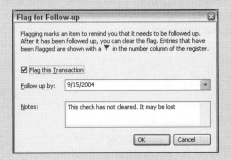

You cannot delete an online payment that has been sent to Online Services. You can, however, send instructions to cancel the payment, as long as you do so within a couple of days of sending it. (See Chapter 18 for more information.)

Moving a Transaction from One Account to Another

Suppose that you discover an error that has nothing to do with incorrect categories, amounts, or payee names. Suppose that you committed the grievous error of entering a transaction in the wrong account register. Before you are put in leg irons, move the transaction to the correct account.

Money gives you two ways to move transactions between accounts:

✔ **From an account register:** If you find the errant transaction in a register, right-click it and choose Move to Account from the shortcut menu. You see the Account dialog box. In the Select New Account for Transaction list, select the name of the account to which you want to move the transaction; then click OK.

✔ **From the Find and Replace dialog box:** If you find the errant transaction by way of the Tools⇨Find and Replace command (the "Finding a transaction so that you can fix it" section a few pages back explains how), double-click it to open the Edit Transaction dialog box. Then click the down arrow on the Account drop-down list box and choose the name of the account in which the transaction rightfully belongs.

After you move a transaction to a different account, go to the other account and make sure that the transaction landed correctly. Very likely, the transaction needs to be renumbered or given a new date.

Printing a Register

Besides fretting over income taxes in April, you also have to print all your account registers from the previous year. Your accountant, if you have one, wants to see them. Even if you don't have an accountant, you should still print the account registers and tuck them away with copies of your income tax forms. Leaving behind a paper trail is important in case a posse from the IRS comes to track you down.

Follow these steps to print all or part of an account register:

1. **Open the account register that you want to print (see the section, "Opening an Account Register," earlier in this chapter).**

2. **Choose File⇨Print or press Ctrl+P.**

   You see the Print Report dialog box, shown in Figure 4-15. Theoretically, you can print part of a register from this dialog box by entering page numbers in the From and To text boxes. However, it is impossible to tell by looking at a register what page you are on or how many pages are in the register altogether. Oh well, so much for printing a handful of pages, although you can blindly try your luck with the From and To text boxes if you want.

3. **If you want to try your luck with printing less than the entire register, select the Pages radio button and enter page numbers in the From and To text boxes.**

4. **Click OK.**

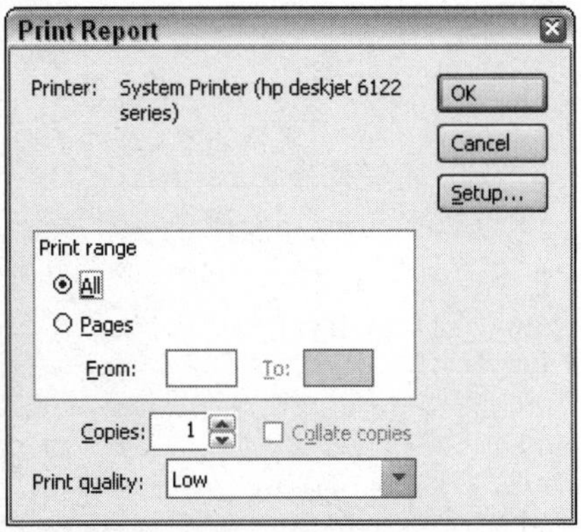

Print Report ⊠

Printer: System Printer (hp deskjet 6122
series)

[OK]
[Cancel]
[Setup...]

Print range
⦿ All
○ Pages
From: [   ]   To: [   ]

Copies: [1 ▲▼] ☐ Collate copies
Print quality: [Low   ▼]

Figure 4-15:
Printing an
account
register.

If the register doesn't print correctly, the problem could be that Money and
your printer aren't on speaking terms. (See Chapter 15 for more information.)

To solve the problem of printing part of a register, create an Account
Transactions report and customize it so that only transactions from a certain
year or other time period appear. (See Chapter 15 for more information.)

Part II
Banking with Money

The 5th Wave
By Rich Tennant

"And tell David to come in out of the hall. I found a way to adjust our project budget estimate."

In this part . . .

Part II explains how to do banking chores with Money. Who likes to do banking chores? Not me. But at least Money takes some of the tedium out of banking.

In this part, you find out how to categorize your spending and income so that reports, budgets, and financial projections that rely on categories are more meaningful to you. You also discover how to balance a bank account. And for people whose handwriting is impossible to decipher, Part II explains how to print checks.

Chapter 5

Categorizing Your Spending and Income

You've probably withdrawn money from an ATM, noticed the dwindling account balance, and asked yourself, "Where did the money go?" Or perhaps you balanced a checking account and scratched your head, asking, "Why did I write so many checks?"

Money can help you find out. By assigning each transaction to a category, you can discover a great deal about your spending habits and sources of income. You can generate a report or graph and find out how much you spent on clothing and dining and office supplies. You can find out how much you earned in interest income and how much you earned from different clients. You can even find out how much you are allowed to deduct for income tax purposes.

This chapter explains how to categorize and classify transactions in account registers. You figure out how to choose categories and how to create meaningful categories that work for you. You also explore how to rename categories, delete categories, and recategorize transactions. You may still have to write the same number of checks, but at least you'll have a better idea why.

Looking at the Ways to Categorize Income and Spending

Money offers four ways to categorize a financial transaction. What are the four ways? You can categorize a transaction by category, subcategory, classification, and tax-related status.

By category

By assigning transactions to categories, you can create neat-looking charts that give you the big picture on your spending, as shown in Figure 5-1. (See Chapter 15 for more about charts.) You can see where all your money is spent and where the money comes from.

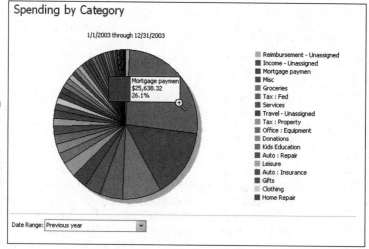

Figure 5-1: Each slice in this pie chart represents spending in a different category.

By subcategory

Divide a category into subcategories when you want to closely examine spending or income. The report in Figure 5-2 shows yearly expenses in three Automobile subcategories: Repair, Insurance, and Fuel. After you have used Money for a while, try running a report like this one to show how much it costs to drive your car for one year.

Spending by Category

1/1/2003 through 12/31/2003

Subcategory	Total
Expense Categories	
Auto : Repair	1,863.12
Auto : Insurance	1,680.56
Auto : Fuel	1,184.56
Total Expense Categories	4,728.24
Grand Total	(4,728.24)

Figure 5-2:
A sub-category report.

By classification

Most people don't need to bother with classifications, but they can be useful for tracking things such as rental properties. As the owner or manager of an apartment building or office building, you need to know precisely how much income the property generates and how much it costs to maintain. The only way to track income and costs, which fall into lots of different expense and income categories and subcategories, is to create a classification.

By tax-related status

By giving a category tax-related status, you can tell Money to include categories and subcategories in tax reports. An accountant may need two or three hours to examine account registers, find all the tax-related transactions, and total them — time that you will be charged for. Money can do it in about six seconds. (Chapter 14 looks at tax preparation with Money.)

Setting Up Your Own Categories and Subcategories

Money gives you a set of generic categories and subcategories so that you can start entering transactions right away. The list is fine and dandy, but sooner or later you have to give serious thought to which categories and subcategories suit you, especially if you use Money to manage a business or track tax-deductible expenses. If you don't see what you need in the generic lists, you can create your own!

Sit down and compose a list of all the categories and subcategories that you need for your business or personal finances *before* you begin creating categories and subcategories. That way, you get it right from the start and you lower the odds of having to recategorize transactions later on.

Money offers two different ways to create categories and subcategories. You can make them up as you go along with the fast-but-dicey method, or you can thoughtfully create them all at one time in the New Category dialog box. The following sections describe the thorough way and the fast way to create categories and subcategories.

Creating a new category in the New Category dialog box

Follow these steps to set up a new category in the New Category dialog box:

1. **Open the Set Up Your Categories window.**

   - Press Ctrl+Shift+C.

   - Click the Banking tab, click the Account Tools button, and then select Categories & Payees.

   If you don't see the Categories list, click the Categories link on the left side of the window.

   Figure 5-3 shows the Categories list. While you're viewing the window, you may want to scroll down the list of categories and subcategories and examine the ones that are already there. Expense categories appear at the top of the list, and Income categories appear at the bottom.

2. **Click the New button at the bottom of the screen.**

   The New Category dialog box appears.

3. **The Create a New Category option button is already selected, so click the Next button.**

   As shown in Figure 5-4, the New Category dialog box offers places for entering a category name and category type.

4. **Type a name for the category in the Name box.**

   The name that you enter will appear in the Category drop-down list when you record transactions, so be sure to choose a meaningful name.

5. **Select the Income or Expense option button and click the Next button.**

   All categories fall under the Income or Expense heading. Income categories describe sources of income; expense categories describe how you spend money.

Banking

Change views

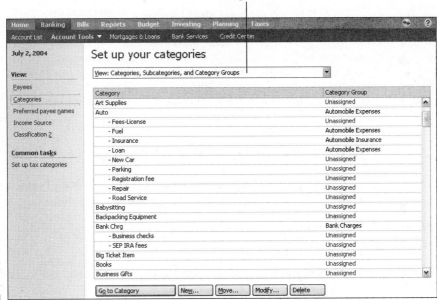

Figure 5-3:
Categories
and sub-
categories.
Sub-
categories
are indented
and appear
below their
parent
categories.

6. Select a category group from the list.

A *category group* is a broad means of defining the category. Money uses
category groups to make calculations in budgets and in tax estimations
(see Chapters 12 and 14). When you select a category group, a description appears on the right side of the dialog box.

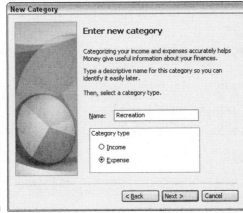

Figure 5-4:
Create new
categories
to describe
your
spending
and income.

7. Click the Finish button.

There it is — your new category, alive and kicking in the Set Up Your Categories window.

Open the View menu in the Categories window and experiment with the different views (refer to Figure 5-3). In Figure 5-3, I chose Categories, Subcategories, and Category Groups from the View menu. The other options can be useful when you are looking for a category in the list.

Creating a new subcategory

The best way to create a new subcategory is to go straight to the Set Up Your Categories window and start from there. Follow these steps:

Banking

1. Open the Set Up Your Categories window:

- Press Ctrl+Shift+C.

- Click the Banking tab, click the Account Tools button, and then choose Categories & Payees.

If necessary, click the Categories link to view categories. You can find this link on the left side of the window under View.

2. Select the parent category of the subcategory that you want to create.

In other words, to create a subcategory of the Education category, scroll to and select Education in the Categories window.

3. Click the New button.

You see the New Category dialog box.

4. Select the Add a Subcategory to an Existing Category option button; then click the Next button.

5. Enter a name for the subcategory in the Name box; then click the Next button.

6. Select a category group.

Category groups are another one of those bold attempts by Microsoft to do your thinking for you. They are used in budget projections and tax estimations.

7. Click the Finish button.

Check it out — your new subcategory appears in the Categories window underneath its parent category.

The fast-but-dicey way to set up categories

When you're in a hurry, you can create a category as you enter a transaction. I don't recommend doing this, because you don't get a chance to look at the big picture. You can't see where your new category or subcategory goes in the Category list or whether your new category or subcategory is really necessary. Anyhow, if you're a daredevil, follow these steps to create a category as you enter a transaction:

1. **Enter the entire transaction on the transaction form, except for the category and subcategory.**

   In other words, enter numbers or letters in the Number, Date, Amount, Pay To, From, and Memo text boxes.

2. **In the Category text box, enter the name of the new category.**

Or, to create a new subcategory, choose a category, type a colon (:), and then type a subcategory name.

3. **Press Tab.**

   You see the New Category dialog box. I hope it looks familiar.

4. **Make sure that the name you entered appears correctly in the dialog box; then click the Next button.**

5. **Select a category group.**

6. **Click the Finish button.**

   The name of the category that you created takes its place in the Category drop-down list so that you can select it in the future.

Editing and Refining a Category or Subcategory

To change a category name, assign it to a new category group, view transactions that were assigned to the category, or do a number of other activities that pertain to a category, Money offers the Category window. Figure 5-5 shows the window for a category called Groceries that tracks money spent at the supermarket. Follow these steps to visit a Category window:

Banking

1. **Open the Set Up Your Categories window.**

   You can get there by pressing Ctrl+Shift+C or by clicking the Banking tab, clicking the Account Tools button, and then choosing Categories & Payees.

2. **Select a category, and then click the Go to Category button at the bottom of the window.**

   You see a Category window like the one shown in Figure 5-5. You can also get to this window by double-clicking a category in the Categories window.

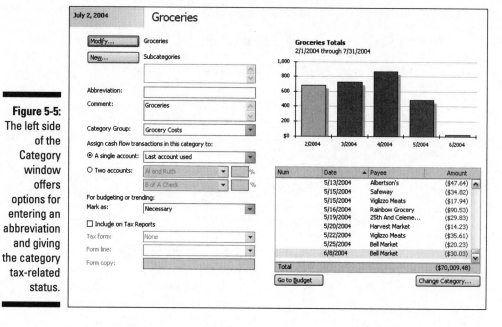

Figure 5-5:
The left side
of the
Category
window
offers
options for
entering an
abbreviation
and giving
the category
tax-related
status.

The window presents a bunch of different amenities. For example, you can see a graph showing how much you spent or took in, as well as a miniregister that shows account activity in the category. Here are some things you can do in a Category window:

✔ **Change category names:** Click the Modify button, and in the Modify Category dialog box, enter a new name for the category. When you change a category name, names in transactions that you've already entered are changed as well.

✔ **Use abbreviations instead of category names:** The Abbreviation box represents an alternate way to assign a category to a transaction. Besides selecting a category from the drop-down list on the transaction form or typing the first few letters of the category name, you can type a two- or three-letter abbreviation. After you type the two or three letters and press Tab to move to the next part of the transaction form, Money enters the entire category name for you. (Big deal, I say. It's not as if selecting from the drop-down list or typing the first few letters of a category name is very difficult.)

✔ **Enter comments:** The Comment box is worth visiting. Enter a few words to describe the category and why you created it. That way, if you forget what the new category is for, you can always come back to the Categories window and find out.

✔ **Assign a category group:** When you draw up a budget, you are given the choice of declaring how much you will spend or earn in each category or in each category group. Budgeting by category is hard work because there are so many categories. Many people opt to budget by category group to save time. You may choose a new category group from this drop-down list. (Chapter 12 explains budgets.)

✔ **Project your cash flow:** Money can project how much money you will have at future dates. The program does its soothsaying by examining the amount of money in different accounts over time. If earning or spending in the category that you just created is done mostly by way of a certain bank account, choose it to help with cash-flow projections. (See Chapter 12.)

✔ **Mark for budgeting:** When you draw up a budget (see Chapter 12), you are also asked to declare by category which spending is necessary and which is discretionary. Choose one or the other if you intend to get Money's help with budgeting.

✔ **Include categories in tax reports:** Select the Include on Tax Reports check box if you want transactions that are made under this category to be calculated in tax reports.

Setting Up and Defining a Classification

At the beginning of this chapter, I explain that a classification is an umbrella grouping under which you track income and expenses in many different categories and subcategories. You can create two classifications in each Money file. When you generate some types of reports, you can ask Money to tell you everything it knows about transactions assigned a certain classification.

Classifications permit you to track income or expenses in several different categories and subcategories simultaneously. A property manager, for example, can create a class named after each building that he or she manages. As well as categorizing expenses for building repairs and income from rent, the manager may classify them by property. Then, from time to time, the manager may run classification reports to see precisely how much each property generates in income and costs in upkeep.

The following sections explain how to set up a new classification. You also find out how to define the *classes* and *subclasses* that go into the classification. When you enter a transaction, you can select a class and subclass from special drop-down lists on the transaction form. In Figure 5-6, the user has named the classification Properties, the class in question is the building at 1020 Lakeshore Drive, and Apt. 2 is a subclass. The transaction records a check that was written to cover plumbing repairs done to Apartment 2 at 1020 Lakeshore Drive.

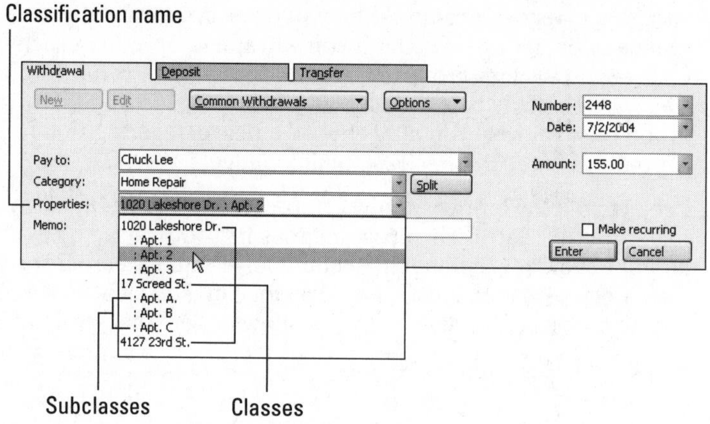
Classification name
Withdrawal
Deposit
Transfer
New
Edit
Common Withdrawals
Options
Number: 2448
Date: 7/2/2004
Pay to: Chuck Lee
Category: Home Repair
Split
Properties: 1020 Lakeshore Dr. : Apt. 2
Amount: 155.00
Memo:
1020 Lakeshore Dr.
: Apt. 1
: Apt. 2
: Apt. 3
17 Screed St.
: Apt. A.
: Apt. B
: Apt. C
4127 23rd St.
Make recurring
Enter
Cancel
Subclasses
Classes

Figure 5-6: Choosing a subclass from the Classification drop-down list.

Setting up a classification

As with categories and subcategories, the starting point for setting up a classification is the all-purpose Set Up Your Categories window. Follow these steps to set up a classification:

Banking

1. **Press Ctrl+Shift+C or click the Banking tab, click the Account Tools button, and then choose Categories & Payees.**

   If necessary, click the Categories link to view categories. You can find this link on the left side of the window under View.

2. **Click the Classification 1 link.**

   You see the Add Classification dialog box, as shown in Figure 5-7.

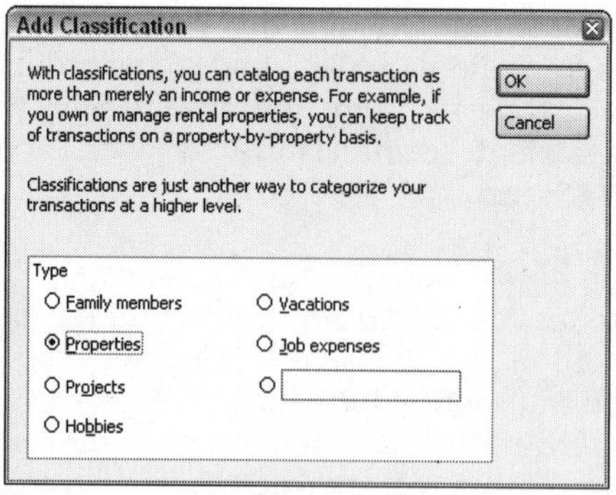
Add Classification
With classifications, you can catalog each transaction as more than merely an income or expense. For example, if you own or manage rental properties, you can keep track of transactions on a property-by-property basis.
Classifications are just another way to categorize your transactions at a higher level.
OK
Cancel
Type
Family members
Vacations
Properties
Job expenses
Projects
Hobbies

Figure 5-7: To name the classification, either select a name or click the last option button and enter your own name.

3. **Select one of Money's names by clicking an option button or click the last option button and enter an original name for the classification.**

   Money's six suggestions for naming the new classification appear next to the six option buttons. If you click the Properties option button, for example, the new classification is called Properties, and the word *Properties* appears on your transaction forms (refer to Figure 5-6).

   If you don't like Money's suggestions for a name, you can always click the last option button and enter a name of your own in the text box.

4. **After you select or enter a name, click OK.**

   You return to the Set Up Your Classification window, where the name that you chose or entered appears on the left side of the window on a button below the Categories button.

The next step is to define classes and perhaps subclasses for the new classification. By the way, if you set up two classifications in a Money file, you get two sets of classification drop-down lists on the transaction forms that appear in the account registers.

Defining classes and subclasses

Starting in the Set Up Your Category window, follow these steps to define the classes and subclasses that appear in the first classification drop-down list on transaction forms:

1. **Click the classification link that is named after the classification to which you want to add the classes.**

   In other words, to create classes for the Properties classification, click the Properties link. The Set Up window lists classes and subclasses in the classification, if you have already created any, as shown in Figure 5-8.

2. **If you are creating a subclass, click the class under which you want to define a subclass.**

   For example, to define a subclass called Apt. 1 that is to be subordinate to the 1020 Lakeshore Drive class, select 1020 Lakeshore Drive.

3. **Click the New button.**

   You see the New Class or Subclass dialog box, as shown in Figure 5-8.

4. **Under Add, select the first option button to create a new class; select the second option button to create a new subclass.**

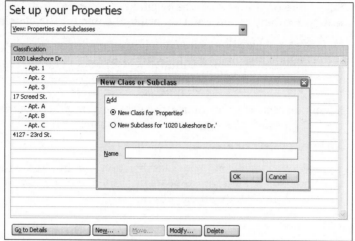

Figure 5-8:
Classes and
subclasses,
as well as
the New
Class or
Subclass
dialog box
for creating
classes and
subclasses.

5. **Enter a name for the class or subclass in the Name text box, and click OK.**

   The name that you enter appears in the Set Up Your Classification window.

To rename a class or subclass, right-click its name in the Set Up Your Classification window, choose Rename from the shortcut menu, enter a new name in the Modify Class or Modify Subclass dialog box, and click OK.

Correcting Transactions that Were Recorded in the Wrong Category

Don't feel foolish if you record transactions in the wrong category or subcategory. It happens all the time. Luckily for you, Money offers a special button called Move for reassigning all the transactions in one category to another category. And if you need to reassign only a handful of transactions, you can use the Find and Replace command to reassign transactions one at a time.

The Move button is very powerful indeed. When you use the Move button to reassign all the transactions in one category to another category, you delete the first category as well. For example, suppose that you assigned the Vacation category to a bunch of transactions when you should have assigned the Leisure category. If you use the Move button to move all the Vacation transactions to the Leisure category, you delete the Vacation category from the Categories list as well as move the transactions. Use the Move button only when you want to drop one category altogether and move all its transactions elsewhere.

Another point about the Move button: If you attempt to move transactions in one category to another category and the category that you want to move includes subcategories, you lose the subcategory assignments when you make the move. However, you can move subcategory assignments from one subcategory to another subcategory with the Move button.

Moving all transactions from one category to another category

To change category or subcategory assignments throughout your account registers, follow these steps:

1. **Press Ctrl+Shift+C or click the Banking tab, click the Account Tools button, and then choose Categories & Payees.**

   You land in the Set Up Your Categories window. If necessary, click the Categories link to make category and subcategory names appear.

   To see the categories and subcategories, you may need to open the View menu and choose Categories and Their Subcategories.

2. **Scroll down the list and select the name of the category or subcategory whose transactions you want to reassign.**

   For example, if you erroneously assigned transactions to the Education: Kids subcategory when you should have assigned them to the Childcare category, select the Education: Kids subcategory from the list.

   Remember, the category or subcategory that you select is deleted from the Categories window after you finish reassigning the transactions. Be sure to examine transactions carefully before you delete anything.

3. **Click the Move button.**

   As shown in Figure 5-9, you see the Move Transactions dialog box. This is where you tell Money where to reassign the transactions in the category or subcategory that you selected in Step 2.

4. **In the Category text box, select the category or subcategory to which you want to reassign the transactions.**

5. **Click OK.**

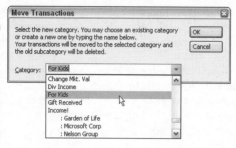

Figure 5-9:
Assigning
transactions
to a
different
category.

In the Categories list, the category or subcategory that you selected in Step 2 has been deleted. Meanwhile, all transactions in your registers that were assigned the old category or subcategory are assigned the one that you chose in Step 4.

Reassigning transactions to new categories

Instead of making a wholesale reassignment of one category or subcategory to another, you may decide to examine transactions one at a time and choose which ones need reassigning. To do that, you have to search for transactions in the account registers, examine each transaction, and then either choose a new category or subcategory or move on without moving the transaction.

Chapter 4 explains everything that you need to know about finding transactions. However, here are shorthand instructions to find and fix transactions that were assigned the wrong category or subcategory:

1. **Choose Tools⇨Find and Replace, or press Ctrl+F.**

   You see the Find and Replace dialog box.

2. **Select Category from the In This Field drop-down list; then, from the Find This Text drop-down list, select the category or subcategory whose transactions need reassigning; finally, click the Next button.**

   As shown at the top of Figure 5-10, the Search Results list shows transactions that are assigned to the category you selected. At this point, you can reassign the transactions one at a time or click the Replace button to reassign several transactions simultaneously.

3. **Assign the transactions to new categories:**

   • **One at a time:** Double-click a transaction that needs a new category. You see the Edit Transaction dialog box, as shown at the bottom of Figure 5-10. Choose a new category or subcategory from the drop-down list, and click the OK button.

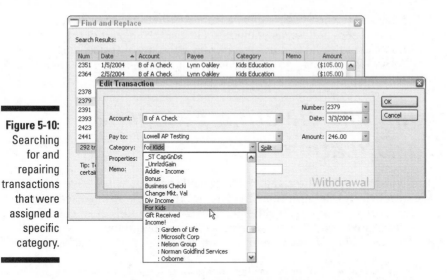

Figure 5-10:
Searching
for and
repairing
transactions
that were
assigned a
specific
category.

• **Several at one time:** Click the Replace button. You see the Find and Replace dialog box, as shown in Figure 5-11. Select the check box next to each transaction that needs a new category assignment, select Category from the Replace drop-down list, select a new category from the With list, and click the Next button. Then click the Finish button on the next screen, which asks whether you really want to make the reassignment.

Choose category.

Choose a new category.

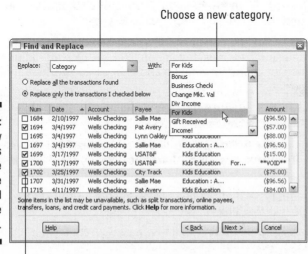

Figure 5-11:
Assign new
categories
en masse
from the
Find and
Replace
dialog box.

Click transactions that need reassigning.

By the way, when you reassign a transaction that has been reconciled, Money beeps and warns you not to change the amount of the transaction you are about to edit. Don't worry about the warning. You are concerned with the category assignment, not the amount of the transaction.

Renaming and Deleting Categories and Classifications

After you have worked with Money for a while and you have refined the list of categories and classifications that you want to work with, you can delete unnecessary categories and classifications. And if a category or classification isn't descriptive enough, you can rename it. The following sections explain how to delete and rename categories, subcategories, and classifications.

After you rename a category or classification, transactions throughout the account registers that were assigned the old category or classification name are automatically given the new name. So, when you rename, you also change the names of category, subcategory, or classification assignments throughout your registers.

Renaming a category or subcategory

Follow these steps to rename a category or subcategory:

Banking

1. **Press Ctrl+Shift+C or click the Banking tab, click the Account Tools button, and then choose Categories & Payees.**

   If necessary, click the Categories link in the window to see the list of categories and subcategories. If you don't see subcategory names but need to see them, open the View menu and choose Categories and their Subcategories.

2. **Scroll down the list and select the category or subcategory whose name you want to change.**

3. **Click the Modify button or right-click and choose Modify (choose Rename if you are dealing with a subcategory) from the shortcut menu.**

   You see either the Modify Category dialog box or the Modify Subcategory dialog box.

4. **Enter a name in the New Name text box, and click OK.**

Renaming a classification

Follow these dance steps to change the name of a classification:

1. **Press Ctrl+Shift+C or click the Banking tab, click the Account Tools button, and then choose Categories & Payees.**

2. **On the left side of the window, click the link named after the classification whose name you want to change.**

3. **Click the Rename Classification link.**

   Look for the link under Common Tasks on the left side of the window. The Rename Classification dialog box appears.

4. **Enter a name in the New Name text box and click OK.**

   Back in the Categories window, the button that you clicked in Step 2 has a new name. Classification assignments throughout your account registers have new names as well.

Deleting a category or subcategory

When you no longer need a category or subcategory, you can delete it. However, be careful, because if you delete a category or subcategory to which transactions are assigned, the transactions lose their category assignments. In other words, you end up with transactions to which no category is assigned — and that defeats one of the primary reasons people use Money, which is to categorize their spending and income to find out where the money came from and where it went.

Try to delete a category or subcategory to which categories are assigned, and you see the Delete Category dialog box. From this dialog box, you can assign transactions to a different category before you delete the category in question, but do you really want to do that? Suppose that some transactions belong in one category and others belong in another category. No, reviewing the transactions one at a time before you delete the category to which they are assigned is wiser. The section "Reassigning transactions to new categories," earlier in this chapter, explains how to review transactions as you change their category or subcategory assignments.

After you reassign the transactions whose category you want to delete, follow these steps to delete a category or subcategory:

1. **Press Ctrl+Shift+C or click the Banking tab, click the Account Tools button, and then choose Categories & Payees.**

2. **Click the Categories button in the window, if necessary, to see the list of categories and subcategories.**

   If you intend to delete a subcategory, you may need to open the View menu and choose Categories and their Subcategories to see subcategories.

3. **Scroll through the list, and select the category or subcategory that you want to delete.**

4. **Click the Delete button, or right-click and choose Delete from the shortcut menu.**

That's all she wrote — the category is gone from the Categories window. However, if you try to delete a category with subcategories underneath it, a dialog box warns you that deleting a category also deletes its subcategories. If you try to delete a category to which transactions are assigned, you see the Delete Category dialog box.

Whatever you do, don't cavalierly delete a category with subcategories. Investigate the matter first and find out whether you need the subcategories for tracking your finances.

Deleting a classification

After you delete a classification, all transactions throughout the registers that were assigned the classification are no longer assigned to it. Therefore, I suggest that you think twice before deleting a classification. Think twice and think hard. Going back through the registers and reassigning transactions to a classification that you deleted is hard work that you'll want to avoid.

Follow these steps to delete a classification that you no longer need:

Banking

1. **Press Ctrl+Shift+C or click the Banking tab, click the Account Tools button, and then choose Categories & Payees.**

2. **Select the classification that you want to delete.**

3. **Click the Delete Classification link.**

   You can find this link under Common Tasks on the left side of the window. A dialog box warns you of the drastic nature of what you are about to do.

4. Ignore the dialog box and click the Yes button to delete the classification.

Back in the Set Up Your Categories window, the classification link now has the generic name Classification 1 or Classification 2, and all class and subclass names have disappeared from the screen.

You can delete a class or subclass by right-clicking it and choosing Delete from the shortcut menu.

A fast way to remove deadwood categories

When you install Money on your computer, the program gives you a bunch of generic categories that you may or may not need. Very likely, you don't need many of them. To quickly remove them, you can use a special button called Remove Unused Categories. After you click this button, Money removes all categories and subcategories on the Categories list to which no transaction has been assigned.

Follow these steps to remove deadwood categories that take up space on the Categories list:

1. **Choose Tools⇨Settings.**

2. **In the Settings window, scroll to and click the Categories link. The Categories tab of the Options dialog box appears.**

3. **Make sure that the Ask Me Before Removing Each Category check box is selected.**

4. **Click the Remove Unused Categories button. A dialog box asks whether you want to remove a certain category.**

5. **Click the Yes or the No button.**

6. **Keep clicking the Yes or the No button until you ax all the deadwood categories and subcategories.**

Chapter 6

Reconciling or Balancing an Account

In This Chapter

▶ Finding out what reconciling is and how to do it in Money

▶ Reconciling a savings or checking account

▶ Recognizing and fixing reconciliation problems

▶ Forcing an account to balance

▶ Reconciling a credit card account

*U*ntil I started using Money, I never *reconciled,* or balanced, my checking or savings accounts, not to mention my credit cards. But Money makes balancing an account very easy indeed. No kidding — you can do it in four or five minutes.

This chapter explains what reconciling is, how to reconcile the transactions in your records with the bank's records, and what to do if you can't get an account to reconcile. Because reconciling a credit card account can be slightly tricky, you can find instructions in this chapter for reconciling credit card accounts as well as checking and savings accounts. *Bon voyage!*

How Reconciling Works

Reconciling is your opportunity to examine your records closely to make sure that they are accurate. When you reconcile an account, you compare your records to the bank's, fix any discrepancies you find, enter transactions that appear on the statement that you forgot to enter in the register, and click in the C (for Cleared) column next to each transaction that appears both in the register and on the bank statement.

In an account register, transactions that have cleared the bank — transactions that you have reconciled with the bank's records — show an R (for Reconciled) in the C (for Cleared) column, as shown in Figure 6-1. Here, you can see that some transactions have cleared the bank and some are still waiting to clear.

These transactions have cleared the bank.

Figure 6-1: An R appears in the C (for Cleared) column when a transaction has cleared the bank.

Account Register						
B of A Check						
Change register view						
All Transactions covering All Dates, Sorted by Date (Increasing)						
! Num	Date ▲	Payee	C	Payment	Deposit	Balance
2435	6/7/2004	Cal State Auto Insurance	R	191.00		6,742.27
ATM	6/7/2004	Withdrawal	R	100.00		6,642.27
ATM	6/8/2004	Withdrawal	R	200.00		6,442.27
2436	6/9/2004	James Lick PTA	R	110.89		6,331.38
2437	6/9/2004	Owen Barker Flyn		250.00		6,081.38
2438	6/11/2004	Susan Thackery		400.00		5,681.38
ATM	6/12/2004	Withdrawal	R	100.00		5,581.38
DEP	6/14/2004	Wilderness Express	R		6,000.00	11,581.38
	6/15/2004	Bank Of America Credit Card		1,299.54		10,281.84
	6/15/2004	Bank Of America	R	1,908.90		8,372.94
2439	6/15/2004	Homecomings Financial		244.17		8,128.77
2440	6/15/2004	Vector Marketing Corp.		107.42		8,021.35
ATM	6/15/2004	Withdrawal	R	200.00		7,821.35
	6/16/2004	Interest Earned	R		0.57	7,821.92
ATM	6/20/2004	Withdrawal		40.00		7,781.92
ATM	6/21/2004	Withdrawal		100.00		7,681.92
2441	6/23/2004	Lynn Oakley		210.00		7,471.92
2442	6/23/2004	SBC		39.24		7,432.68
2443	6/23/2004	PG & E		86.91		7,345.77
2444	6/23/2004	American Honda Financial Corp		180.66		7,165.11
☐ Show transaction forms						
New	Edit	Delete			Ending Balance: $5,717.37	

These have not been reconciled yet.

Balancing an Account

Balancing an account is a two-step business. First, you tell the program how much interest the account earned (if it earned any) and how much you had to pay the bank for checks, ATM withdrawals, and other services (if you had to pay anything). Then you move ahead to the Balance Account window, where you make your records jibe with the bank's and click off each transaction that appears both on your bank statement and in the register.

Before you begin comparing the register to the bank statement, lay the bank statement flat on your desk. And you may want to put checks in numerical order (if you intend to reconcile a checking account) and your ATM slips in date order (you *have* been saving your ATM slips, haven't you?). With a little luck, you can reconcile without having to glance at checks and ATM slips. But if something goes amiss, you may have to examine the paperwork closely.

What does *reconcile* mean, anyway?

In financial terms, *reconcile* means to compare one set of records to another for the sake of accuracy. When you reconcile an account in Money, you compare the transactions on the statement that the bank or brokerage house sent you to the transactions that you entered in the Money register.

If you find a discrepancy between your records and the bank's, you can be pretty sure that the error was made on your side. Not that it doesn't happen, but banks don't err very often when recording financial transactions. Yes, bank lines move too slowly and banks have been known to nickel-and-dime their customers with all kinds of petty charges, but banks are sticklers for accuracy. If you find a discrepancy between your records and the bank's, chances are the error was made on your side, not the bank's.

Telling Money which transactions cleared the bank

Open the register of the account that you want to reconcile, and follow these steps to tell Money to reconcile the account:

1. **Click the Balance This Account link.**

   You see a Balance dialog box like the one in Figure 6-2. This dialog box is where you enter information from the bank statement. The Starting Balance text box shows the amount of money in the account as of the last time you reconciled it (or the account's opening balance, if you recently opened the account).

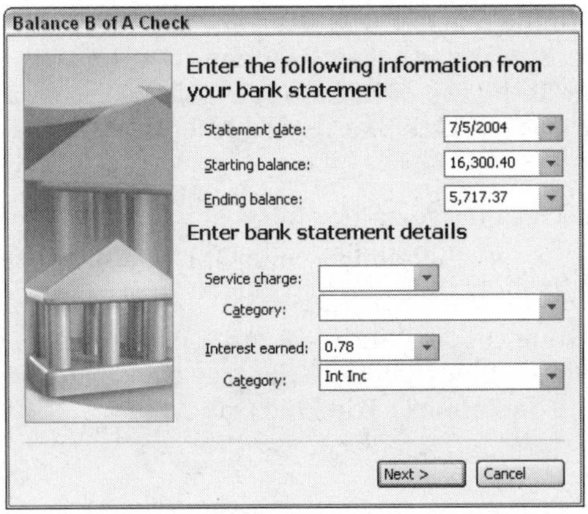

Figure 6-2:
The Balance dialog box, where you tell Money what the bank told you.

Balance B of A Check

Enter the following information from your bank statement

Statement date: 7/5/2004
Starting balance: 16,300.40
Ending balance: 5,717.37

Enter bank statement details

Service charge:
Category:
Interest earned: 0.78
Category: Int Inc

Next >   Cancel

2. **At the top of the Balance dialog box, enter information from your bank statement:**

   • **Statement date:** Enter the date listed on the bank statement.

   • **Starting balance:** If this number is incorrect, enter the starting balance from your bank statement. If you reconciled this account last month, the correct number is already listed.

   • **Ending balance:** Enter the closing balance from the bank statement.

3. **At the bottom of the Balance dialog box, enter any service charges or interest income that is listed on your bank statement:**

   • **Service charge:** If you have to pay a service charge, enter it in this text box. Banks are like mosquitoes: They like to bite. Banks do it by charging customers all sorts of miscellaneous fees. The fees appear on bank statements. You may get charged for ordering checks, calling for information, using an ATM, or sneezing too loudly. Scour the statement for evidence of service charges, and enter the sum of those charges in the Service Charge text box. For a category, choose Bank Charges: Service Charge or something similar. (For more on categorizing, turn to Chapter 5.)

   • **Interest earned:** If the account earned any interest, enter the amount and categorize the interest payment.

   Before you click the Next button to move ahead, compare what you entered in this dialog box to what is on your bank statement one last time. Entering numbers incorrectly in this dialog box is one of the primary reasons that people have trouble reconciling their bank accounts.

4. **Click the Next button to move ahead to the Balance Account window, as shown in Figure 6-3.**

   Only transactions in the register that have not been reconciled appear in the window. Deposits and other transactions that brought money into the account appear at the top of the window; following that are withdrawals and other transactions that record when money was taken out of the account.

   If you entered a service charge and/or interest payment in the Balance dialog box (in Step 3), the amounts already appear in the window, along with a check mark to show that they have been cleared.

   Many people think that reconciling accounts is easier when transactions are shown on one line rather than two. To show transactions on one line, open the View menu and choose Top Line Only.

Click here when a transaction also appears on the bank statement.

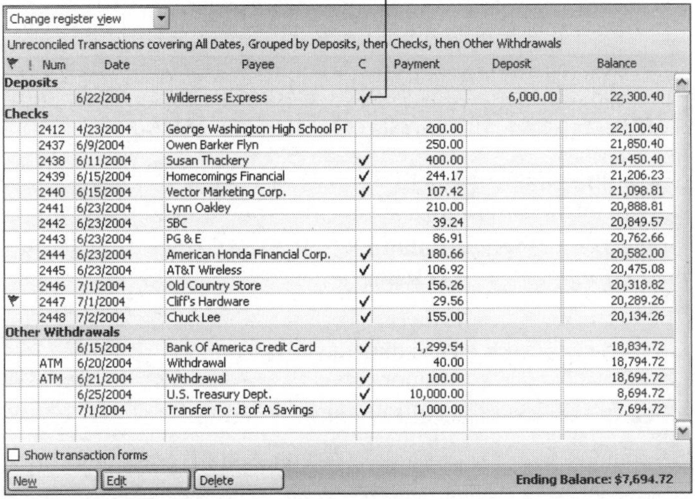

Figure 6-3:
Compare
transactions
in the
register to
transactions
on the bank
statement to
balance an
account.

	Num	Date	Payee	C	Payment	Deposit	Balance
Change register view ▼							
Unreconciled Transactions covering All Dates, Grouped by Deposits, then Checks, then Other Withdrawals							
Deposits							
		6/22/2004	Wilderness Express	✓		6,000.00	22,300.40
Checks							
	2412	4/23/2004	George Washington High School PT		200.00		22,100.40
	2437	6/9/2004	Owen Barker Flyn		250.00		21,850.40
	2438	6/11/2004	Susan Thackery	✓	400.00		21,450.40
	2439	6/15/2004	Homecomings Financial	✓	244.17		21,206.23
	2440	6/15/2004	Vector Marketing Corp.	✓	107.42		21,098.81
	2441	6/23/2004	Lynn Oakley		210.00		20,888.81
	2442	6/23/2004	SBC		39.24		20,849.57
	2443	6/23/2004	PG & E		86.91		20,762.66
	2444	6/23/2004	American Honda Financial Corp.	✓	180.66		20,582.00
	2445	6/23/2004	AT&T Wireless	✓	106.92		20,475.08
	2446	7/1/2004	Old Country Store		156.26		20,318.82
	2447	7/1/2004	Cliff's Hardware	✓	29.56		20,289.26
	2448	7/2/2004	Chuck Lee	✓	155.00		20,134.26
Other Withdrawals							
		6/15/2004	Bank Of America Credit Card	✓	1,299.54		18,834.72
	ATM	6/20/2004	Withdrawal		40.00		18,794.72
	ATM	6/21/2004	Withdrawal	✓	100.00		18,694.72
		6/25/2004	U.S. Treasury Dept.	✓	10,000.00		8,694.72
		7/1/2004	Transfer To : B of A Savings	✓	1,000.00		7,694.72

☐ Show transaction forms

New   Edit   Delete   **Ending Balance: $7,694.72**

5. **Examine your bank statement, and click the C column next to each transaction on the statement that also appears in the register.**

   The left side of the window lists the difference between the ending balance on your bank statement (you listed it in the previous dialog box) and the amount as tabulated by Money. When you click the C column in the register to clear transactions, this amount changes. Gradually, as the account is reconciled, the number approaches 0.00.

   To remove a check mark in the C column, click the column again. The next section in this chapter explains how you can fix mistakes in the register while you reconcile. The section after that offers strategies for recognizing and fixing reconciliation problems.

   If you have trouble finding a transaction in the register, open the Change Register View menu and choose Sort By⇨Sort by Date or Sort By⇨ Sort by Number. The Sort by Date command lists transactions in date order, and the Sort by Number command lists them in numerical order in the Num column.

6. **Click the Next button when the difference amount is 0.00 and you are satisfied that the account is reconciled correctly.**

   You can find the Next button in the lower-left corner of the window. A Balanced! screen appears and tells you that your account is balanced.

7. **Click the Finish button.**

   Back in the register, all those check marks in the Balance Account window turn to *R*s in the register. The transactions that you clicked off in the Balance Account window have cleared the bank and are reconciled with your records.

If the reconciling business makes you tired or if you find something better to do, click the Postpone button. Later, you can pick up where you left off by clicking the Balance This Account button in the Account window.

Fixing mistakes as you reconcile

Glancing at the bank statement, you discover that you made a mistake when you entered a transaction in a register — you entered the wrong amount or check number. Or perhaps you forgot to enter a transaction altogether. It happens. Cash withdrawals from ATMs, which usually are made on the spur of the moment, often fail to get recorded in account registers.

Follow these steps to fix a mistake in a transaction:

1. Click the transaction that needs correcting.

If you need to enter a brand-new transaction, go straight to Step 2.

2. Select the Show Transaction Forms check box.

As shown in Figure 6-4, a transaction form appears in the window. The form looks and works like the transaction forms that you know and love in account registers.

3. Fix the error or enter a new transaction:

- **Repair an error:** Click the Edit button, enter the correct amount, check number, date, or anything that needs correcting.

- **New transaction:** Click the New button, and enter the transaction.

4. Click the Enter button.

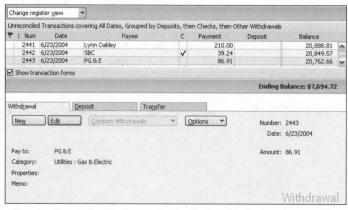

Figure 6-4:
Fixing an entry error in the Balance Account window.

Help! The Darn Thing Won't Reconcile!

Not being able to reconcile a bank account is frustrating. You pore over the bank statement. You examine checks and ATM slips. You gnash your teeth and pull your hair, but still the thing won't reconcile. No matter how hard you try, the Difference figure, which lists the difference between the cleared amount and the statement amount, cannot be brought to 0.00.

To help get you out of the jam you are in, Money offers techniques for recognizing and fixing reconciliation problems. And Money also has a gizmo called AutoReconcile (which gets its own section later in this chapter) that may be able to help you reconcile your bank account.

A checklist of things to do if you can't reconcile

If an account won't balance, a number of different things can be wrong. The following sections explain how to recognize and fix reconciliation problems.

A transaction wasn't entered

The primary reason that accounts don't reconcile is because a transaction that is listed on the bank statement has not been entered in the register. ATM withdrawals, for example, are easy to forget and often do not get entered in account registers.

Remedy: Look for a transaction on the bank statement that is equal to the Difference amount in the Balance Account window. For example, if the Difference amount is $35.20, chances are you forgot to record a $35.20 transaction in the register. Look for a $35.20 transaction on the bank statement and, if necessary, select the Show Transaction Forms check box to display a form and enter the transaction. Be sure to enter the date correctly. If the difference is $20.00, $40.00, or another round number, you probably forgot to enter an ATM withdrawal.

An amount in the register is incorrect

Another reason accounts don't reconcile is that amounts were entered incorrectly in the register. This problem is a sticky one and is hard to track down. Look for transposed numbers and numbers that were entered backward. For example, $32.41 and $34.21 look alike at a glance, but there is a difference of $1.80 between the numbers.

Here's an old accountant's trick: If the difference between what you have and what you should have is evenly divisible by 9, you probably transposed a number.

Remedy: Click the transaction, select the Show Transaction Forms check box, and change the amount on a transaction form.

A transaction was entered twice

Look for duplicate transactions in the register to make sure that no transaction was entered twice.

Remedy: Delete one of the transactions by right-clicking it and choosing Delete from the shortcut menu.

A check was entered as a deposit or vice versa

Making an error like this is easy. Fortunately, detecting it is easy, too.

Remedy: Clear your checks and withdrawals first; then clear your deposits. During this process, you'll notice whether a deposit, check, or withdrawal is missing. Click the transaction, and then select the Show Transaction Forms check box. On the transaction form, click the Options button, choose Change Transaction Type To, and choose Withdrawal or Deposit.

The Ending (statement) balance is incorrect

If you enter the Ending balance incorrectly in the Balance dialog box (refer to Figure 6-2), you cannot reconcile an account, no matter how hard you try.

Remedy: Return to the Balance dialog box (refer to Figure 6-2), and enter a correct Ending balance figure. To do so, click the Postpone button to return to the Accounts window, click the Balance This Account link, and then click the Next button. You see the Balance dialog box again, where you can enter a correct Ending balance this time. Click the Next button again to return to the Balance Account window.

A service charge or interest earned amount is incorrect

Besides entering the ending balance incorrectly, you may have entered an incorrect amount in the Service Charge or Interest Earned text box in the Balance dialog box (refer to Figure 6-2). Compare the interest and service charges on your statement to the ones in the Balance Account window to see whether an amount is incorrect.

Remedy: Click the service charge or interest entry in the Balance Account window, select the Show Transaction Forms check box, and enter a correct figure on the transaction form.

The bank statement wasn't flipped over

I'm embarrassed to admit it, but one or two times I wasn't able to reconcile an account because I forgot to turn over the bank statement and examine the transactions listed on the other side of the page — very stupid of me.

Remedy: Turn the page, note the transactions, and click to put a check mark next to them.

"AutoReconciling" an account

If all else fails, you can try using Money's AutoReconcile gizmo to find out why the account won't balance. This contraption scours the register for transactions that it thinks were entered incorrectly and gives you the chance to enter them correctly so that the account can be reconciled. Follow these steps to try the AutoReconcile feature:

1. **Click the Next button in the Account Register window.**

   Although the account isn't balanced, click the Next button as though it is in balance. You see the Balance dialog box, as shown in Figure 6-5.

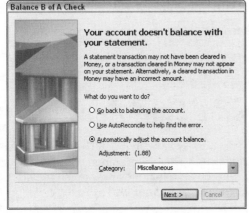

Figure 6-5: Forcing an account to balance.

2. **Select the second option button, Use AutoReconcile to Help Find the Error.**

   If you are in luck and Money can find the error, the Possible Error dialog box appears.

3. **Read the description of the error, and click the Yes or the No button to change the transaction in question or to let it stand.**

Forcing an account to balance

If, despite your detective work, you can't find the problem that keeps your account from balancing, you can force the account to balance. Forcing an account to balance means entering what accountants call an "adjustment transaction" — a fictitious transaction, a little white lie that makes the numbers add up. Don't tell anybody that I said so, but if the difference between what your statement says and what the Balance Account window says is just a few pennies, enter the adjustment transaction and spare yourself the headache of looking for the error. A few pennies here and there never hurt anybody.

The words *Account Adjustment* appear in the register on the Payee line when you force an adjustment transaction. Money gives you the chance to categorize the transaction on your own. After you have torn out your hair trying to discover why an account doesn't balance, follow these steps to force an adjustment transaction:

1. **Click the Next button in the Balance Account window.**

   Click the Next button even though the account has not been reconciled. The Balance dialog box appears (refer to Figure 6-5). It tells you that the account isn't in balance and asks what you want to do about it.

2. **Select the Automatically Adjust the Account Balance option button.**

3. **Choose a category from the Category drop-down menu.**

4. **Click OK.**

Reconciling a Credit Card Account

Reconciling a credit card account is done in much the same way as reconciling a checking or savings account. The only difference is in the Balance dialog box (refer to Figure 6-2), where you tell Money how much the statement says that you owe.

When you reconcile an account, you clear credits as well as charges made to your credit card. Before you start reconciling, make sure that the credits the card issuer owes you have been entered in the credit card register.

Open the credit card account register and follow these steps to reconcile a credit card account:

1. **Click the Balance This Credit Card Account link.**

   The link is located under Common Tasks on the left side of the window.

You see the Balance dialog box, as shown in Figure 6-6. The amount you owed as of the last time you reconciled the account appears in the Total Amount You Owed Last Month text box.

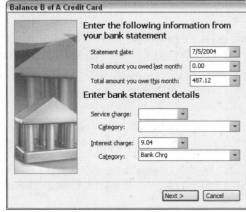

Figure 6-6:
When you reconcile a credit card account, start by telling Money how much you owe this month.

2. **At the top of the Balance dialog box, enter information from your credit card statement:**

   • **Statement date:** Enter the date listed on your credit card statement.

   • **Total amount you owed last month:** You don't have to enter anything here. This text box lists how much you owed as of the last time you reconciled your credit card account.

   • **Total amount you owe this month**: Enter the amount that the statement says you owe, including all service and interest charges. In other words, enter the amount that you would have to pay if you were to pay off all debt you owe to the credit card issuer.

3. **At the bottom of the Balance dialog box, enter any service charges or interest charges listed on your credit card statement:**

   • **Service charge:** Some credit card issuers charge an annual fee. Record an annual fee in the Service Charge box. For a category and subcategory, choose Bank Charges: Service Charge or a similar category.

   • **Interest charge:** Enter the amount that you must pay in interest to service the credit card debt. Most people don't pay off their credit card debt each month, so they have to pay an interest charge. And if you take out cash advances, you have to pay interest for those, too. For a category and subcategory, choose Bank Charges: Interest Paid or a similar category.

4. **Click the Next button.**

   You see the Balance Account window, which lists all transactions in the register that have not been reconciled. If the Balance Account window looks familiar, that is because it looks and works exactly like the Balance Account window for reconciling savings and checking accounts (refer to Figure 6-3).

5. **Examine your credit card statement, and click the C column next to each transaction on the statement that also appears in the register.**

   To change the amount of a charge or credit, click it in the register and then select the Show Transaction Forms check box. That step opens the transaction form so that you can alter the transaction.

6. **Click the Next button after the account is reconciled.**

   A Balanced! screen appears.

7. **Click the Pay Bill Later button to pay the credit card bill later on, or click the Pay Bill Now button to open the Edit Transaction dialog box and record a bill payment.**

Guess what? You can use the same techniques for fixing reconciliation problems in credit card accounts as you can in checking and savings accounts. See the section "Help! The Darn Thing Won't Reconcile!" earlier in this chapter, to find out how to fix reconciliation problems, or use the AutoReconcile gizmo to find and fix errors.

Chapter 7

Writing and Printing Checks

. . . .

In This Chapter

▶ Identifying the different kinds of checks

▶ Ordering checks

▶ Preparing your printer to print checks

▶ Recording checks that you intend to print in registers

▶ Printing practice checks

▶ Printing a full or partial sheet of checks

▶ Reprinting checks that didn't print correctly

. . . .

*N*ot every Money user needs to print checks. Checks are expensive, for one thing. If you order checks from Microsoft Money Checks by Deluxe, the official vendor, an order of 500 checks can cost between $70 and $89.50, depending on the kind of check you order, whereas most banks charge about $15 for that many checks. So, printing checks with Money costs five to six times as much as writing checks by hand.

But printing checks with Money can save time, especially if you run a small business and print lots of checks. When you write a check by hand, you have to write it twice (once when you record it in a register and once when you scribble on the paper check). When you print a check with Money, you enter it only once when you record it in a register. The printer handles the rest. What's more, you can *batch-print* checks (print a dozen or so at one time). Small-business owners who print lots of payroll checks or monthly expense checks ought to seriously consider printing checks with Money.

Another advantage of printing checks is being able to itemize the payment on the check stub. As long as you print checks on wallet-size or voucher checks (I explain those shortly), you can itemize the payment by splitting it (as I discuss in Chapter 4). The split-transaction information appears on the check stub.

But the best reason for printing checks has nothing to do with saving time or itemizing — it has to do with appearances. Printed checks are more professional looking. They make a good impression on creditors and clients. A printed check says "I mean business," whereas a handwritten check with spidery lettering says "Thank you, kind sir or madam, for honoring my little check." Everyone who works in a profession where appearances count — supermodels, for example — ought to print checks.

This chapter explains everything you need to know about printing checks — from choosing the right type of checks to ordering checks, telling your printer how to print checks, and adjusting checks that don't print correctly. You also discover how to record checks in a register, print a full sheet or a partial sheet of checks, and print addresses on checks. By the way, if you came to this chapter to find out how to record a check in a register, you came to the wrong place. You should be in Chapter 4.

Deciding What Kind of Check to Order

Your first decision is what kind of check to order. Checks are printed on sheets and loaded into your printer like sheets of paper. As shown in Figure 7-1, the choices are wallet-size, standard business, or voucher checks. Checks and check envelopes are available in standard as well as European sizes. Most companies that make checks offer the opportunity to print company logos on checks and customize the checks in other ways. Table 7-1 compares and contrasts the three types of checks that you can print with Money. These prices come from Microsoft Money Checks by Deluxe, the Microsoft affiliate that offers checks for use with Money.

Figure 7-1:
The three types of checks: wallet-size (left), standard business (middle), and voucher (right).

Table 7-1		Checks for Use with Money		
Name	*Size*	*Checks per Sheet*	*Cost per 500/ Cost per Check**	*Description*
Wallet-size	2.83" x 8.5"	3 checks	$70/14¢	The smallest check. It includes a 2.5" stub for tracking expenses. This check is for individuals, not businesses.
Standard	3.5" x 8.5"	3 checks	$75/15¢	The largest check. It does not include a stub, although you can list tax-deductible expenses on the Memo line. For small businesses.
Voucher	3.5" x 8.5"	1 check	$89.50/18¢	Includes ample room — two-thirds of a page — for listing expenses. For small businesses that need to itemize checks in detail.

* Prices listed here are from Microsoft Money Checks by Deluxe, are for standard-color checks, and are current as of July 2004. Premier-color checks, which come in a variety of colors, cost more. You can buy checks in sets of 250, 500, 1,000, or 2,000. Third-party vendors offer different prices for checks.

Ordering the Checks

Besides ordering from Microsoft Money Checks by Deluxe, you can order checks from third-party vendors. Table 7-2 lists vendors whose checks are compatible with Money. Checks are available in many different colors and designs, so shop around. Perhaps you can find checks in soft lilac, paprika, icy periwinkle, and the other chichi colors whose names grace clothing catalogues.

Table 7-2	Vendors Offering Checks for Use with Money	
Company	*Phone*	*Internet Address*
Best Checks	800-521-9619	www.bestchecks.com
Compuchecks	800-356-5581	www.compuchecks.com
EiPrinting	800-245-5775	www.checksforless.com
Microsoft Money Checks by Deluxe	800-432-1285	www.microsoftchecks.com
PC Checks & Supplies	800-322-5317	www.checkstomorrow.com

After you know how many checks you want and in what size you want them, your next step is to contact a company that sells checks. Do that by calling the company or visiting its Web site (refer to Table 7-2). I recommend calling the company, because the friendly human on the other side of the phone connection can likely answer all your questions.

When you order checks, you will be asked for the following information, most of which appears on the face of a check:

✔ Your name, address, and phone number.

✔ Your bank's name and the city, state, and zip code in which it is located.

✔ Your bank's *fractional number,* also known as the *routing number.* When you deposit a check, you usually list the first four numbers of the fractional number on the deposit slip. Here's an example of a fractional, or routing, number: 66–55/4321.

✔ Your checking account number.

✔ The starting check number. See the sidebar, "Choosing a starting number for the checks," to discover the ins and outs of choosing a number.

✔ The size of the checks — wallet-size, standard business, or voucher.

✔ Whether you have a laser printer, an ink-jet printer, or an antique continuous-feed printer.

Choosing a starting number for the checks

When you choose a starting number for the checks, be sure to choose one that won't conflict with the numbers on checks that you write by hand. Bankers frown and even call you on the telephone when you write two checks with the same check number. And if you try to record two checks with the same number in a checking register, a dialog box asks whether you really want to do that.

Writing checks with duplicate numbers is a faux pas, but it is easy to do when you write checks and print checks from the same account. Your spouse, checkbook in hand, could be on a shopping spree while you are at home printing checks. Or, you could write a few checks from the checkbook, forget to record them in Money, and then print checks with the same numbers without thinking about it.

To keep from writing checks with duplicate numbers, choose a starting number for the printed checks that is far, far removed from the check numbers in your checkbook. For example, if the checks in your checkbook are numbered 601 to 650, choose 1501 as the starting check number for printed checks. That way, you can't write and print checks with duplicate numbers.

Printing the checks that you order isn't absolutely necessary. You can always tear one off and write it by hand when you buy a pillbox hat at the thrift store or pay for a pizza.

Getting Your Printer Ready to Print Checks

To print checks, Money and your computer have to be on speaking terms. They have to understand each other and be able to work together. And your printer has to know which kind of check to print — a wallet-size check, standard business check, or voucher check.

Very likely, Money and your printer have already been introduced. When you install Money, the program gets information about your printer from the Windows operating system. You probably don't have to tinker with the printer settings, but you do need to tell the printer what kind of check to print.

Follow these steps to open the Check Setup dialog box and tell your printer everything it needs to know to print checks, including which font to use:

1. **Choose File⇨Print Setup⇨Check Setup.**

   You see the Check Setup dialog box, as shown in Figure 7-2.

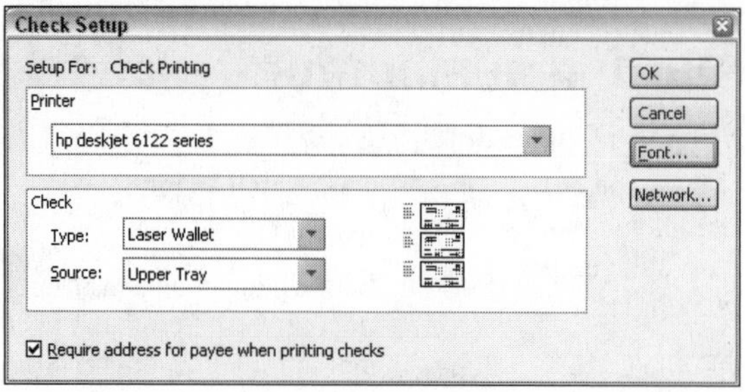

Figure 7-2:
Telling
Money
about your
printer and
the style of
check that
you intend
to print.

Check Setup

Setup For: Check Printing

Printer

hp deskjet 6122 series

Check

Type: Laser Wallet
Source: Upper Tray

OK
Cancel
Font...
Network...

☑ Require address for payee when printing checks

2. **In the Printer drop-down list, select which printer to print the checks with, if necessary.**

   More than one printer appears in the drop-down list if you or someone else has set up a second or third printer to work with your computer. Select the printer from which you will print the checks.

3. **Click the down arrow on the Type drop-down list, and select which style of check you will print.**

   Select an option from the top of the list if you have a laser printer. Choices for continuous-feed printers, also known as pinwheel printers, appear at the bottom of the list. (If you migrated to Money from Quicken, additional choices appear in the Type drop-down list for printing on Quicken check forms. For more details, see Chapter 22.)

4. **If necessary, click the down arrow on the Source drop-down list and select the tray through which you will feed checks to the printer.**

   Don't bother with the Source drop-down list if your printer has only one tray.

5. **Click the Font button, and choose a font for printing your checks, if you want.**

   A *font* is a typeface design. Unless you choose otherwise, checks are printed in Courier New font in 12-point type. But you can choose a more stylish font or different type size in the Check Printing Font dialog box. Click OK when you're done.

6. **Select the Require Address for Payee When Printing Checks check box if you want payee addresses to appear on your checks.**

   As long as an address is on file for a person or business to which you write a check, the address appears on the check — that is, it appears if you select this check box. As Chapter 11 explains, Money gets addresses from the Set Up Your Payees window. If you ordered window envelopes along with checks, you can print addresses on the checks, insert the checks in window envelopes, and save yourself the trouble of having to address envelopes. (Later in this chapter, the sidebar "Including addresses on checks" explains how to enter a payee's address.)

7. **If your computer is connected to a network and you intend to print checks on a network printer, click the Network button and select the printer in the Connect to Printer dialog box.**

8. **Click OK to close the Check Setup dialog box.**

Recording Checks That You Intend to Print

Recording a check that you intend to print is not very different from recording a handwritten check. The only difference is that you select Print This Transaction from the Number drop-down list on the Withdrawal form rather than enter a check number, as Figure 7-3 shows.

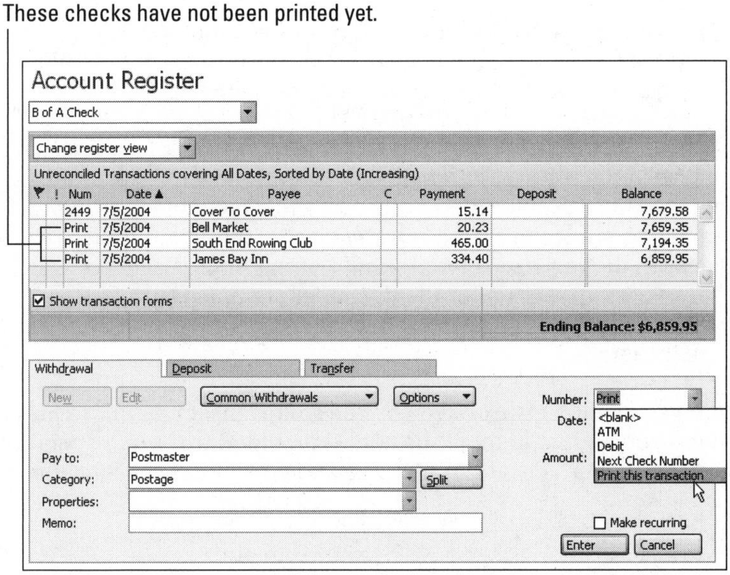

These checks have not been printed yet.

Figure 7-3: Select Print This Transaction from the Number drop-down list to record a check that you want to print.

Chapter 4 explains everything you need or care to know about recording a check, but here are the raw details:

1. **Open the checking account register from which you want to write the check.**

2. **Click the New button.**

3. **From the Number drop-down list, choose Print This Transaction.**

4. **Enter the date that you want to appear on the check in the Date text box.**

5. **Enter the name of the person or business that you are paying in the Pay To text box.**

    If you have paid this person or party before, you can enter the payee's name by typing the first couple of letters and pressing Tab.

6. **Enter the amount of the check in the Amount text box.**

7. **Describe the transaction by selecting a category and subcategory.**

8. **If you want, enter a word or two in the Memo box.**

    The words that you type in the Memo box appear on the printed check.

9. **Click the Enter button (or press Enter).**

    The Print Address dialog box appears.

10. **If you want to record an address along with the check, fill out the Print Address dialog box and click OK.**

    If you prefer not to see the Print Address dialog box each time you record a check that will be printed, select the Don't Show Me This Again check box in the Print Address dialog box.

"When does the check get numbered?" you may ask. The check number is entered in the register automatically after the check is printed. Until the check number is entered, the word Print appears in the Num column of the register, as shown in Figure 7-3. Meanwhile, the To Do notice tells you that checks in the register need printing. On the Home Page, the words Print checks also appear under the Reminders notice. (Turn to Chapter 2 to see how to make the Reminders notice appear on the Home Page if it doesn't appear there.)

When you split a check payment, the split-transaction information appears on the voucher, or stub, of the check, provided that you're printing on wallet-size or voucher checks. (Wallet-size and voucher checks include a stub.)

Testing to See Whether Checks Print Correctly

Practice makes perfect. The following pages explain how to print a practice check and make adjustments, if necessary, to the way checks are printed.

Printing a practice check

After you've recorded a check to print, `Print Checks` appears in the Reminders notice on the Home Page and under "To Do" on the checking register page (refer to Figure 7-3). You're ready to go.

Before you print your first check, however, print a practice check. Insert a thin, transparent piece of paper into the printer. After you're done experimenting, you can lay the sheet of paper over a sheet of real checks and hold both sheets to the light to see whether the text landed in the right places.

Follow these steps to do a test run and see whether your printer handles checks correctly:

1. **Open the checking register, if it is not already open.**

2. **Click the words `Print Checks` under the To Do notice, or choose File⇨Print Checks.**

   You see the Print Checks dialog box, as shown in Figure 7-4. For now, don't worry about the confusing options in this dialog box. You're interested only in the Print Test button.

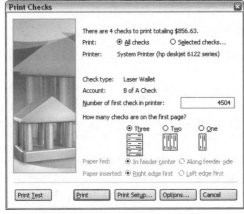

Figure 7-4: Click the Print Test button to make sure that the printer handles checks correctly.

3. **Click the Print Test button.**

4. **Click the Cancel button to close the Print Checks dialog box.**

   Money prints a check with a bunch of *X*s on it and the words `This is a VOID check`. How does it look? If all is well, you don't need to read the next part of this chapter. It explains how to realign checks so that they print correctly.

As I explain in the section "Printing partial sheets of checks," later in this chapter, to print a partial sheet of checks, you have to load the partial sheet into your printer as if you were loading an envelope. If you want to test how partial sheets print, follow the instructions here, but click the Two or the One option button in the Print Checks dialog box before running the test. Then tear off a practice check or two (or cut off part of the practice piece of paper that you're using), load the partial sheet into your printer, and click the Print Test button.

Making adjustments to the text alignment

So, everything is slightly out of whack on your check? You can do something about that if you're using a laser printer. Visit the Print Checks tab in the Options dialog box and change the vertical and horizontal alignment settings. (If you're using a dot-matrix printer, you can fix the problem the old-fashioned way — by adjusting the sprockets on the printer.)

Take note of roughly how far out of position the text is, and then do the following to realign the text so that it falls correctly on your checks:

1. **Click the words** Print Checks **under the To Do notice at the left of the register, or choose File⇨Print Checks to see the Print Checks dialog box.**

2. **Click the Options button.**

   As shown in Figure 7-5, you see the Print Checks tab in the Options dialog box.

   At the bottom of the tab are four text boxes for changing the horizontal (side-to-side) and vertical (up-and-down) alignment of text on sheets with all three checks and on partial sheets. The horizontal boxes move the text left or right on the check. The vertical boxes move it up or down.

3. **Enter a number or numbers in the text boxes.**

   Enter a **1** to move text by a sixteenth of an inch, enter a **2** to move it by an eighth (two-sixteenths) of an inch — you get the idea.

   To move text side to side, click in one of the horizontal text boxes and enter a positive number to move the text toward the right or a negative number to move it toward the left.

   To move text up or down, click one of the vertical text boxes and enter a positive number to move the text down or a negative number to move it up.

4. **Click OK when you're done.**

   You return to the Print Checks dialog box.

5. **Click the Print Test button.**

Adjust text on full sheets.   Adjust text on partial sheets.

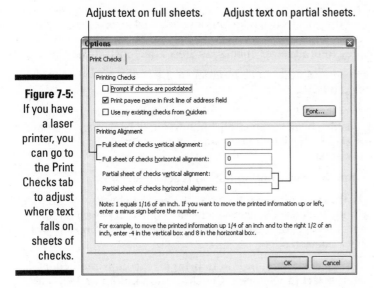

Figure 7-5:
If you have
a laser
printer, you
can go to
the Print
Checks tab
to adjust
where text
falls on
sheets of
checks.

I hope the check prints correctly this time. If it doesn't, return to the Options dialog box and keep trying. As the prelate said to the layman, "Persistence and perseverance made a bishop of his reverence."

Printing Your Checks

The moment of truth has now arrived. You're ready to print the checks. If only printing money were this easy. These pages explain how to print a full sheet of checks and a partial sheet of checks. If you use wallet-size or standard business checks, the day will arrive when you have only one or two checks left on a sheet. Printing a partial sheet of checks requires a little extra work.

Printing a full sheet of checks

Take note of the number on the first check that you intend to print on, load a sheet or two of checks into the printer, and then follow these steps to print on a full sheet of checks:

1. **Open the checking register and click the words** `Print Checks` **under the To Do notice, or choose File⇨Print Checks.**

   You see the Print Checks dialog box (refer to Figure 7-4).

The top of the dialog box lists how many checks need printing and how large of a bite the checks will take out of your checking account. If the bite is too large, you can always click the Selected Checks option button and tell Money to print fewer checks, as Step 4 demonstrates.

2. **If necessary, enter a new check number in the Number of First Check in Printer text box.**

   The Number of First Check in Printer text box lists what Money thinks is the next available check number. This number may be wrong. Compare it to the first paper check that you loaded in the printer, and enter a new number, if necessary.

3. **Make sure that the Three option button is selected.**

   The Three button tells Money to print a full sheet of checks. By the way, if you're printing voucher checks, which come one to a page, you don't see the Three, the Two, or the One option button because you can print only one check on each page.

4. **Select the All Checks option button to print all the unprinted checks in the register; select the Selected Checks option button to pick and choose which ones to print.**

   Selecting the Selected Checks option button opens the Select Checks dialog box, as shown in Figure 7-6. To begin with, all the checks are selected, or highlighted, in the dialog box.

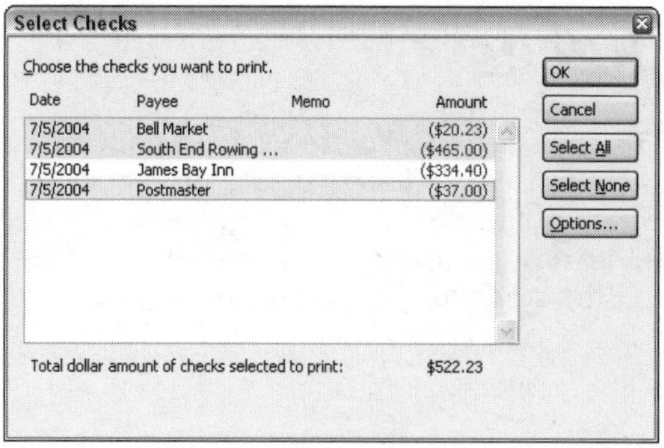

Figure 7-6:
Select
which
checks to
print in this
dialog box.

Select Checks				
Choose the checks you want to print.				OK
Date	Payee	Memo	Amount	Cancel
7/5/2004	Bell Market		($20.23)	Select All
7/5/2004	South End Rowing ...		($465.00)	Select None
7/5/2004	James Bay Inn		($334.40)	Options...
7/5/2004	Postmaster		($37.00)	
Total dollar amount of checks selected to print:			$522.23	

To print a handful of these checks, either click the Select None button to deselect all the checks and then click each one that you want to print, or simply click each check that you *don't* want to print to take its highlighting away and deselect it. Click OK to return to the Print Checks dialog box.

5. **Click the Print button.**

   The Print Checks dialog box shows you the numbers of the checks that "*should* have printed correctly." Examine the checks to see whether they printed correctly.

6. **Click the Finish button if the checks printed correctly; click the Reprint button if they didn't print correctly.**

   If, woe is me, you have to click the Reprint button, then turn a couple of pages ahead to the section "Whoops! My Checks Didn't Print Correctly." That section explains what to do next.

Compare the numbers on the printed checks to the numbers in the Num column of the checking register to make sure that the numbers match. And be sure to sign the checks.

Printing partial sheets of checks

Wallet-size and standard business checks come three to a sheet, which makes printing them slightly problematic. After you print the first check on the sheet, for example, you are left with two blank checks. It would be a shame to waste them, so Money offers options in the Print Checks dialog box for printing on partial sheets.

To take advantage of the partial sheet options, you may have to get out the dreary manual that came with your printer. You have to find out how your printer accepts envelopes. Find out whether envelopes are fed to your printer in the center or along the side of the paper tray. Find out as well whether envelopes are fed right-edge first or left-edge first. The settings that apply to envelopes also apply to partial sheets of checks.

The previous section in this chapter explains how to print a full sheet of checks. The only difference between printing a full sheet and a partial sheet of checks is that you have to do three important things in the Print Checks dialog box (refer to Figure 7-4):

✔ Select the Two or the One option button to tell Money how many checks remain on the sheet.

✔ Select the Paper Fed option button that describes where on the paper tray the paper is fed to your printer (in the center or on the side).

✔ Select the Paper Inserted option button that describes which edge of the paper is inserted in your printer first (right or left edge).

Including addresses on checks

As long as an address is on file for a person or business to which you write a check, the address appears on the check — that is, it appears on the check as long as you select the Require Address for Payee When Printing Checks check box in the Check Setup dialog box. To get to that dialog box, choose File⇨ Print Setup⇨Check Setup.

Money gets addresses from the Payees Details window, as Chapter 11 explains. To enter or view a payee's address, follow these steps:

1. **Click the Banking tab to go to the Account List window.**

2. **Click the Account Tools button and choose Categories & Payees.**

3. **Click the Payees link.**

   You can find this link on the left side of the window. You see a list of payees after you click it.

4. **Either double-click the payee for whom you want to enter an address or select the payee and then click the Go to Payee button.**

   You see the Payees window, with boxes for entering addresses and other kinds of juicy information.

5. **Enter an address.**

   The address that you enter appears on printed checks if you instruct your printer to print addresses.

As someone who writes and edits computer books, I shouldn't admit it, but I have a phobia of printers. I hate them. Rather than dicker with the options for printing on partial sheets of paper, I always try to print checks three at a time. That way, I never have to agonize over the partial sheet options. You can easily find a second or third bill that needs paying and use it to round out a check sheet. And if I can't find a second or third bill, I simply tear out the extra checks, carry them to a store, and use them like handwritten checks.

Whoops! My Checks Didn't Print Correctly

If you had to click the Reprint button in the Print Checks dialog box because your checks didn't print correctly, all is not lost; Money gives you a second chance to print the checks. When you click the Reprint button, the Select Checks to Reprint dialog box, shown in Figure 7-7, appears. From this dialog box, you tell Money which checks to reprint.

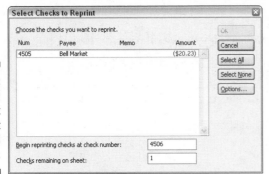

Figure 7-7:
Reprinting
checks that
didn't get
printed
correctly.

Before you reprint wallet-size or standard business checks that didn't print correctly, you may have to load the sheets sideways in your printer. Wallet-size and standard business checks come three to a sheet, so you have to load them sideways when only one or two checks remain on a sheet. The previous section of this chapter explains all the issues that pertain to printing on partial sheets.

After you click the Reprint button in the Print Checks dialog box, follow these steps to reprint checks:

1. **Select the checks that need reprinting.**

   As you click each check in the Select Checks to Reprint dialog box, the check is highlighted.

2. **Make sure that the number in the Begin Reprinting Checks at Check Number text box is correct, and if it isn't, enter a new number.**

   This number should match the number on the first check that is loaded in your printer.

3. **Make sure that the number in the Checks Remaining on Sheet text box is correct, and enter a new number if necessary.**

4. **Click OK.**

   The Print Checks dialog box appears.

5. **Examine your checks and click the Finish button if the checks printed correctly; click the Reprint button if they didn't print correctly.**

   As someone who has had to battle with printers, I hope that you don't have to click the Reprint button again.

Be sure to write VOID on checks that didn't print correctly and file them away with your canceled checks. That way, you have a record of what happened to them.

And on the subject of checks that didn't print correctly, what happens if you have to reprint three or four checks and you end up with a three- or four-check gap in the checking register? If you're a stickler for keeping good records, enter a transaction in the checking register for each check that needed reprinting and void it. In other words, if you botched check 1501 and reprinted it, enter a check transaction, give it number 1501, right-click the transaction, and choose Mark As⇨Void from the shortcut menu (or press Ctrl+V).

Part III
Money for Investors

"Oh yeah, he's got a lot of money. When he tries to check his balance online, he gets a computer message saying there's 'Insufficient Memory' to complete the task."

In this part . . .

1 hope you didn't come to this part of the book expecting to find 10-, 20-, and 50-dollar bills folded between the pages. No, you have to get money for your investments elsewhere. After you do, though, you can use Microsoft Money to track your investments.

In Part III, you discover how to record the sale and purchase of mutual fund shares, stock shares, and bonds. You find out how to set up an electronic investment portfolio and examine the investments in the portfolio in different ways. You also discover how to update your investment and research investments online.

Chapter 8

Setting Up Investment Accounts

· ·

In This Chapter

▶ Understanding the Portfolio Manager window

▶ Setting up an account to track your investments

▶ Setting up an account to track your retirement investments

▶ Setting up an account to track employee stock options

▶ Creating a Watch account so that you can monitor securities

· ·

*I*n order to track investments, you have to set up accounts. Investment accounts work much like checking or savings accounts. Each transaction — each sale or purchase of stock shares, for example — is recorded in an account register. After you set up investment accounts, you can start recording your investment activity.

In this chapter, you find out how to set up an electronic investment portfolio with investment accounts, accounts for tracking your retirement investments, and accounts for tracking employee stock options. You also find out how to create a Watch account — an account for monitoring stocks, bonds, and mutual funds you don't own but are curious about.

Your Own Electronic Portfolio Manager

A *portfolio* is a collection of investments. After you set up investment and retirement accounts, you can click the Investing tab and see an electronic version of your portfolio, as shown Figure 8-1. After you have set up a portfolio like this one, recording investment transactions is easy. What's more, the Portfolio Manager window is an excellent place to start analyzing your investments.

Names of accounts

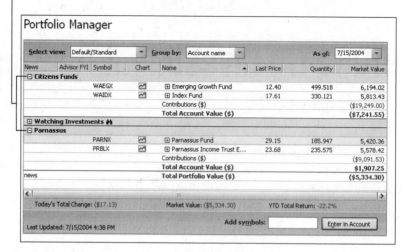

Figure 8-1:
The
Portfolio
Manager
window
offers many
different
ways of
examining
your
investments.

Looking at Figure 8-1, you can see the following:

- **The names of the investment or retirement accounts:** Create one investment or retirement account for each statement you receive from a brokerage house, each financial institution you buy certificates of deposit (CDs) or other investments from, and each retirement plan that you participate in. Doing so makes keeping the records easier because you can enter data in the account straight from the brokerage or bank statement and even reconcile your account from the statements that you receive in the mail.

- **The names of the individual investments:** After you set up the accounts, you list the names of the securities — the stocks, bonds, mutual funds, CDs, and so on — that belong in the account. You can then record purchases, sales, share reinvestments, capital gains, dividends, stock splits, and so on in the register.

- **The grand total value of your investments:** This sum appears at the bottom of the window, along with year-to-date return of your investments.

When your portfolio is complete, you can see at a glance the market value and price of each investment. By changing views, you can see how your investments perform, how they have changed in value, and how you have allocated them, among other things. By clicking the Analyze My Portfolio link, you can analyze investments in various ways.

Before you can analyze your investments, you need to set up an investment account, retirement account, or Employee Stock Option account:

- ✔ Create a retirement account to track as 401(k)s, Keoghs, SEPs (Simplified Employee Pensions), and IRAs.

- ✔ Create an investment account to track stocks, bonds, securities, annuities, treasury bills, precious metals, real estate investment trusts (REITs), and unit trusts.

- ✔ Create an Employee Stock Option account to track stock options you receive from the company you work for.

Setting Up an Investment Account for Tracking Securities

The first step in tracking investments is to create a new account for each institution or brokerage house that you trade securities with. After you set up an investment account, you describe the securities that the account tracks. Spread the last statement from the bank or brokerage house across your desk and follow these steps to set up an investment account:

> Investing

1. **Click the Investing tab to go the Investing window.**

   After you set up your investment account, its name appears in this window.

2. **Click the Portfolio Manager link.**

   You see the Portfolio Manager window (refer to Figure 8-1). You can also reach this window by clicking the Investment Tools button and choosing Portfolio Manager on the drop-down menu.

3. **Click the Work with Accounts link, and on the submenu that appears, choose Add an Account.**

   The Choose an Account Type window, shown in Figure 8-2, appears. This is your starting point for creating investment, retirement, and employee stock option accounts.

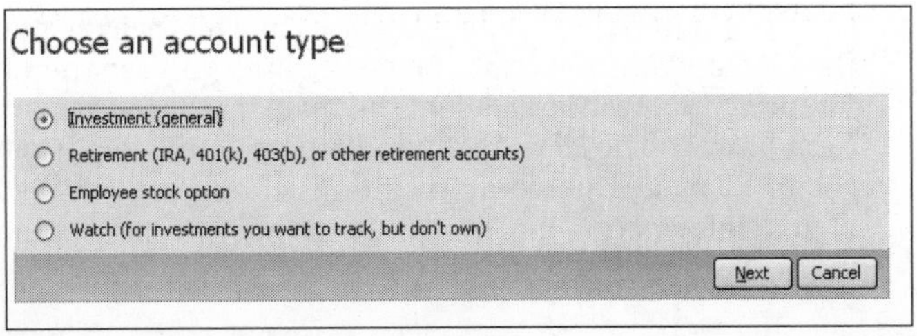

Figure 8-2:
Setting
up an
investment
account.

Choose an account type

- ⊙ Investment (general)
- ○ Retirement (IRA, 401(k), 403(b), or other retirement accounts)
- ○ Employee stock option
- ○ Watch (for investments you want to track, but don't own)

[Next] [Cancel]

4. **Click the Investment option button, and then click the Next button.**

The Select a Bank or Brokerage window appears. In this window, you tell Money the name of the brokerage house or bank where you maintain your investment account.

Money has made arrangements with some brokerages and banks so that you can enter investment-account transactions into your Money investment-account register by downloading transaction records from your bank or brokerage house. This spares you the trouble of entering the transactions yourself. If your bank or broker has this arrangement with Money and you want to be able to download transactions from your bank or broker, you may be asked to supply the password that your broker or bank gave you in the steps that follow.

Regardless of whether Money has made an arrangement with your broker or bank to download transactions, everyone can update the price of securities online as long as the securities are publicly traded (Chapter 9 explains how to update security prices online). In other words, everyone who uses Money can update the price of the securities they own by downloading the prices from the Internet. The only advantage of being able to download directly from a broker or bank is that you don't have to enter buy or sell transactions yourself.

5. **Click the first letter in the name of your brokerage house or bank, select the name from the list, and click the Next button.**

What happens next depends on whether your brokerage house or bank is on the list and whether you can download transaction information straight from your bank or broker:

• **Name on the list, can download directly:** You see the Do You Already Have Sign In Information? window. Collect the User ID and password information you received from your bank or broker, and click the Yes button. In the windows that follow, you enter your User ID and password, and you tell Money what kind of data you want to download from your bank or broker.

If you don't have your User ID, password, or other necessary information, click the Finish Later button. After you obtain this information, go to the Account List window and click the Provide Sign-in Information link next to your investment account's name. Then fill in the windows to provide the information.

• **Name on the list, settings change needed:** You see the Settings Change Required for Online Updates at This Bank window. Click the Update Your Accounts Manually link. You see the Choose an Account Type window. Select the Investment option, and click the Next button. The New Account dialog box appears. Go to Step 6. (Later, to make the required settings changes, click the Provide Sign-in Information link next to your investment account's name in the Account List window.)

- **Name on the list, can't download directly:** You see the Choose an Account Type window. Select the Investment option, and click the Next button. The New Account dialog box appears. Go to Step 6.

- **Name not on the list:** Click the My Bank or Brokerage Isn't Listed link (it is located at the bottom of the window). The Choose an Account Type window appears. Select the Investment option, and click the Next button. The New Account dialog box appears. Go to Step 6.

6. **Enter a name for your account in the New Account dialog box, and click Next.**

   The name you enter will appear in the Account List window after you finish setting up the account. For convenience' sake, you may want to enter the name of the brokerage house where you keep the account.

7. **Click the Taxable or Tax Deferred or Tax Free option button to specify whether the money you track in this account is tax deferred; then click the Next button.**

   Tax deferred means that you don't have to pay income tax on the money that the account generates until you begin withdrawing it at retirement age. Probably the option to select is Taxable. Most tax-deferred accounts are retirement accounts (how to set up a retirement account is explained shortly).

8. **In the next dialog box, click the No, I'll Do This Later option button; then click Next.**

   Chapter 9 explains how to record security transactions in an Investment account.

9. **In the next dialog box, enter the approximate value of the account in the Investments text box, as shown in Figure 8-3.**

   Don't worry about being accurate with these figures — they are used for planning and estimating purposes only. You can get the estimated value of the investments in the account from your most recent statement. Don't include cash in the estimated value of the account if you keep cash as well as investments in the account. If you recently sold a security or made a deposit in the account, it likely includes a bit of cash.

10. **Enter the amount of money in the account in the Cash text box.**

    As the dialog box explains, you can estimate the amount of money in the cash account if you want. The amounts you enter in the dialog box are used for planning purposes.

11. **Click the Finish button.**

    You go to the Account List window.

Know the tax status of your investment

Don't confuse tax-deferred income with tax-exempt income. Income from a tax-deferred account is not taxed until you start withdrawing money from the account. In contrast, you never have to pay any tax on tax-exempt income. Most retirement accounts are tax deferred, not tax exempt.

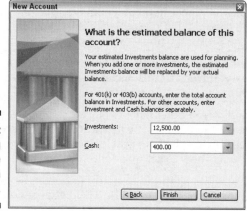

Figure 8-3:
Estimating
the balance
of an
account.

After you set up the investment account, right-click its name in the Account List window and choose See Account Settings on the shortcut menu. You go to the Change Account Settings window, where you can enter the name and phone number of your broker. You need that information in case you need to call your broker. You can enter other useful information in the window as well.

Setting Up a Retirement Account for Tracking Retirement Savings and Investments

Create a retirement account to track stocks, mutual funds, and bonds you own as part of a 401(k) plan, Keogh plan, SEP (Simplified Employee Pension) fund, or IRA. Income from these accounts is tax deferred. You don't have to pay taxes on the income until you start withdrawing it at retirement age.

Follow these steps to set up an account for tracking the tax-deferred investments you have made for your retirement:

1. **Click the Investing tab to go the Investing window.**

   The name of your retirement account will appear in this window after you have set it up.

2. **Click the Portfolio Manager link.**

   You see the Portfolio Manager window (refer to Figure 8-1). You can also get to this window by clicking the Investment Tools button and choosing Portfolio Manager on the drop-down menu.

3. **Click the Work with Accounts link, and on the submenu, choose Add an Account.**

   The Choose an Account Type window appears (refer to Figure 8-2).

4. **Select the Retirement option button, and then click the Next button.**

   You see the Select a Bank or Brokerage window, where you tell Money the name of the brokerage house or bank where you maintain your investment account.

   Some brokerages and banks permit you to enter retirement-account transactions into your Money investment account register by downloading transaction records from your bank or brokerage house. Downloading the transactions spares you from having to enter the transactions yourself. If your bank or broker can download transactions to your computer, you may be asked to supply the password that your broker or bank gave you in the steps that follow.

   Regardless of whether your broker or bank permits you to download transactions, you can update the price of securities online as long as the securities are publicly traded (Chapter 9 explains how to update security prices online). Everyone who uses Money can update the price of the securities they own from the Internet.

5. **Click the first letter in the name of your brokerage house or bank, select the name from the list, and click the Next button.**

   What you do next depends on whether your brokerage house or bank is on the list and whether you can download transaction information straight from your bank or broker:

   • **Name on the list, can download directly:** You see the Do You Already Have Sign In Information? window. Collect the User ID and password information you received from your bank or broker, and click the Yes option button. In the windows that follow, you enter your User ID and password, and you tell Money what kind of data you want to download from your bank or broker.

If you don't have your User ID, password, or other necessary information, click the Finish Later button. After you obtain this information, go to the Account List window and click the Provide Sign-in Information link next to your investment account's name. Then fill in the windows to provide the information.

- **Name on the list, settings change needed:** You see the Settings Change Required for Online Updates at This Bank window. Click the Update Your Accounts Manually link. You see the Choose an Account Type window. Select the Investment option, and click the Next button. The New Account dialog box appears. Go to Step 6. (Later, to make the required settings changes, click the Provide Sign-in Information link next to your investment account's name in the Account List window.)

- **Name on the list, can't download directly:** You see the Choose an Account Type window. Select the Investment option, and click the Next button. The New Account dialog box appears. Go to Step 6.

- **Name not on the list:** Click the My Bank or Brokerage Isn't Listed link (it is located at the bottom of the window). The Choose an Account Type window appears. Select the Investment option, and click the Next button. The New Account dialog box appears. Go to Step 6.

6. **Enter a name for the account in the New Account dialog box, and click the Next button.**

   The name you enter will appear in the Account List window after you finish setting up the account.

7. **In the next dialog box, shown in Figure 8-4, select the type of retirement account you want to set up; then click the Next button.**

   If you aren't sure what kind of retirement account you are dealing with, refer to the glossary or click an account type and read its description in the dialog box.

8. **In the next dialog box, select the No, I'll Do This Later option button; then click Next.**

   In Chapter 9, I show you how to record transactions in the account.

9. **In the next dialog box, enter the approximate value of the account in the Investments text box.**

   These figures are used strictly for planning and estimating purposes. You will be given ample opportunities to enter the exact numbers later on. Check your recent statement for the estimated value of the investments in the account. If cash is in the account at present, don't include it in the estimated value.

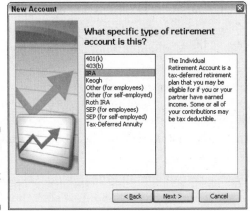

Figure 8-4:
Setting up a
retirement
account.

10. **Enter the amount of money in the account in the Cash text box.**

    As the dialog box explains, you can estimate the amount of money in the cash account if you want.

11. **Click the Finish button.**

    You go to the Account List window, where the name of your new account appears in all its glorious splendor.

Right-click the name of your new retirement account in the Account List window and choose See Account Settings on the shortcut menu. You go to the Change Account Settings window, where you can enter your broker's name and phone number and other useful information.

Setting Up an Account to Track Employee Stock Options

If you are fortunate enough to work for a company that offers stock options to its employees, you can track the value of that stock with Money. To do so, create an investment account (see the section "Setting Up an Investment Account for Tracking Securities," earlier in this chapter), fill in the New Account dialog boxes, and choose Employee Stock Option when you are asked what kind of account you want to set up (refer to Figure 8-3).

Follow these steps to set up an account for tracking your employee stock options:

Investing

1. **Click the Investing tab to go to the Investing window.**

   The name of the employee stock option account will appear in this window after you have set it up.

2. **Click the Portfolio Manager link.**

   The Portfolio Manager window appears (refer to Figure 8-1). You can also see this window by clicking the Investment Tools button and choosing Portfolio Manager on the drop-down menu.

3. **Click the Work with Accounts link, and on the submenu, choose Add an Account.**

   The Choose an Account Type window appears (refer to Figure 8-2).

4. **Click the Employee Stock option button, and then click the Next button.**

   The Choose Level of Detail window appears, as shown in Figure 8-5.

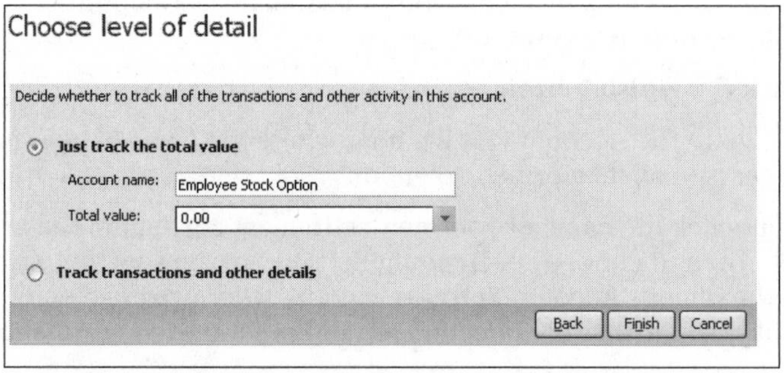

Figure 8-5:
Setting
up an
employee
stock option
account.

Choose level of detail

Decide whether to track all of the transactions and other activity in this account.

⊙ **Just track the total value**

   Account name: Employee Stock Option

   Total value: 0.00

○ **Track transactions and other details**

   [Back] [Finish] [Cancel]

5. **Enter a name for the account in the Account Name text box.**

6. **Select the first option button (and enter the value of your company stock in the Total Value text box) if you simply want to track the stock's value; select the second option and click the Next button if you want to update the stock's value online or you want to track the value of the stock as you are vested in company shares.**

   In most companies, employees are not given stock outright. Instead, they become vested in the stock they own over a period of time.

   If you selected the first option, Just Track the Total Value, click the Finish button.

   If you selected the second option, you see the first of several New Employee Stock Option dialog boxes. Proceed to Step 7.

7. **Speed-read the dialog box, which tells you how you will suffer through the next seven steps, and click the Next button.**

8. **Enter the stock's name, and click the Next button.**

9. **Enter the stock's ticker symbol if you know it, and click the Next button.**

   If stock in your company is not publicly traded — if your company is held in private hands — the stock doesn't have a ticker symbol yet. You can click the Find Symbol button to look up the ticker symbols of publicly traded companies.

10. **Click the Online Quotes button if you suspect that the stock has been split recently; then click the Next button.**

   A stock split is when shares are divided to lower the share price. In a 2-for-1 split, for example, stock owners are given twice as much stock, but the value of individual shares is half of what it was before the split.

11. **Enter the strike date, how many shares you were granted, and the strike price in the following dialog box; then click the Next button.**

   The *strike price* is the closing price of the stock on the day it was given to you. Be sure to correctly enter the date you were given the stock. Money needs that date to correctly calculate the value of the stock over time.

12. **Enter a name for the stock grant in the Grant Name text box, and click the Next button.**

13. **Describe how your company's plan calls for you to be vested in the stock you were granted, and click the Next button.**

   As shown in Figure 8-6, the next New Employee Stock Option dialog box is for telling Money how quickly or slowly the stock grant becomes yours. Typically, employees do not receive their stock option grant all at once. They earn it over a period of months or years.

14. **Click the Finish button.**

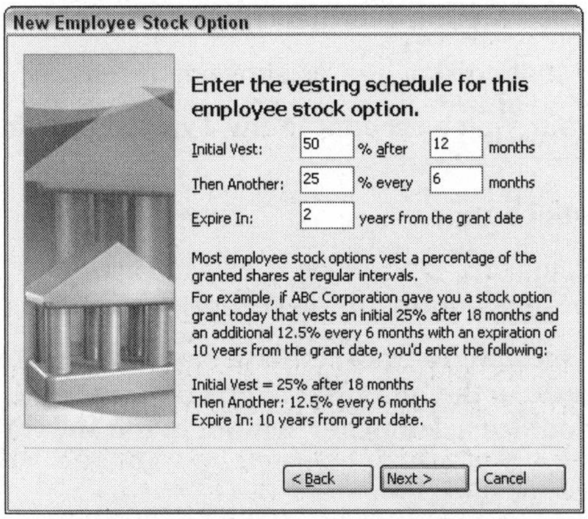

Figure 8-6:
Fill in the text boxes to describe how, slowly but surely, you become the owner of the stocks your company has granted you.

New Employee Stock Option

Enter the vesting schedule for this employee stock option.

Initial Vest: 50 % after 12 months

Then Another: 25 % every 6 months

Expire In: 2 years from the grant date

Most employee stock options vest a percentage of the granted shares at regular intervals.

For example, if ABC Corporation gave you a stock option grant today that vests an initial 25% after 18 months and an additional 12.5% every 6 months with an expiration of 10 years from the grant date, you'd enter the following:

Initial Vest = 25% after 18 months
Then Another: 12.5% every 6 months
Expire In: 10 years from grant date.

[< Back] [Next >] [Cancel]

When you finish setting up the account, open its register. If you set up a vesting schedule for the ownership of your stocks, you see future entries that describe when you will receive new stock as part of the vesture. As you update the stock price in this register, it shows the stock's value.

Tracking Securities You Don't Own in a Watch Account

Suppose that you want to track a stock, mutual fund, money market fund, or other security that you don't own, perhaps to decide whether you want to buy it later. You can do that by placing the security in the Watch account, a special investment account that Money maintains for monitoring security prices.

Getting price quotes for securities on the Watch List is a great way to find out from day to day or week to week how a potential investment performs. You can even download index prices in order to compare and contrast the securities you own to the performance of an index.

Follow these steps to create a Watch account:

1. **Click the Investing tab to go the Investing window.**

2. **Click the Portfolio Manager link.**

   The Portfolio Manager window appears (refer to Figure 8-1).

3. **Click the Work with Accounts link, and on the submenu, choose Add an Account.**

   The Choose an Account Type window appears (refer to Figure 8-2).

4. **Click the Watch option button, and then click the Next button.**

   You see the New Account dialog box, as shown in Figure 8-7.

5. **Enter a name for your Watch account in the Type a Name for the Account text box.**

6. **Click the Find Symbol button.**

   The Find Symbol dialog box appears, as shown in Figure 8-8. Use this dialog box to find ticker symbols for the securities you want to track.

7. **For each security you want to track, enter a stock, mutual fund, option, or index name in the Enter Name text box; click the Find button; and then double-click a ticker symbol in the Make Your Selection box.**

   The ticker symbols appear in the New Account dialog box.

Figure 8-7:
Listing
securities in
a Watch
account.

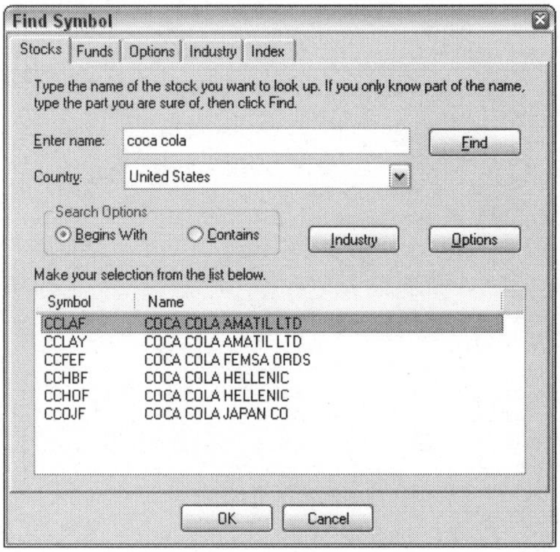

Figure 8-8:
Finding a
ticker
symbol.

8. **If you want, you can play being an investor by selecting the Make This Account a Model Portfolio check box and making choices in the bottom half of the New Account dialog box.**

   Select an option button to pretend you own 100 shares of each security, pretend you own $10,000 worth of each security, or pretend that all the securities you are tracking are worth $10,000 (or another sum you enter in the Total Value text box).

9. **Click the Finish button.**

   Your Watch account appears alongside all your other accounts in the Account List window. In the Portfolio Manager window, the Watch account is marked with a binoculars icon.

Next time you download quotes from the Internet, you can see how the investment has performed. Right-click a security and choose See Price History to see a chart that shows how well or poorly the security has performed in the past six months.

Chapter 9

Tracking the Value of Your Investments

After you have gone to the significant trouble of setting up investment and retirement accounts, the next step is to describe the investments you own and track in your investment and retirement accounts. For each investment, you tell Money what kind of security you are dealing with — stocks, mutual funds, or bonds. You enter the value of the security and, if possible, a ticker symbol so that Money can track the security's value by downloading prices from the Internet.

This chapter explains how to trade — how to buy, sell, redeem, disburse, and record interest payments from — different types of securities. When you are finished reading this chapter, you will know precisely how much your investments are worth. You will be able to track the value of your investments and determine whether they are performing like nags or thoroughbreds.

Recording Payments to (and Disbursements from) Brokers

It might seem kind of odd, but when you write a check to your broker so he or she can purchase securities on your behalf, or when you make a contribution to a retirement account, you record the check in Money as a transfer from your checking account to the account where you track your investments or retirement savings.

Follow these steps to record the check that you write to your brokerage house or bank for securities purchases:

1. **Open the checking account register where you will record the check.**

2. **In the transaction form, click the Transfer tab.**

   Figure 9-1 shows the transfer tab.

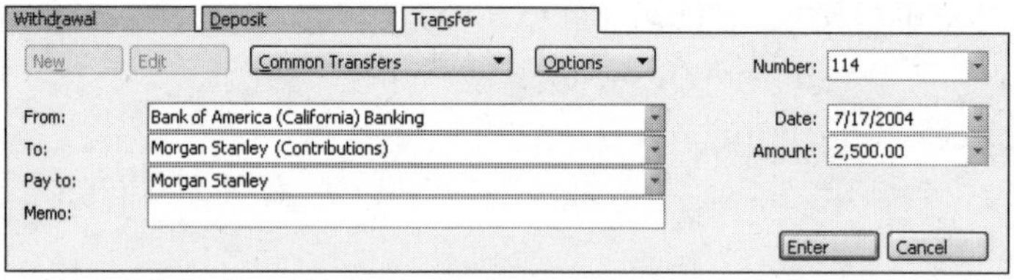

Figure 9-1:
Record payments to brokers as money transfers.

3. **Enter the check number in the Number text box.**

4. **In the To drop-down list, select the name of the investment or retirement account where you track investment activity.**

5. **In the Pay To text box, enter the name of your broker or bank.**

   Enter the name that you will write on the check.

6. **Enter the amount you are contributing to your investment or retirement account in the Amount text box.**

7. **Click the Enter button.**

On the other side, in the investment or retirement account, the transfer is recorded as a deposit. The cash in investment and retirement accounts is used to pay for stock, bond, and other security purchases. To open the investment or retirement account register where you transferred the money, right-click the transfer transaction in your checking account register and choose Go to Account on the shortcut menu.

Similarly, when you sell or collect interest on a security, the proceeds are recorded as a cash deposit in the Deposit column of the investment or retirement account. Suppose that you decide to take money out of an investment or retirement account. When the check comes from your broker and you deposit it in your bank account, record the transaction as a transfer from your investment or retirement account to your checking or savings account. For example, if you sell a stock and the proceeds come to $400, record the transaction as a $400 transfer from your investment account to the checking account where you deposit the $400.

You can click the Cash Transactions link (found on the left side of the register window) when you are looking at an investment or retirement account to see money transfers in and out of the account.

Describing the Securities in Investment and Retirement Accounts

After you set up an investment or retirement account, you must describe each security in the account. *Securities* are the stocks, mutual funds, certificates, bonds, or other financial instruments that the account tracks. Gather the paperwork and follow these steps to describe each security that you own. If you just purchased more shares of a security that you already own and have already described in an investment or retirement account, skip ahead to "Handling Stocks" or "Handling Mutual Funds," later in this chapter.

Investing

1. **Click the Investing tab.**

2. **In the Investing window, click the Portfolio Manager link.**

   You land in the Portfolio Manager window. You can also get there by clicking the Investing Tools button and choosing Portfolio Manager from the drop-down menu.

3. **Click the Work with Investments link, and then choose Add an Investment from the drop-down menu.**

   You'll find the Work with Investments link under Common Tasks on the left side of the window. After you click it, the first New Investment dialog box appears.

4. **Click the down arrow to open the Account drop-down list, and select the investment or retirement account where you track the security; then click Next.**

   If no account names appear on the menu, you haven't set up an investment or retirement account yet. Chapter 8 explains how to do that.

5. In the Investment Name text box, enter the name of the security; then click Next.

The name you enter will appear in the Portfolio Manager window. You see the Create New Investment dialog box, as shown on the left side of Figure 9-2. In this dialog box, you tell Money what kind of investment you are tracking.

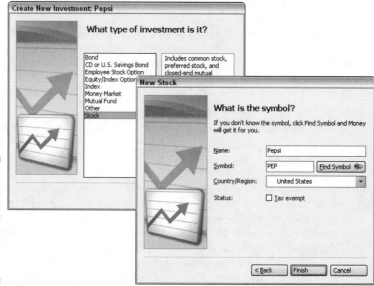

Figure 9-2:
Telling Money what kind of security you are dealing with.

6. Select an option to describe the security, and then click Next.

Which dialog box you see next depends on which option you selected. In Figure 9-2, I chose the Stock option, so the New Stock dialog box asks me to enter the stock's symbol. Except for bonds, Money asks for your investment's ticker symbol. In the case of a bond, you will be asked for the coupon rate, interest paid, maturity date, and call date.

7. Fill in the New dialog box or boxes, and then click the Finish button.

If you can, enter the ticker symbol for your mutual fund, stock, or money market fund in the New dialog box (refer to Figure 9-2). That way, you can update the security's price from the Internet and save a lot of time that you would otherwise spend updating the price by hand. If you don't know the ticker symbol, look for it carefully on your brokerage statement — you can usually find it there. Or try clicking the Find Symbol button to go on the Internet and find the ticker symbol.

If you are describing a bond you purchased, see "Recording the purchase of a bond," later in this chapter.

8. **In the following dialog box, shown in Figure 9-3, enter in the Quantity text box the number of shares of the security you own.**

   For mutual funds and stocks, enter the number of shares you own. If you are describing the purchase of a single CD or bond, enter **1**. For investments such as precious metals, enter the number of ounces or other unit of measurement.

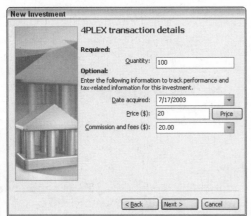

Figure 9-3:
Describing
the value of
the security.

   You don't have to fill in the bottom three boxes in the New Investment dialog box, but do so if you intend to track the value of the security from the day you purchased it. By filling in these boxes, you can analyze your investment to see how it has grown or shrunk over time.

9. **In the Date Acquired text box, enter the date that you purchased the security; enter the price per unit you paid in the Price text box; enter the commission if you paid one in the Commission and Fees text box; click the Next button.**

   When you enter share prices of stock, you can enter fractions. For example, you can enter 50½ or 10¼. Money converts the entry to a decimal.

   If you are tracking the value of this security from the day you bought it, be sure to enter data about your original purchase. You may have bought more shares in the security or sold shares in the past. The value may have gone up or down. You need to enter purchase data as of the date you entered back in the Date Acquired text box.

10. **Click the Finish button if you are done entering securities in the account; if other securities you track in this account need listing, click the Yes button, click the Next button, and return to Step 3.**

    Do not pass Go and do not collect $200.

Repeat Steps 5 through 9 for each security that your investment or retirement account tracks.

Handling Stocks

Keeping track of stocks is probably the most problematic task you will ever undertake with Money. Merely figuring out what a short sell is, not to mention a margin buy and a stock split, is hard enough to begin with. How can you record these strange events in an investment or retirement account register?

Read on, friend, and you can discover how to record everything from stock sales and purchases to short sells and margin buys.

Recording a purchase of stocks

When you purchase shares of a stock, follow these steps to record the purchase:

Investing

1. **Click the Investing tab.**

2. **In the Investing window, click the Investing Tools button and choose Portfolio Manager from the drop-down menu.**

   The Portfolio Manager window appears.

3. **Click the Work with Investments link, and then choose Record a Buy from the drop-down menu.**

   You see the Edit Transaction dialog box.

4. **On the Inv. Account drop-down menu, select the name of the investment or retirement account where you want to record the purchase of the stock shares.**

5. **In the Date text box, enter the date you purchased the stocks.**

   Be sure to enter the date correctly. Money needs this date to calculate the stock's value over time.

6. **In the Investment drop-down menu, click the arrow and select the stock from the drop-down list.**

   If this is the first time you have purchased shares of this stock, you see the Create New Investment dialog box (refer to Figure 9-2). The section "Describing the Securities in Investment and Retirement Accounts," earlier in this chapter, explains how to handle the Create New Investment dialog boxes.

7. **Select Buy from the Activity drop-down list.**

   New text boxes — Activity, Transfer From, Quantity, Price, Commission, and Total — appear for describing the stock purchase, as shown in Figure 9-4.

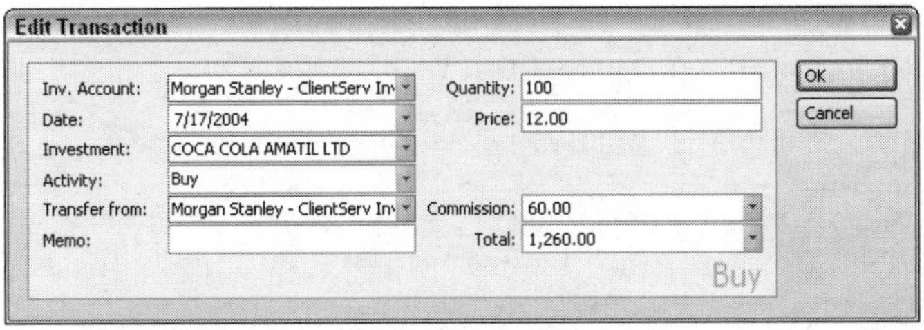

Figure 9-4:
Describing
the pur-
chase of
stocks.

Edit Transaction		
Inv. Account:	Morgan Stanley - ClientServ Inv	Quantity: 100
Date:	7/17/2004	Price: 12.00
Investment:	COCA COLA AMATIL LTD	
Activity:	Buy	
Transfer from:	Morgan Stanley - ClientServ Inv	Commission: 60.00
Memo:		Total: 1,260.00

OK   Cancel   Buy

8. **In the Quantity text box, enter the number of stock shares that you purchased.**

   When you enter share prices of stock, you can enter fractions. For example, you can enter 50½ or 10¼. Money converts the entry to a decimal.

9. **In the Price text box, enter the price per share of the stock.**

10. **In the Commission text box, enter the commission (if you paid one).**

    The amount in the Total text box should now equal the total purchase price for the stock that is listed on your statement. If the amount isn't correct, review your statement and enter the correct quantity, price, and commission.

11. **Click OK.**

    The purchase of the stock is entered in your account register.

Recording the sale of stocks

Except for the problem of lots, recording the sales of stocks is pretty simple. A *lot* is a group of securities purchased at the same time for the same price (and also a nephew of Abraham whose wife got turned into a saltshaker, but that's another story). Suppose that you buy 10 shares of Burger Heaven at $10 per share in January, and then buy 10 more shares of the same company at $20 per share in February. In March, you sell 15 shares. How many shares you sell from the $10 lot and the $20 lot is important in determining how much profit you make and how much you have to pay in capital gains taxes. Fortunately, Money can help you decide which shares to sell.

TIP

To see which stock lots you have purchased, click the name of the stock in the Portfolio Manager window. You see a miniregister with recently made transactions, as shown in Figure 9-5. Click the More Investment Data button in the miniregister, and choose View Lots from the pop-up menu. As shown in Figure 9-5, the View Lots dialog box shows you which lots you purchased and how much you paid for the stock in each lot.

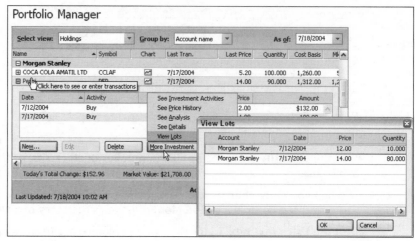

Figure 9-5:
Finding out
whether you
purchased
stock in lots.

Follow these steps to record the sale of stock shares:

1. **Click the Investing tab and, in the Investing window, click the Portfolio Manager link.**

   You land in the Portfolio Manager window.

2. **If necessary, click the name of the account where you track the stock you want to sell.**

   To see the name of stocks and other investments in an account, you click the account's name, unless the investment names are already displayed, in which case you don't have to click an account name.

3. **Click the name of the stock you sold.**

   A miniregister showing recently completed transactions appears.

4. **Click the Work with Investments link, and then click Record a Sell on the submenu.**

   As shown in Figure 9-6, the Edit Transaction dialog box appears. Because you selected the stock you are selling in Step 3, the correct Inv. Account, Investment Name, and Activity options are already selected. However, if you want, you can bypass Steps 2 and 3 by clicking the Work with Investments link and choosing Record a Sell on the submenu. You see the Edit Transaction dialog box straightaway, but you have to choose an Inv. Account and Investment Name in the dialog box.

5. **In the Quantity text box, enter the number of shares that you sold; enter the price per share in the Price text box.**

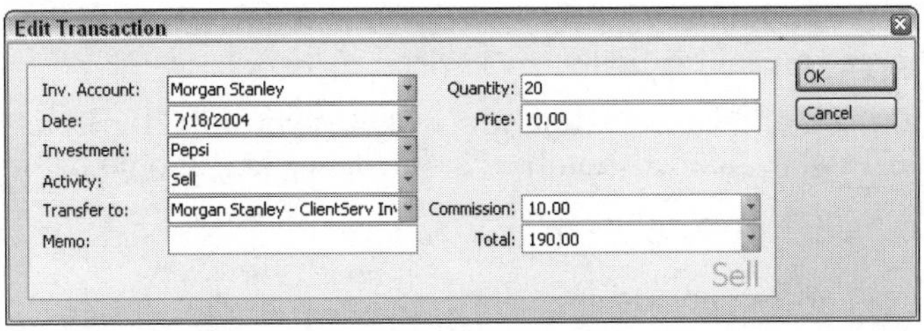

Figure 9-6:
Selling a
stock.

6. **If a commission was charged on the sale, enter the amount of the commission in the Commission text box.**

   Money enters the total amount of the sale in the Total text box. If the figure is incorrect, double-check the Quantity and Price text boxes to make sure that you entered the numbers correctly.

7. **Click OK.**

   An Advisor FYI Alerts message box informs you whether you need to pay capital gains taxes or the sale resulted in a capital loss. The proceeds from the sale are deposited in your investment or retirement account. See "Recording Payments to (and Disbursements from) Brokers," earlier in this chapter, to find out how to handle profits from a sale of stock in your account registers.

That's all there is to it — unless you purchased the shares in different lots. In that case, you see the What Shares Should I Use? dialog box after you click OK. Unless you tell it otherwise, Money assumes that you want to sell the shares in the lot that you purchased first. To do that, simply click the Finish button. But if you want to sell shares from different lots, follow these steps to tell Money which shares you want to sell:

1. **Click the first option, Let Me Specify Which Shares to Sell or Transfer, and then click the Next button.**

   You see the Allocate Lots dialog box.

   In this dialog box, you can select shares yourself from the lots, as the following steps demonstrate; you can click the Maximum Gain button to sell lots and pay the most capital gains taxes; or you can click the Minimum Gain button to sell lots to minimize your capital gains.

2. **In the top of the dialog box, click one of the lots from which you sold shares.**

3. **Enter the number of shares you sold from the lot in the Enter Shares to Allocate from Lot Above text box.**

4. **Select another lot and repeat Steps 2 and 3 to tell Money how many shares you sold from it.**

   After you're done declaring which shares you sold, the Total Selected and Total to Allocate numbers in the dialog box should be the same.

5. **Click the Finish button.**

Be sure to notify your broker of which shares you want to sell. If you forget to do that, your broker may assume that you want to sell shares beginning with the first lot you purchased. Chapter 14 explains how to investigate the capital gains tax you have to pay on the sale of a security.

If you incorrectly allocated shares from different lots you purchased, right-click an investment name and choose Reallocate Lots from the shortcut menu.

Recording and reinvesting dividends from stocks

Most stocks pay dividends, which means that you have to record dividends as they arrive. And some stocks, rather than pay dividends in cash, give share-holders the opportunity to buy more shares with their dividends as part of a DRIP (dividend reinvestment program). The advantage of reinvesting a dividend is that you often don't have to pay a broker's commission to purchase the new stock.

To record a dividend or the reinvestment of a dividend, start from the Portfolio Manager window and click the name of the stock that paid a dividend. Then, in the miniregister, click the New button. You see the Edit Transaction dialog box. Select Dividend or Reinvest Dividend from the Activity drop-down list and do one of the following:

- ✔ **Recording a dividend:** In the Total text box, enter the amount of the dividend. Make sure the correct account name appears in the Transfer To drop-down list. For a category, choose Investment Income: Dividends. Click OK when you're done.

- ✔ **Recording a dividend reinvestment:** Enter the number of shares you purchased with the dividend in the Quantity text box, the price per share in the Price text box, and any commission in the Commission text box. Make sure that the total in the Total text box is correct before you click the OK button.

Recording stock splits, short sells, margin purchases, and other esoterica

The stock market, it seems, has a hundred different ways to trade stock, handle stock sales, and handle stock purchases. I suspect that the brokers like it that way because it makes them appear indispensable. Fortunately, you can use Money to record certain kinds of oddball stock trades and sales.

Stock splits

Occasionally, stock shares are split to lower the price of individual shares and make them more attractive to investors. In a 2-for-1 split, for example, investors are given twice as much stock, but the value of individual stocks is half what it was before, so the owner of 100 shares worth $2,000 now owns 200 shares worth the same amount, $2,000.

Follow these steps to record a stock split:

1. **Starting from the Portfolio Manager window, click the Record a Special Activity link and then choose Record a Split from the submenu.**

   You see the Split Shares dialog box.

2. **Click the Investment down arrow and select the stock that was split from the drop-down list.**

3. **Enter the date that the stock was split in the Date text box.**

4. **In the Split the Shares text boxes, enter the ratio of new stocks to old ones.**

   For example, in a 2-for-1 split, enter **2** in the first box and **1** in the second box.

5. **Click OK.**

   In the Portfolio Manager window, Money calculates and enters the number of shares you own. The total value of those shares, however, remains the same.

Short sells

A *short sell* is when you believe that a stock will fall in price and you attempt to profit by borrowing shares from a broker, selling them at a high price, and then buying shares when the price drops and using those low-priced shares to replace the ones you borrowed.

Suppose, for example, that you think that ABC Corporation's shares will fall below their current price of $20 a share. You borrow ten shares from your broker and sell those shares for $200. When the price drops to $15 a share, you buy ten shares on your own, pay $150 for them, and give the broker back his or her ten shares. By selling the shares that didn't belong to you first (for $200) and buying them later (for $150), you earn a $50 profit. Of course, if the stock rises in price, you end up paying the broker back out of your own pocket, not from the proceeds of the sale.

To record a short sell, fill in the Edit Transaction dialog box as you normally would, but select Short Sell from the Activity drop-down list. Typically, brokers charge interest for the shares you borrow. The interest is reported in the Commission text box.

Return of capital

A *return of capital* is a return of part of the price you paid for stock. Sometimes a return of capital is paid to investors in lieu of a dividend. You'll know when you have been paid a return of capital because your statement tells you so. To record a return of capital, select Return of Capital from the Activity drop-down list in the Edit Transaction dialog box. Enter the amount of the return in the Total text box and select the account where you will stash it from the Transfer To drop-down list.

Margin purchases

Brokers gladly lend money to buy stocks and bonds. Buying a stock or bond with money you borrowed from a broker is called *buying on the margin*.

To record stocks or a bond you purchased on the margin, record it as you would a buy, but select Other Expense from the Activity drop-down list. When you select Other Expense, a category box appears on the transaction form so that you can categorize the expense. Select an expense category from the category drop-down list to describe the interest you had to pay your broker for the loan.

Corporate mergers

When one corporation merges with another and the two swap stocks, you need to record how many shares are being issued for each share of the parent company and the share price that the parent company has to pay for each share of the company that it has swallowed.

When you own stock that is involved in a swap, go to the Portfolio Manager window, click the Record a Special Activity link, choose Record a Merger, and fill in the Record a Merger dialog boxes.

Corporate securities spin-off

When a corporation spins off, drops off, or lops off part of itself and you own shares in the corporation, you need to record how many new shares the corporation is issuing for each old share. To do that, go to the Portfolio Manager window, click the Record a Special Activity button, and choose Record a Spin-Off from the submenu. Then fill in the Record a Spin-Off dialog boxes.

How to record brokerage account fees

Brokers charge fees. Not a few of them have been known to nickel-and-dime their customers to death. How do you record brokerage fees in Money? The answer: You record transactions in the investment or retirement account register and select Other Expense from the Activity drop-down list on the transaction tab.

When you select Other Expense, the Category drop-down list appears so that you can categorize the brokerage fee. If the expense is associated with a particular security, select the security from the Investment drop-down list; otherwise, leave the Investment box blank. And make sure that the account from which you paid the fee appears in the Transfer from box.

Handling Mutual Funds

Mutual funds seem to be everybody's favorite investment. A *mutual fund* is an investment company that raises money from shareholders and invests the money in a variety of places, including stocks, bonds, and money market securities. With a mutual fund, you let experts do the work of deciding what to invest in. All you have to do is collect the profits, count them, and hide them under your mattress.

Recording the sale or purchase of mutual funds

You record the sale or purchase of a mutual fund the same way as you record the sale or purchase of stock shares. Earlier in this chapter, the sections "Recording a purchase of stocks" and "Recording the sale of stocks" explain how.

When you buy shares in the fund, select Buy from the Activity drop-down list; when you sell shares, select (duh) Sell. Be sure to accurately describe the number of shares you purchased or sold in the Quantity text box. And don't forget to enter the price per share correctly in the Price text box, either.

Recording dividends and distributions

From time to time, mutual fund managers send dividend distributions. More than likely, however, dividends are paid in the form of *reinvestments.* Instead of profits that your shares have made coming to you in a check, the profits are used to purchase more shares in the fund. Following are instructions for recording a dividend payment and for recording a mutual fund distribution.

Mutual fund dividend distributions

Follow these steps to record the receipt of mutual fund dividend distributions:

1. **Go to the Portfolio Manager window and click the name of the fund from which you received a dividend distribution.**

   A miniregister appears showing transactions you made in the mutual fund.

2. **Click the New button.**

   You see the Edit Transaction dialog box.

3. **Enter the date that the dividend was disbursed in the Date text box.**

4. **From the Activity drop-down list, select the option that describes the dividend distribution.**

   Look on your mutual fund statement to find out which option to select:

   • **Interest:** An interest distribution

   • **Dividend:** A dividend distribution

5. **Enter the amount of the dividend in the Total text box.**

   Make sure that the account into which you deposited the distribution appears in the Transfer To box.

6. **Click the OK button.**

Mutual fund reinvestment distributions

Follow these steps when the profits from a mutual fund are used to purchase more shares in the fund:

1. **In the Portfolio Manager window, click the name of the mutual fund.**

   As shown on the top of Figure 9-7, a miniregister appears with transactions you made in the mutual fund.

2. **Click the New button.**

3. **Enter the date of the reinvestment in the Date text box.**

4. **From the Activity drop-down list, select Reinvest Dividend or Reinvest Interest.**

   Your mutual fund statement tells you which of these options to select. Text boxes appear for recording how many mutual fund shares were reinvested and the value of those shares, as shown in Figure 9-7.

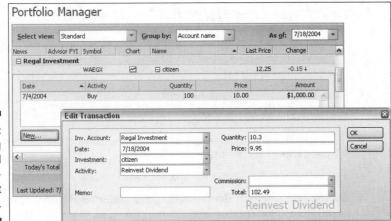

Figure 9-7:
Recording
a mutual
fund re-
investment
distribution.

5. In the Quantity text box, enter the number of shares that the reinvestment purchased.

6. In the Price text box, enter the price of shares in the mutual fund.

7. If necessary, enter a commission you had to pay in the Commission text box.

One of the advantages of reinvesting mutual fund profits is *not* having to pay a commission to purchase the shares. Most funds do not require you to pay a commission when you reinvest. If your fund makes you pay a commission, complain about it to the fund manager.

8. Click the OK button.

Handling Bonds

A bond is really a loan that you make to a government agency or private corporation. During the life of the loan, the government agency or corporation pays you interest, known as the *coupon rate.* Interest payments are usually made twice yearly. Bonds are considered safer investments than stocks because the amount of the bond is paid back at the end of the loan term, known as the *maturity date.* Instead of owning part of the company, which is the case with stocks, bondholders own a debt that the company or government agency that issued the bond is obliged to pay back.

Read on to find out how to track bond purchases and interest distributions with Money.

Recording the purchase of a bond

When you purchase a bond, follow these steps to record its purchase:

`Investing`

1. **Click the Investing tab.**

2. **Click the Portfolio Manager link.**

   The Portfolio Manager window appears.

3. **Click the Work with Investments link, and then choose Record a Buy on the drop-down menu.**

   The Edit Transaction dialog box appears.

4. **On the Inv. Account drop-down menu, select the name of the investment or retirement account where you want to record the purchase of the bond.**

5. **In the Date text box, enter the date you purchased the bond.**

   Be sure to enter the date correctly. Money needs this date to calculate the bond's value over time.

6. **On the Investment drop-down menu, enter a name for the bond and click the Tab button.**

   After you enter the name, you see the Create New Investment dialog box.

7. **Select Bond in the What Type of Investment Is It list, and click the Next button.**

   You see the first of several New Bond dialog boxes.

8. **Select the type of bond, and click the Next button.**

   If you can't find the kind of bond you are dealing with in the list, select the Other Bond Type option.

9. **Make sure that the name you entered is correct in the Name text box, choose a country in the Country/Region drop-down list, and click the Next button.**

   Now you're getting somewhere. You see the Enter a Few More Bond Details dialog box, as shown in Figure 9-8.

10. **Describe the bond, and click the Next button.**

    To describe the bond, enter information in these text boxes:

    - **Rating:** Moody and Standard & Poor's rate bonds according to their reliability. If you know the rating, choose it from the drop-down menu. You can generate Money reports on the basis of bond ratings.

    - **Coupon Rate:** Enter the annual interest rate that the bond pays.

    - **Interest Paid:** From the drop-down menu, choose the frequency with which interest income from the bond is paid.

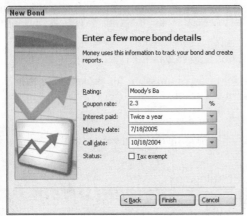

Figure 9-8:
Describing a
bond you
purchased.

- **Maturity Date:** Enter the date at which the bond falls due and is to be paid back to you.

- **Call Date:** Enter the earliest date that the bond can be redeemed. If the bond is redeemable at more than one date, enter the earliest date. You are only guaranteed interest payments up to the call date.

- **Status:** Select the Tax-Exempt check box if interest income from the bond is exempt from federal taxes. This is the case with most municipal bonds.

11. **Click the Finish button.**

   You return to the Edit Transaction dialog box.

12. **On the Transfer From drop-down menu, choose the account in which you track the value of the bond.**

   Money to pay for the bond is transferred from the cash reserves in your investment or retirement account. At the start of this chapter, the section "Recording Payments to (and Disbursements from) Brokers" explains how to transfer money from a checking or savings account to an investment or retirement account to pay for securities.

13. **In the Quantity text box, enter the face value of the bond.**

   The *face value*, also called the *par value*, is the value of the bond when it matures. Most bonds have a $1,000 face value. The face value is used to calculate interest payments. For example, a 5 percent bond with a face value of $1,000 pays $50 interest annually.

14. **In the Price text box, enter the price of the bond.**

   The price of a bond is stated as a percentage of the bond's face value.

15. **In the Accrued Int. text box, enter how much interest income, if any, has accumulated between the last interest payment date and the date of the sale.**

    Enter **0** if you have not sold this bond yet.

16. **If you paid your broker a commission for purchasing this bond, enter it in the Commission text box.**

17. **Click OK.**

    Your bond is listed in the Portfolio Manager window.

Recording interest payments from bonds

Periodically, creditors pay interest on bonds you own, and when they pay up, follow these steps to record interest income from a bond:

Investing

1. **Click the Investing tab and, in the Investing window, click the Portfolio Manager link.**

    You see the Portfolio Manager window.

2. **If necessary, click the name of the account where you track the bond from which you received an interest payment.**

    To see the name of bonds and other investments in an account, you click the account's name, but if the investment names are already displayed, you don't have to click an account name.

3. **Click the name of the bond.**

4. **Click the New button.**

    A transaction form appears.

5. **On the Activity drop-down menu, choose Interest.**

6. **Enter the amount of the interest payment in the Total text box.**

7. **Click OK.**

    The interest payment is recorded in the miniregister.

Other Kinds of Investments

The tail end of this chapter is for investors who believe in precious metals and certificates of deposit. How do you handle those types of investment with Money? Read on.

Precious metals

To track precious metals in an investment account, treat the metal as you would stock shares and describe the investment by units of measurement. For example, to describe the purchase of two ounces of gold, record the purchase as you would a purchase of two stock shares.

You can use the same method to track commodities. For example, if you are the proud purchaser of five bushels of wheat, record the purchase as you would a stock purchase and count the five bushels as five shares.

Certificates of deposit

You can track the value of a certificate of deposit (CD) in an investment or retirement account by selecting Certificates of Deposit in the Create New Investment dialog box. As the CD accumulates interest, record the interest payments by selecting Interest from the Activity drop-down list.

Editing and Deleting Investment and Retirement Account Transactions

Suppose that you enter a transaction in an investment or retirement account incorrectly. It can happen. And when it does happen, you will be glad to know, you can edit or delete it by using the same techniques you use in a checking account or savings account — by going into the account register and making the change.

To edit or delete an investment or retirement account transaction, open the Portfolio Manager window, locate the investment in question, and click its name. You see a miniregister like the one shown in Figure 9-9. Select the transaction and edit or delete it:

- **Editing a transaction:** Click the Edit button. The Edit Transaction dialog box appears so you can change the particulars of the transaction.

- **Deleting a transaction:** Click the Delete button, and click Yes in the message box that asks whether you really want to go through with it.

If working in the miniregister is too much trouble for you, open the register of the account where the transaction that needs editing or deleting is located. To do so, start in the Portfolio Manager window, click the Work with

Accounts link, and choose the name of an account on the drop-down menu. The Account Register window opens. Select the transaction and edit or delete it:

- ✔ **Editing a transaction:** Click the Edit button in the transaction form and change the particulars of the transaction.

- ✔ **Deleting a transaction:** Right-click the transaction and choose Delete on the shortcut menu.

Click an investment to open the miniregister.

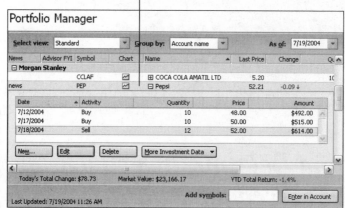

Figure 9-9:
Editing or deleting investment transactions.

Updating the Price of Securities

For investors who dabble in stocks, mutual funds, and bonds, being able to download share prices from the Internet with Money is too good to be true. Rather than update share prices yourself by entering numbers in text boxes, all you have to do is plug into the Internet, grab the numbers, and be done with it. No fooling — downloading share prices from the Internet with Money takes about two minutes. It's free, too. By tracking changes in the value of a security, you can analyze the performance of your investments and then track the value of your portfolio over time (see Chapter 10). Money offers two ways to update security prices — from the Internet and on your own. Both techniques are described here.

Chapter 17 explains how to tell Money about your Internet connection so that the program knows how to download security prices. If you have trouble downloading prices, consult Chapter 17.

Making sure you have the right ticker symbol

While you're describing the securities in an investment or retirement account, Money gives you the opportunity to enter ticker symbols, but if you chose not to enter them or you entered the wrong symbol, you can follow these steps to assign a ticker symbol to a stock or mutual fund and be able to download its current price from the Internet:

1. **In the Portfolio Manager window, right-click the name of the security that needs a ticker**

symbol, and choose **Investment Details** on the shortcut menu.

You see the Details window was shown in the figure.

2. **Enter the ticker symbol in the Symbol text box.**

If you're running any version of Money except the Standard version, you can find out a company's ticker symbol by clicking the Find Symbol button in the Details window.

Pepsi details

Use this page to change the investment details for Pepsi.

Investment name:	Pepsi Rename...
Investment type:	Stock
Status:	☐ Ta_x exempt
Symbol:	PEP Find Symbol
Comment:	
Country/Region:	United States

Downloading stock and mutual fund quotes from the Internet

You can download stock, mutual fund, and bond prices as long as you have access to the Internet through an Internet service provider and you have entered ticker symbols for your investments. A ticker symbol is an abbreviated company name that is used for tracking the performance of stocks, mutual funds, and bonds. You can usually find these symbols on the statements you receive from brokers. Unless Money has a company's ticker symbol on file, you can't download the current price of a stock, bond, or mutual fund.

Follow these steps to update the prices of stocks, bonds, money market funds, and mutual funds in your portfolio:

Investing

1. **Click the Investing tab and, in the Investing window, click the Portfolio Manager link.**

You land in the Portfolio Manager window.

2. **As shown in Figure 9-10, click the Update Prices link and choose an option from the submenu to update the price of the securities in your portfolio from the Internet.**

   The window offers two ways to update the price of securities:

   • **Update the price of all securities:** Click the Update Prices Now option.

   • **Update the price of a handful of securities:** Click the Pick Quotes to Download option. You see the Pick Quotes to Download dialog box (refer to Figure 9-10). Uncheck the securities whose prices you *don't* want to update and click OK.

The Update Prices submenu also offers an option called Update Prices Manually. Choose this option to enter prices on your own, as explained in the next section of this chapter.

By default, security prices are updated every 30 minutes as long as your computer is connected to the Internet. If you prefer to update prices only when you give the command to do so, go to the Portfolio Manager window, click the Update Prices link, and deselect the Update Automatically (Every 30 Minutes) option on the submenu.

Figure 9-10:
Click the
Update
Prices link
and choose
how you
want to
download
security
prices.

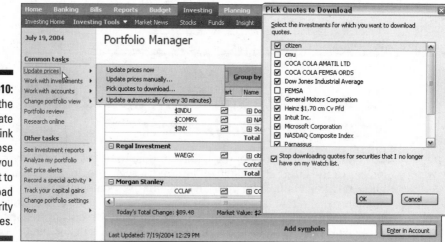

Updating the price of securities on your own

If a security you're tracking doesn't have a ticker symbol or you believe in tracking securities the old-fashioned way, follow these steps to manually update the price of a security in your portfolio:

1. **Open the Portfolio Manager window.**

   To get there, click the Investing tab and, in the Investing window, click the Portfolio Manager link.

2. **Click the Update Prices link and choose Update Prices Manually from the submenu.**

   You see the Update Price dialog box, also shown in Figure 9-11.

3. **Click the arrow to open the Investment drop-down list and select the investment whose price you want to update.**

4. **In the Date box, enter the date that the price changed.**

5. **Enter the new price in the Price ($) text box.**

6. **Click the Update button.**

   The new price is entered in the price history list. Note in Figure 9-11 that the Source column says `Online` next to some entries. When you enter a price yourself, the column says `Update`, but it says `Online` when you get prices from the Internet.

7. **If you want to record the price history of a security, keep entering new dates and new security prices; otherwise, select a new security from the Investment drop-down list and update its price.**

8. **Click the Close button when you're done.**

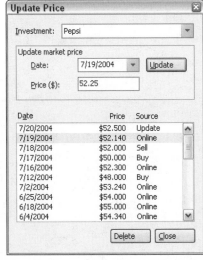

Figure 9-11:
Report
changes in
the price of
a security in
the Update
Price dialog
box.

Chapter 10

Researching and Analyzing Your Investments

*A*re you a good investor? Choosing profitable investments requires a bit of luck, knowledge of the markets, and the wherewithal to look past the hype and see what a company or mutual fund is really about.

One of the advantages of Money to investors is being able to get information quickly and find out at a moment's notice how the investments you already own are performing. Using Money, you can analyze your investments, compare your investments to one another, and compare your investments to securities you don't own. You can also get advice for diversifying your investments and tell Money to alert you when a security falls within a certain price range. Because Money was designed to work hand in glove with the MoneyCentral Web site, you can do all kinds of research at MoneyCentral without leaving the Money program. Better read on.

Analyzing Your Investments

The fun begins after you enter the securities and list their prices in investment and retirement accounts. Now you can examine your investments in different ways. Like peering into the different windows of a house (with the occupants' permission, of course), you can stare into your investments from different angles and see whether you gain any insights that way.

Investing

The simplest way, although not necessarily the most revealing way, to start analyzing your investments is to click the Investing tab and go to the Investing window. As shown in Figure 10-1, this window lists the current value of your different investment and retirement accounts. You can also see how much each account has gained or lost in value.

Figure 10-1:
The
Investing
window.

Investing Accounts			
Account Name	Current Value	Value on 6/19/2004	Gain/Loss
Citizens Funds	11,866.42	17,214.30	(5,347.88)
Parnassus	10,963.19	12,350.00	(1,386.81)
Total	22,829.61	29,564.30	(6,734.69)
View my portfolio		Last updated: 7/19/2004 4:44 PM Update now	

More revealing than the Investing window is the Portfolio Manager window, as shown in Figure 10-2. To get there from the Investing window, click the Portfolio Manager link under My Investing Tools, click the Investing Tools button, and choose Portfolio Manager on the drop-down menu, or click the View My Portfolio link.

Change view   Arrange in different ways.

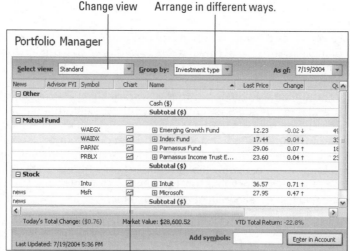

Figure 10-2:
The
Portfolio
Manager
window.

Interactive charts icon

Under each retirement or investment account name, the Portfolio Manager window lists the latest price of each security, the securities' market value, and how much each has increased or decreased in value. Here are the basics of getting around in the Portfolio Manager window:

✔ Click the plus sign (+) next to an account name to view the securities that are tracked by the account. Click the minus sign next to an account name to hide the securities.

✔ Click a security name to open a miniregister and view transactions made with the security.

✔ Choose an option from the Select View drop-down menu (or click the Change Portfolio View link and choose an option) to analyze your investments in different ways. Table 10-1 describes the 11 different views from which you can choose. Test them all and see whether you can gain any insights and be a better investor.

✔ Choose an option from the Group By drop-down menu to arrange securities in the window under account names, by investment type, by capitalization (large cap and small cap), by currency, from least risky to most risky, or by position from worst earner to best earner.

The status bar at the bottom of the Portfolio Manager window lists the securities' daily total change of value, the market value of all the securities, and the year-to-date percentage return. You can decide what appears on the status bar. Click the Change Portfolio Settings link, and on the Status Bar tab of the Preferences dialog box, choose options from the Position 1, 2, and 3 drop-down menus.

Table 10-1	Views in the Portfolio Manager Window
View Option	*What You See*
Standard	Securities arranged by account. Choose this view to see in which accounts you keep securities.
Asset Allocation	Securities arranged by type — stocks first, then mutual funds, CDs, bonds, and so on. Choose this view to see whether you incorrectly placed all your investment eggs in the same basket.
Performance	Performance data, including how much you have profited or lost on each investment, the gain or loss by percentage, and the annual return by percentage.

(continued)

Table 10-1 *(continued)*

View Option	What You See
	Return-on-investment projections for the coming week, four weeks, year, and three-year period. Money makes these calculations based on investment type. Choose this view to see how the wizards at Microsoft think your investments will grow or shrink.
Valuation	Value information about your securities, including their cost bases, appreciation, and increase in value.
Quotes	Market data on each investment, including its latest price, latest change in price, and daily and yearly high and low.
Holdings	The latest price, number of units you own, and market value of your investment holdings.
Fundamental Data	Historical price information, including 52-week high and low prices and P/E ratios.
Options	Stock options in alphabetical order.
Employee Stock Options	Stocks options you have acquired from your place of employment.
Bonds	Bonds in your portfolio.

When you see the Interactive Charts icon in the Portfolio Manager window, you can click the icon to go to the MoneyCentral Web site (www.money central.com) and see a chart showing how the security has performed in the past year. Click the Customize Chart link to change the date range or compare the security against a stock index such as NASDAQ or the S&P 500.

Charting the Performance of an Investment

If you want to press your nose to the glass and get a very, very close look at an investment, double-click its ticker symbol (not its name) in the Portfolio Manager window. That action takes you to the Price History window, where a chart shows you precisely how well the security is performing, as shown in Figure 10-3.

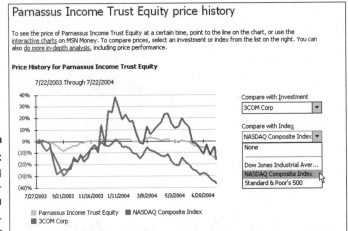

Parnassus Income Trust Equity price history

To see the price of Parnassus Income Trust Equity at a certain time, point to the line on the chart, or use the interactive charts on MSN Money. To compare prices, select an investment or index from the list on the right. You can also do more in-depth analysis, including price performance.

Price History for Parnassus Income Trust Equity

Figure 10-3:
Charting the performance of an investment.

In the Price History window, make selections from the drop-down lists to compare an investment's performance with another one of your investments or with an index. The chart in Figure 10-3 compares the performances of two different stocks and the NASDAQ Composite Index over a one-year period.

If you have the Deluxe version of Money, you can click the Interactive Charts link or the Do More In-Depth Analysis link in the Price History window to go to the MoneyCentral Web site and research your investment even further.

Reviewing Your Portfolio

If you pay an investment counselor to review your portfolio, he or she may give you good advice about changing your investment plan. Whether the advice is good or bad, the investment counselor will most certainly charge you a lot for the service. In the interest of saving money on investment counselors, Money offers an investment counselor in a can. The canned counselor reviews your portfolio and gives you a report showing how your investments are allocated, your tax liability, your investments' performance, and how much risk you are exposing yourself to, as shown in Figure 10-4.

Investing

To put the investment counselor to work, click the Investing tab and, in the Investing window, click the Portfolio Review link. That's all there is to it. Scroll through the Portfolio Review window to see what's what with your investments.

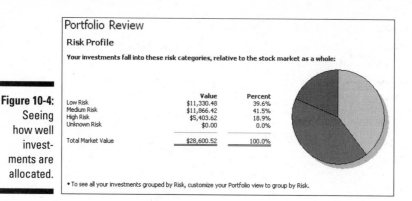

Figure 10-4:
Seeing
how well
invest-
ments are
allocated.

Seeing How Well Your Investments Are Allocated

On the theory that you shouldn't put all your eggs in one basket, many investment counselors advocate diversifying investments across many different investment classes. By allocating your investments this way, you minimize investment risks, because if one class of investments falters, the others will pick up the slack.

In the Portfolio Manager window, open the Select View drop-down menu and choose Asset Allocation to view your investments by investment class — stocks, mutual funds, bonds, and so on. If the majority of your investments fall in one or two classes, consider using the Assert Allocation Manager to get advice about diversifying your investments.

To use the Asset Allocation Manager, either click the Investing tab to go to the Investing window and then click the Asset Allocation link, or click the Investing Tools button and choose Asset Allocation from the drop-down menu. You see the Welcome to Asset Allocation window. Click the Learn link to embark on a lesson in asset allocation and develop a plan for diversifying your investments. As you go from window to window, clicking the Next button as you go along, you can see how well your investments are allocated, get Money's advice for reallocating your investments, and devise a plan for diversifying your investments. Figure 10-5 shows an Allocation Manager window comparing existing investments and Money's target plan for creating a more diversified portfolio.

Another way to see how your investments are allocated is to run an Asset Allocation report. In the Portfolio Manager window, click the See Investment Reports link and choose Asset Allocation on the submenu. Chapter 15 explains reports in detail.

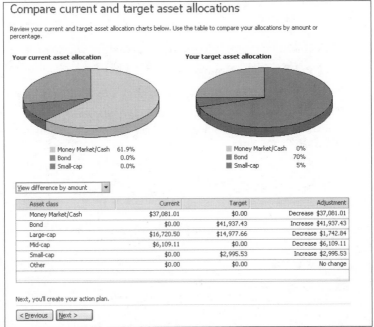

Figure 10-5:
Developing
an asset
allocation
plan.

Generating Investment Reports

To make it easy for you to generate investment reports, the Portfolio Manager window offers the See Investment Reports link. Click this link to see a submenu with all the investment reports that you find in the Reports window. There are ten investment reports in all. Chapter 15 explains how to generate and customize reports.

Being Alerted When a Security Hits a Certain Price

As Chapter 13 explains, you can make Advisor FYI alerts appear on the Home Page when an important event occurs. By clicking an alert, you can go to the Review the Advisor FYI Details window, where you can find out why you are being alerted. Besides being alerted to account balances, your monthly spending in different categories, and important dates, you can be alerted when a stock or mutual fund reaches a certain price range.

Follow these steps to be alerted to changes in the price of a security you are tracking with Money:

Investing

1. **Click the Investing tab to go to the Investing window.**

2. **Click the Portfolio Manager link.**

3. **In the Portfolio Manager window, click the Set Price Alerts link.**

    You can find this link under Other Tasks. After you click it, you see the Investment Alerts tab of the Advisor FYI Options dialog box, as shown in Figure 10-6.

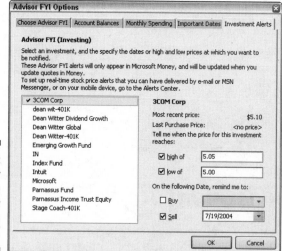

Figure 10-6:
Tell Money
to alert you
to security
price
changes.

4. **Select the security for which you want to be alerted.**

5. **In the High Of and Low Of text boxes, enter figures to describe a price range.**

6. **If you want the alert to instruct you to buy or sell the security when its price falls within the range, select the Buy or the Sell check box and enter the date by which you want to be alerted.**

7. **Click OK.**

    If you want to be alerted to price changes of securities you don't own or don't track with Money, enter those securities in a Watch account (see Chapter 8). Watch account securities can also be placed on the Advisor FYI list.

Researching Investments at MoneyCentral

You may not realize it, but Money has a split personality. Besides being a program for tracking financial activity, Money is a Web browser. Clicking many links in the Money program takes you to the MoneyCentral Web site. However, the Web site appears inside the Money window, not in a browser window. To confuse matters even further, the MoneyCentral Web site looks much like the Money program. To see what I mean, open your browser and go to this address: www.moneycentral.com. You will find yourself at a Web site that looks deceptively like Money itself!

Because Money and the MoneyCentral Web site are on such friendly terms, it is easy to research investment opportunities on the MoneyCentral Web site while you are working in Money:

✔ In the Investing window, click one of the links under Markets, Stocks, Funds, Insight, or Brokers on the left side of the screen to go to MoneyCentral and research the markets, a stock, or a mutual fund.

✔ In any Investing window, click one of the five buttons — Market News, Stocks, Funds, Insight, or Brokers — to go to the MoneyCentral Web site and conduct your research. Figure 10-7 shows the MoneyCentral Web page for researching stocks. Notice the ubiquitous advertisement. Is there any escaping advertisements?

Click here...   ... or here to go to MoneyCentral.

Figure 10-7: Researching stocks at Money Central.

Other Ways to Research Investments Online

It goes without saying, but MoneyCentral isn't the only place on the Internet to research investments. You are hereby encouraged to get investment advice from as many places as you possibly can. In my opinion, there are no experts when it comes to handing out investment advice. They are just people with opinions. The following pages unscrew the inscrutable. They show you where to go on the Internet to research mutual funds and stocks.

Researching mutual funds on the Internet

Before you start dabbling in mutual funds, you need to know about how fees are levied, the different kinds of funds, and the risks. After you know that, you can start looking for a fund that meets your needs. Here are some Web sites where you can acquire the basics of mutual fund investing:

- **Brill's Mutual Funds Interactive:** An all-purpose Web site for mutual fund investing. Here, you can read about mutual fund investing or search for funds by name and read about them. Address: `www.funds interactive.com`

- **Mutual Fund Investor's Center:** An excellent Web site with articles about mutual fund investing. This site ranks mutual funds in various ways. You can also search for mutual funds by using different criteria. Address: `www.mfea.com`

- **CNNMoney:** Offers advice about choosing, buying, and selling mutual funds. Address: `money.cnn.com`

At last count, investors could choose from among 10,000 mutual funds. After you know what you want in a mutual fund, check out MoneyCentral to search for a mutual fund that fits your investment strategy. You can also search at these Web sites:

- **Morningstar.com:** The granddaddy of mutual fund analysis, this company offers reports on 7,000 mutual funds. You can get fund profiles, performance reports, financial statements, and news articles. Address: `www.morningstar.com`

- **SmartMoney.com:** Offers a sophisticated search engine for pinpointing mutual funds. Address: `www.smartmoney.com`

Researching stocks on the Internet

The stock market, it has been said, is 85 percent psychology and 15 percent economics. And that's only half the problem. The other half has to do with the market's hard-to-understand terminology and the numerous confusing ways to buy and sell stock.

To get general-purpose information about stocks and stock markets, read stock tips, and discover stock-picking strategies, try these sites, which are good starting places:

✔ **Briefing.com:** Get stock quotes, reports, and historical charts. Address: www.briefing.com

✔ **DailyStocks.com:** Provides links to market indexes, news sources, earnings figures, and newsletters. Address: www.dailystocks.com

Part IV
Getting Your Money's Worth

"Get ready, Mona — here come the stats."

In this part . . .

Part IV shows you how to get the most out of Money. You find out how to draw up a budget, schedule bills so that you can pay them on time, and get ready for tax season. Oh, and you also pick up a handful of housekeeping hints, such as backing up your data files, that make your trip to Moneyland more enjoyable.

Chapter 11

Some Important Housekeeping Chores

This chapter explains a handful of housekeeping chores that you must do from time to time. Sorry. Nobody likes housekeeping chores, but they have to get done.

In this chapter, you find out how to back up your data file so that you have a spare copy if your computer fails. You also discover how to restore a file — that is, load a backup copy of a file onto your computer. This chapter explains how to delete old bank accounts, create a second file for storing transactions, delete a file, and rename a file. You also find out how to archive a file to keep records of past transactions. For spies, secret agents, and people who often glance over their shoulder, this chapter also explains how to clamp a password on a Money file.

Backing Up and Restoring Money Files

Computers are wonderful machines — until they break down. If a computer breaks down entirely, it's worse than useless because the data on its hard drive can't be recovered. It can't be recovered, I should say, unless someone had the foresight to back up the data.

In computerese, *backing up* means to make a second copy of a file so that the data can be recovered if something evil happens to the hard drive where the original file is stored. As long as you have a backup copy of your Money file, it doesn't matter whether your computer is run over by a bulldozer or struck by lightning. It doesn't matter because you can always restore your data from the backup file. *Restoring* means to load the backup copy of a file onto a computer and use it instead of the original file from which the backup was made.

Telling Money how to back up your financial data

Backing up is so important that Money gives you the opportunity to do it when you close the program or close a data file. You may have already noticed the Back Up dialog box, as shown in Figure 11-1. By clicking the Back Up button in this dialog box each time you close Money, you can make a backup copy of your data file.

Figure 11-1:
The Back Up dialog box appears whenever you close Money.

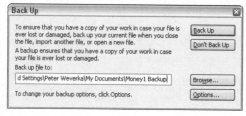

To be accurate, you make a backup copy to the C:\My Documents or the C:\Documents and Settings*Your Name*\My Documents folder on the hard drive. Instead of the data file being copied to a floppy disk that can be dropped in a drawer or filing cabinet, the backup copy is stored on the same computer that stores the original file. If something wicked happens to that computer — if it crashes or is stolen — you lose the Money data you so carefully assembled. You can't restore the file from a backup copy, because the backup copy is also on your computer.

To remedy this problem, you can tell Money that you want to make backup copies to a floppy disk, Zip disk, or other removable disk as well as the hard drive each time you close the program. Backing up this way takes all of five seconds. And by backing up this way, you always have a completely up-to-date copy of your data file on hand in case of an emergency.

Follow these steps to change the backup settings so that you back up your Money file to a floppy disk as well as to the hard drive whenever you close the program:

1. **Open the Backup Options tab of the Options dialog box.**

   You can get there two different ways:

   - Click the Options button in the Back Up dialog box (refer to Figure 11-1).
   - Choose Tools➪Settings, and in the Settings window, click the Backup Options link.

   You see the Backup Options tab, as shown in Figure 11-2.

2. **Select either or both of the Automatically Back Up check boxes.**

   The first Automatically Back Up check box makes a backup copy to a file in your My Documents folder. The second makes a backup copy to a floppy disk or other removable drive. (In Step 6, you tell Money where that removable drive is.) If you select both option buttons, you will have to negotiate two Back Up dialog boxes each time you close Money.

3. **Make sure that the check box called Prompt Me Before Backing Up is selected.**

   This way, you are reminded to make backup copies of your data.

4. **Enter 1 in the Automatically Back Up to Floppy Every X Days text box.**

   Unless you change this setting, you are asked every 14 days whether you want to back up the data file to a floppy disk. But 14 days is not often enough. I think you should back up the data file to a floppy disk or removable drive each day that you finish using the program.

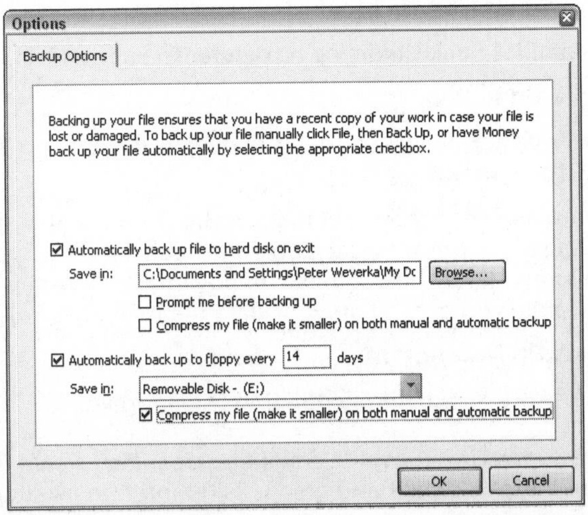

Figure 11-2:
Enter **1** in the Automatically Back Up to Floppy Every *X* Days text box to be reminded each time you use Money to back up your data file to a floppy disk.

Options

Backup Options

Backing up your file ensures that you have a recent copy of your work in case your file is lost or damaged. To back up your file manually click File, then Back Up, or have Money back up your file automatically by selecting the appropriate checkbox.

☑ Automatically back up file to hard disk on exit

Save in: C:\Documents and Settings\Peter Weverka\My Dc   [Browse...]

☐ Prompt me before backing up

☐ Compress my file (make it smaller) on both manual and automatic backup

☑ Automatically back up to floppy every 14 days

Save in: Removable Disk - (E:)

☑ Compress my file (make it smaller) on both manual and automatic backup

[OK] [Cancel]

5. **Click the Browse button and, in the Backup dialog box, choose a folder for storing backup copies of your Money file on the hard drive.**

   Backup copies are stored in the `C:\My Documents` folder by default, but most people reserve that folder for data files that they use on a daily basis. I suggest choosing or creating a more inconspicuous folder. The folder can be anywhere on your hard drive.

6. **Open the Save In drop-down list and choose a removable disk apart from the floppy disk drive (A:) if you want to make backup copies elsewhere.**

   If your computer is equipped with a Zip drive, for example, you can choose Removable Disk - (D:) from the drop-down list to make backup copies to a Zip disk.

7. **Click OK to close the Options dialog box.**

   You're all set. You will be reminded to back up your data file to a floppy disk or other disk whenever you close Money 2005.

Backing up your data file

Money gives you two ways to back up a data file. You can wait until you close the program and negotiate the Back Up dialog box as part of shutting down, or you can choose File⇨Backup to back up the data file without closing the program (see the "Backing up on the fly" sidebar).

Assuming that you want to wait to back up your data, here are instructions for backing up a data file to the hard drive and a floppy disk when you close the program:

1. **Click the Close button (the X in the upper-right corner of the screen) or choose File⇨Exit to close Money.**

   You see the familiar Back Up dialog box (refer to Figure 11-1).

2. **Click the Back Up button.**

   Your computer grinds away and then the deed is done — the file is backed up to the hard drive.

   As long as you followed the instructions earlier in this chapter in the section "Telling Money how to back up your financial data," you see the Back Up to Floppy dialog box. It tells you how many days have passed since the last time you backed up your data file to a floppy disk.

3. **Click the Back Up Now button.**

   That's all she wrote — the file is copied to the floppy disk.

Be sure to put the floppy or removable disk in a safe place. A *safe place* is one where nothing can be spilled on it and no one is tempted to use it for a drink coaster.

Backing up on the fly

You don't have to wait till you shut down Money to back up a data file. To back up in the middle of your work, choose File⇨Backup. In the Back Up dialog box, select an option button to tell Money where to back up your data file; then click OK.

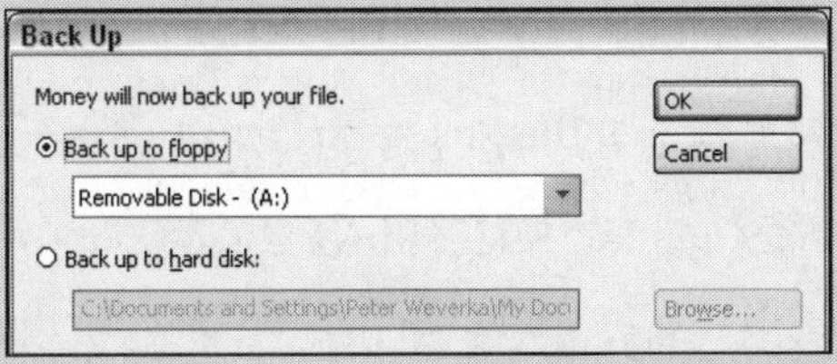

```
Back Up
Money will now back up your file.                          OK
⊙ Back up to floppy                                      Cancel
  Removable Disk - (A:)                    ▼
○ Back up to hard disk:
  C:\Documents and Settings\Peter Weverka\My Doc    Browse...
```

Restoring a file from its backup copy

Suppose that doomsday arrives and you have to restore a data file from its backup copy on a floppy disk, a removable disk, or the hard drive. Perhaps you botched a find-and-replace operation or your computer went momentarily haywire. If that happens, follow these steps to start working with the backup copy of a file instead of the original copy:

1. **If you want to restore your data file from a disk, put the disk with the backup copy of your data file in the A: drive.**

2. **Choose File⇨Restore Backup.**

   You see the Restore Backup dialog box.

3. **Select the Restore from a Backup File option button (if it isn't already selected) and click the Next button.**

   The Restore Backup File dialog box, shown in Figure 11-3, appears. Take a close look at the filename that is listed in this dialog box. What you do in Step 4 depends on whether that file is the one you want to restore.

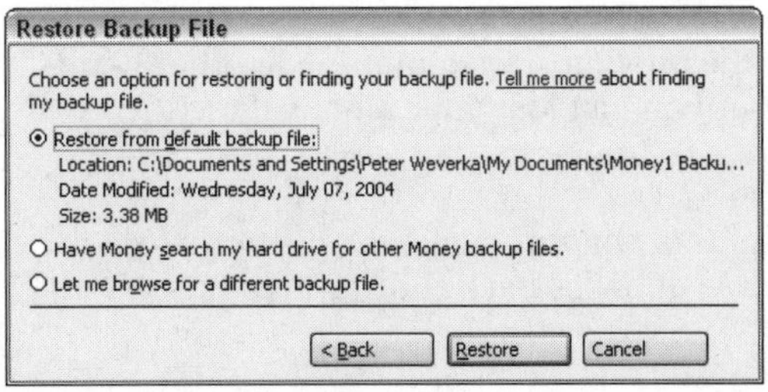

Figure 11-3: In this dialog box, tell Money where the backup file is located.

```
Restore Backup File
Choose an option for restoring or finding your backup file. Tell me more about finding
my backup file.
⊙ Restore from default backup file:
     Location: C:\Documents and Settings\Peter Weverka\My Documents\Money1 Backu...
     Date Modified: Wednesday, July 07, 2004
     Size: 3.38 MB
○ Have Money search my hard drive for other Money backup files.
○ Let me browse for a different backup file.

        < Back      Restore      Cancel
```

4. **Locate the backup file you will use to restore you Money data.**

Money offers three ways to do that:

- **The dialog box lists the backup file:** Select the Restore from Default Backup File option button and then click the Restore button if the file listed in the dialog box is the one you want to restore.

- **You don't know where the file is:** Select the Have Money Search My Hard Drive for Other Money Backup Files option and click the Next button if the dialog box lists the wrong backup file and you don't know where the correct file is. After a moment, you see a list of backup files. Select the one you want to use as the restore file.

- **The dialog box lists the wrong backup file:** Select the Let Me Browse for a Different Backup File option button and click the Next button if you want to restore a different file from its backup copy. In the Restore dialog box, select the correct file and click OK.

Backup files have the word "Backup" in their name and have the extension .mbf.

5. **Make sure that the Restore Backup File dialog box lists the file that you want to restore from its backup copy; then click the Restore button.**

In a moment or two, depending on how large the data file is, the backup file takes the place of the original. Now, all you have to do is enter the financial transactions that you entered between the time you last backed up the file and the time you restored it. I hope there aren't many transactions to enter.

Transferring Your Money File to a New Computer

When you get a new computer, you may well ask yourself, "How do I get my Money data from my old computer to my new computer?" The answer is by backing up the data on your old computer to a floppy disk or Zip disk, loading the Money software on your new computer (if necessary), and restoring the backed-up Money file on your new computer. In other words, pretend on your new computer that you just lost your Money data; then restore the data from a backup file.

The previous section in this chapter explains how to restore data from a backup file. Turn a couple of pages back and start reading. I'll wait for you here.

Pruning the Payees List

As you surely know, Money "remembers" the names of people and businesses that you enter in account registers. When you enter a payee name the second time, you have to type only the first two or three letters. Money enters the full name for you. And if you are the sort of person who would rather click than type, you can enter a payee name in an account register by selecting it from the Pay To drop-down list.

As wonderful as it is, the Payees list has a habit of getting very long. From time to time you need to prune the list to cut it down to size. That way, fewer names appear in the Payee To or From text box and you can find the name you need faster on transaction forms.

When you delete a payee on the list, nothing happens to his, her, or its name in the account registers. The payee's name remains intact for future generations to see and behold. Next time you try to enter the payee's name in a transaction form, however, the name doesn't appear automatically in the Pay To or From text box after you type the first couple of letters.

Follow these steps to remove names from the Payees list:

Banking

1. **Press Ctrl+Shift+C or click the Banking tab, click the Account Tools button, and then choose Categories & Payees.**

2. **Click the Payees link.**

   The Set Up Your Payees window appears, as shown in Figure 11-4. The fastest way to scroll through a long Payees list is to press a letter on your keyboard. Press P, for example, to scroll to the names that begin with the letter P.

Figure 11-4:
Prune the
Payees list
when it gets
too long.

2. **Select a payee name on the list and click the Delete button.**

   A dialog box asks whether you really want to go through with it.

3. **Click the Yes button.**

You can edit information about a payee anytime. Simply go to the Payees list, double-click a payee's name, and change the information on the Payee screen.

Organizing Your Favorite Accounts, Reports, and Web Sites

If you have spent any time in Money, you know how to play favorites. By choosing Favorites⇨Add to Favorites, you can place an account, report, or Web site on the Favorites list. Then all you have to do to go to the account, report, or Web site is choose a command from the Favorites menu: Favorites⇨Favorite Accounts, Favorites⇨Favorite Reports, or Favorites⇨Favorite Web Sites.

Also on the Favorites menu is a command called Organize Favorites. Choose Favorites⇨Organize Favorites when your Favorites lists get out of hand and need reorganizing. Money will take you to a window where you can prioritize your favorite accounts, reports, and Web sites; delete them; or rename them.

The Favorites lists are very convenient devices for getting around in Money. You can even put a list of your favorite accounts on the Home Page and open account registers from there (see Chapter 2). Use the Organize Favorites command to squeeze more pleasure and profit from your Favorites lists.

Protecting Files with Passwords or Passports

Probably the last thing you want is someone snooping in your Money file. To keep jealous colleagues, future biographers, agents of Interpol, or anyone else from opening a file, you can protect it with a password. Money offers two ways to protect a file with a password:

✔ **Conventional password:** Enter the password each time you start Money. Fail to do so and you can't open the Money file.

✔ **Microsoft .NET passport:** Use a .NET passport. Microsoft offers the .NET passport service for free. Instead of having to remember many passwords to many Web sites, you enter one password — your .NET passport — at participating Web sites. The password is "encrypted," a computer term that means "buried so deep in the crypt no one can uncover it."

The following sections explain how to lock a file with a password or .NET passport, open a file that has been given a password, and change or remove passwords.

Locking a file with a password or .NET passport

Connect to the Internet if you want a .NET passport. Follow these steps to clamp a password — conventional or .NET — on a Money file:

1. **If necessary, open the file that needs a password.**

2. **Choose File➪Password Manager.**

   You see the Manage Your Password dialog box, as shown in Figure 11-5.

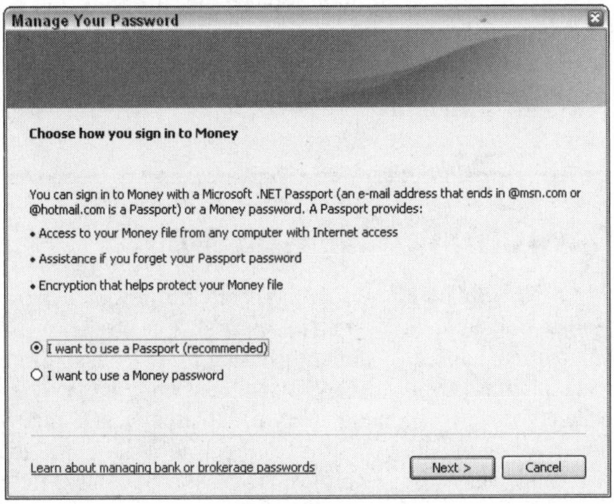

Manage Your Password

Choose how you sign in to Money

You can sign in to Money with a Microsoft .NET Passport (an e-mail address that ends in @msn.com or @hotmail.com is a Passport) or a Money password. A Passport provides:

• Access to your Money file from any computer with Internet access

• Assistance if you forget your Passport password

• Encryption that helps protect your Money file

⦿ I want to use a Passport (recommended)

○ I want to use a Money password

Learn about managing bank or brokerage passwords   [Next >]   [Cancel]

Figure 11-5: Choosing a password.

3. **Click the first option, I Want to Use a Passport, if you've opted for a .NET passport; click the I Want to Use a Money Password option if you favor a conventional password.**

4. Sign on for a conventional password or a .NET passport:

- **Conventional password:** Click the second option, I Want to Use a Money Password, and click Next. Type a password in the New Password text box, type the same password in the Confirm New Password text box, and click Next. It doesn't matter whether a password is uppercase, lowercase, or a combination of upper- and lowercase letters. If the password is Oaxaca, for example, it doesn't matter whether you enter oaxaca, OAXACA, or Oaxaca in the Password dialog box when you open the file.

- **.NET passport:** Click the I Want to Use a Passport option, and click Next. Then enter your e-mail address and password, and click the Sign In button. The password you entered is sent over the Internet to Passport.com, Microsoft's name for the Web site where .NET passports are kept under lock and key. Click the Done button.

It's settled: Whoever tries to open the file next time, or whoever starts the Money program next time, will need the secret password.

Opening a file that has been given a password

When you try to start Money or open a new Money file that has been given a password, you see an opening screen like the one in Figure 11-6 (people with .NET passports see a slightly different screen). I hope that you know the password. If you do, enter it and click the Sign In button.

The Microsoft .NET passport

You have no choice but to use a .NET passport if you intend to record Money transactions online, download information from your bank, or see MoneyCentral information while you browse the Internet (these subjects are covered in Part VI). Here is some good news for people who use Hotmail or have an account with MSN (the Microsoft Network): You already have a .NET passport. The same password that gets you into Hotmail or MSN can double as a password to Money.

Go to this Web site to get a .NET passport: http://register.passport.com. One benefit of using a .NET passport instead of a conventional password is that you can forget the .NET passport and still recover it from Microsoft. If you forget a conventional password, you're plumb out of luck. You can't open your Money file.

Some gratuitous advice about choosing passwords

Everybody has different advice for choosing a password that isn't likely to be forgotten or discovered, and everybody agrees that you shouldn't use your own name or the names of family members or pets, because devious souls try those names first when they try to crack open a file. Here's a good tip for choosing passwords: Pick your favorite foreign city and spell it backward. My favorite foreign city is in Mexico. If I used a password, it would be acaxa0.

People who enter .NET passports can click the Remember Password check box, but clicking this check box sort of defeats the purpose of having a password. Next time you open Money, your sign-in name and password will already be entered on the Welcome screen. All you or a cat burglar has to do is click the Sign In button to access the Money file.

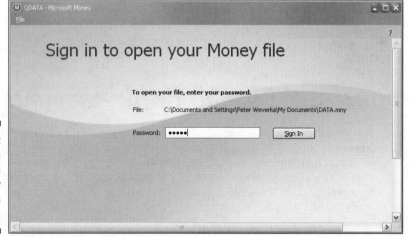

Figure 11-6:
Enter the password for a Money file in this dialog box.

If you don't remember the password and yours is a conventional password, wag your head and proclaim, "Woe is me." All is not lost if yours is a .NET passport. You can go to this Web site on the Internet and recover your stray password: http://memberservices.passport.com. Click the I Forgot My Password link and take it from there.

Changing and removing passwords

How you change or remove a password from a file depends on what kind of password you have. Start by choosing File➪Password Manager to open the Manage Your Password dialog box. Then take the following steps in the Manage Your Password dialog boxes:

- ✔ **Changing a conventional password:** Select the first option, I Want to Change or Remove My Money Password, and click the Next button. Enter your current password in the Old Password text box, and enter the new password in the New Password and Confirm New Password text boxes. Then click Next.

- ✔ **Changing a .NET passport:** Click the Change button. In the following dialog box, click the first option, I Want to Change the Microsoft Passport I Use to Sign in to My Money File, and click Next. Enter an e-mail address, enter a password, and click the Sign In button.

- ✔ **Removing a conventional password:** Select the first option, I Want to Change or Remove My Money Password, and click Next. Enter your password in the Old Password text box, and click the Remove button. Finally, click the Next button to confirm the removal.

- ✔ **Removing a .NET passport:** Click the Remove button. In the following dialog box, click the first option, I Want to Remove My Passport from My Money File, and click Next. Then click the Done button.

Deleting and Closing Bank Accounts

When you close a bank account, you can either delete it or close it in the Accounts window. If the transactions in the account no longer matter for your financial history — and if the IRS wouldn't care whether a history of the account remains in your records — delete the account. More likely than not, however, you need the records in the account for reports, charts, and other financial analyses.

Rather than delete an account, simply close it. You can still view transactions in a closed account. To view them, go to the Account List window, click the Sort Account List By link, and deselect Hide Closed Accounts on the submenu. Then double-click the name of the closed account to see its transactions.

Closing an account

Follow these steps to close an account:

1. **Click the Banking tab.**

   You see the Account List window, as shown in Figure 11-7. If the window is displaying closed accounts, their names are grayed out in the window.

Closed accounts are grayed out.

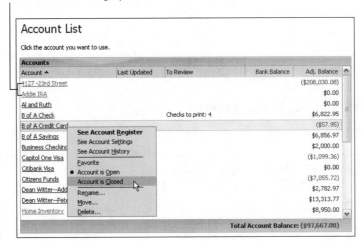

Figure 11-7:
Marking an
account as
closed.

2. **Right-click the account you want to close, and choose Account Is Closed on the shortcut menu.**

   The name of the account is either removed from the window or grayed out, depending on whether the window displays closed accounts.

You can reopen an account that you closed by right-clicking its name and choosing Account is Open from the shortcut menu. To see closed accounts in the Account List window, click the Sort Account List By link and choose and deselect Hide Close Accounts on the submenu.

To close or reopen several accounts at the same time, choose Tools⇨Settings and click the Account Settings (Global) link the Settings window. In the Global Settings window, click the Close or Reopen Accounts button. You see a list of your accounts. Select the ones you want to close; deselect the ones you want to reopen.

Deleting an account

Think twice before deleting an account. You might need the data later on. Follow these steps to delete an account:

Banking

1. **Click the Banking tab to go to the Account List window.**

2. **Right-click the account you want to delete and choose Delete on the shortcut menu (refer to Figure 11-7).**

   A dialog box warns you to think twice before deleting.

3. **Think twice and click the Yes button.**

Creating an Archive File for Past Transactions

An *archive file* stores all the previous transactions to a certain date for safe-keeping. Archive your Money file at tax time, copy it to a floppy disk, and put it away with all your receipts and records from the previous year. That way, you have an electronic record of your financial transactions from the past.

Don't create an archive file on January 1. Wait until you have cleared all transactions from the previous year and filed your income tax returns.

Follow these steps to create an archive file:

1. **Make sure that the file you want to archive is open.**

2. **Choose File➪Archive.**

   You see the Archive dialog box. Never mind all that verbiage; just glance at the text box in the lower-right corner to make sure that it shows January 1. All transactions in your registers prior to that day are copied to the archive file.

3. **If the date box doesn't show January 1, enter January 1 of this year.**

4. **Click OK.**

   You see the Archive dialog box. Money suggests a name for the archive file — it wants to name the file after last year.

5. **In the File Name text box, either enter your own name for the archive file or let Money's name stand.**

6. **Click OK.**

   You see the Archive dialog box.

7. **Select the check box next to the accounts whose transactions you want to include in the Archive file.**

8. **Click OK.**

Creating a Separate File for Financial Activity

You have to create a Money file for tracking a small business with Money. Self-employed people and people who operate very small businesses that require only one bank account can use their personal Money file, but all others need a separate file. As a rule, you need a separate file if you submit a separate income tax report for your business.

Read on to find out how to create a Money file and how to open a file. You also discover how to switch back and forth between the Money file where you track your personal finances and the one where you track your business's finances.

Creating the separate file

Follow these steps to create a new file:

1. **Choose File⇨New⇨New File or press Ctrl+N.**

   You see the Create New File dialog box, as shown in Figure 11-8.

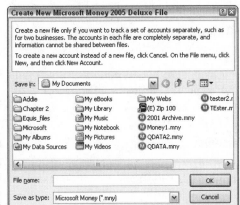

Figure 11-8: Creating a new file.

2. **In the File Name text box, enter a descriptive name for the new file.**

   Be sure to choose a name that is easy to identify. Filenames can be 255 characters long (though it's hard to imagine anyone that longwinded). Filenames *cannot* include the following characters: / \ [ ] : (* | <> = + ; , ? (if you saw these characters in a comic book, you would think that I was swearing at you).

3. **Click OK.**

   The Back Up dialog box appears. Money wants to close the file that is on-screen and open the one you just created, but before it closes files or closes the Money program, it always asks whether you want to back up the file you have been working on.

4. **Click the Back Up button.**

5. **Click the Next button and fill out the Set Up dialog boxes, if you so choose.**

   Chapter 2 explains setting up a new Money file. Click the Decline button if you want to start Money without using a .NET passport.

Opening the Money file you want to work with

The fastest way to go from one file to another is to click File on the main menu and select a filename from the bottom of the menu. But if the name of the file you want to open is not on the File menu, follow these steps to switch from one file to another:

1. **Choose File⇨Open or press Ctrl+O.**

   You see the Open File dialog box.

2. **Find and select the file you want to open.**

3. **Click the Open button.**

   Money insists on backing up a file when you close it to open another, so the Back Up dialog box appears. Earlier in this chapter, I explain all the details about backing up, but suffice it to say that you can click the Don't Back Up button if you're in a hurry.

4. **Click the Back Up button.**

   The new file appears on-screen. You can tell which file you've opened by reading its name on the title bar in the upper-left corner of the window.

Renaming and Deleting Files

In order to rename a file, it must be closed. Follow these steps to rename a Money file or delete one that you no longer need:

1. **Choose File⇨Open or press Ctrl+O.**

   You see the Open File dialog box.

2. **Locate the file that needs renaming or deleting.**

3. **Right-click the file you want to rename or delete.**

   A shortcut menu appears.

4. **Either rename or delete the file:**

   - **To rename:** Click Rename and type the new name over the old one.

   - **To delete:** Click Delete and then click Yes when Money asks whether you are brave enough to really do it.

5. **Click Cancel or press Esc to close the Open dialog box.**

Chapter 12

Pinching Your Pennies

. . . .

In This Chapter

▶ Keeping your spending under control

▶ Scheduling bills so that they are paid on time

▶ Formulating a budget with Money

▶ Tracking your frequent flyer miles

. . . .

"A penny saved is a penny earned," according to Benjamin Franklin. Apart from finding a better-paying job (or a second job), the only way to make more money and stay out of debt is to save and spend wisely. This chapter explains how to get Money's help to do just that.

In this chapter, you find out how to set limits for your spending, plan for a big-ticket purchase such as a house or car, schedule bills so that you pay them on time, put yourself on a budget, and track the frequent flyer miles or points that you earn with credit card purchases.

Being Alerted to Excessive Spending

One way to tighten your belt is to set monthly spending limits and have Money alert you when you spend too freely in a particular category. As soon as you overspend in the category, Money's Advisor FYI tells you as much (this feature is not available in the Standard edition). The clotheshorse in Figure 12-1, for example, has overspent in the Clothing category.

FYI advisories appear on the Home Page, in pop-up boxes when you record a transaction that exceeds a spending limit (refer to Figure 12-1), and in the Advisor FYI Options dialog box. They are hard to miss. Chapter 13 explains the Advisor FYI in detail. For now, follow these steps to see an FYI advisory when you overspend in a category:

1. **Choose Tools⇨Alert Center.**

   You go to the Settings window.

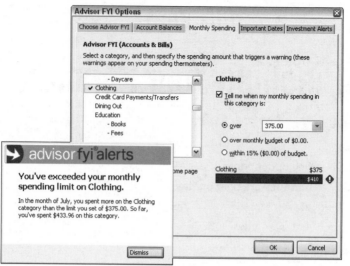

Figure 12-1:
The Advisor
FYI is one
way to
keep your
spending
under
control.

2. **Click the Customize Your Advisor FYI Alerts link.**

   The link is located in the Advisor FYI box. The Advisor FYI Options
   dialog box appears.

3. **Click the Monthly Spending tab.**

   Figure 12-1 shows this tab.

4. **Select the name of a spending category.**

   Choose the category in which your spending — how do I put this deli-
   cately? — is undisciplined. Usually that means the Clothing, Dining, or
   Entertainment category.

5. **Select the Tell Me When My Monthly Spending in This Category Is
   check box.**

6. **Enter a dollar figure in the Over text box.**

   Enter the amount that you want to spend each month in the category.
   Exceed the amount, and the Advisor FYI curls its lip and growls.

7. **Click the Show Thermometer on Money Home Page check box if you
   want a graph showing whether you overspent to appear on the Home
   Page.**

8. **Click the OK button.**

Scheduling Bills So That They're Paid on Time

Everybody forgets to pay a bill now and then. Usually, an envelope with an ominous red warning appears in the mail, you pay the bill, and that's the end of it. But sometimes you have to pay a fee for being late. Credit card issuers, for example, are notorious for charging late fees. Mortgage lenders also do not tolerate tardiness. And if you forget to pay the IRS on time . . . well, I shudder to think what happens if you forget to pay the IRS.

To make sure that you pay bills on time, schedule them in the Bills Summary window. If you want, a list of due and overdue bills can appear in the Money Express window and on the Home Page. (See Chapter 2 to find out how to make the list of bills appear.) On the Home Page in Figure 12-2, for example, one bill is overdue and two are upcoming. Bills are made a part of the budgets that you can create with Money and are used for cash-flow forecasting.

Which bills are candidates for scheduling? Any bill for which you have to pay a late fee. Go ahead and schedule the mortgage payment or rent, vehicle registration fees, credit card payments, alimony payments, and the like. But don't crowd the Bills Summary window with every bill that you receive. The purpose of scheduling bills is to help pay them on time. A crowded Bills Summary window is very discouraging, for one thing. And facing all those bills is hard because, in a long list of bills, it's difficult to identify which ones are the most important and need to be paid first.

Figure 12-2:
You can list overdue and upcoming bills in the Home Page.

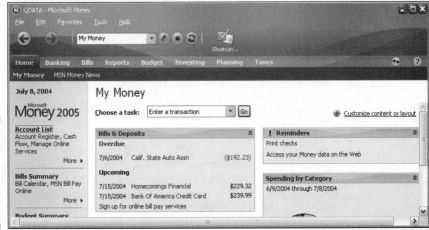

Advanced versus essential bills

Money offers two ways to schedule bills and deposits — advanced bills and essential bills. Both methods permit you to schedule bill payments, track when payments are due, and assign categories to scheduled bills for budgeting purposes. With advanced bills, however, you can schedule deposits as well as bill payments. You can also schedule investment purchases. And you can tell Money to enter scheduled transactions automatically in your registers as well as stop scheduling transactions after a certain amount of time has elapsed.

Personally, I don't think advanced bill scheduling is particularly advanced or that essential billing is particularly essential. You may as well go with advanced bill scheduling. It isn't very much trouble. Follow these steps to switch between advanced bills and essential bills:

1. **Click the Bills tab to go to the Bills Summary window.**

2. **Click the Change Bill Settings link. The Bills and Deposits tab of the Options dialog box appears.**

3. **Click the Switch to Advanced Bills link or the Switch to Essential Bills link.**

4. **Click the Use Advanced Bills button or the Use Essential Bills button.**

By the way, bills aren't the only things that you can schedule. You can also schedule deposits and account transfers. (I show you how in the section "Scheduling a bill payment or deposit," later in this chapter.) If your employer deposits your pay directly into a bank account, you can schedule the deposit. Or, you can simply schedule the deposit to remind yourself to do so and to make your future income a part of the financial projections and budgeting that Money does.

Scheduling a bill payment or deposit

Follow these steps to schedule a bill or deposit:

Bills

1. **Click the Bills tab.**

    You go to the Bills Summary window, as shown in Figure 12-3. You can also get to this window by clicking the Record or Pay Bills link in an Account Register window. The window lists bills, deposits, transfers, and investment purchases that have been scheduled thus far, if you have scheduled any transactions. Days on the calendar appear in boldface when a bill is due or a deposit is expected. (If you don't see the calendar, select the Show Calendar check box.)

2. **If you opted for advanced bills, click the New button and, from the pop-up menu, choose Bill or Deposit. If you opted for essential bills, simply click the New button to schedule a bill.**

Schedule bills and deposits.

Bills Summary

Click New to set up a new scheduled transaction. To pay, enter, or edit an existing
scheduled transaction, select it, and then click a button below.   Customize view...

Payee	Amount	Next Due	▲ Frequency	Payment Method
Calif. State Auto Assn	($192.23)~	7/6/2004	Monthly	Write Check
This transaction is 2 days overdue (1 occurrence past due).				
Homecomings Financial	$0.00 ~	7/15/2004	Monthly	Write Check
Bank Of America Credit ...	$0.00	7/15/2004	Monthly	Write Check
American Honda Financi...	($180.66)	7/23/2004	Monthly	Write Check
South End Rowing Club	($465.00)	2/5/2005	Yearly	Write Check

B of A Check balance: Current: $6,822.95   After: $6,630.72

[Enter in Register...] [Pay Online...] [New ▲] [Edit ▲] [Skip This Occurrence...] [Delete]   ~ Estimate ☑ Show calendar

◄	July 2004	►	August 2004	►	7/8/2004

S	M	T	W	T	F	S
27	28	29	30	1	2	3
4	5	6	7	**8**	9	10
11	12	13	14	**15**	16	17
18	19	20	21	22	**23**	24
25	26	27	28	29	30	31

S	M	T	W	T	F	S
1	2	3	4	5	**6**	7
8	9	10	11	12	13	14
15	16	17	18	19	20	21
22	**23**	24	25	26	27	28
29	30	31	1	2	3	4
5	6	7	8	9	10	11

Figure 12-3:
Scheduled
transactions
are listed in
the Bills
Summary
window.

Click a date to schedule a transaction.

You see the Create a Recurring Deposit window or the Create a Recurring
Bill window (the latter is shown in Figure 12-4). In this window, you
describe the bill or deposit, how frequently it is made, and in which
account register you will record it.

Create a recurring bill

To create a new recurring bill, enter the following information, and then click OK.

Payee Details

Pay to:* [M. Evans Co. ▼]   Address:

Account number:

Payment Information

Pay from:*	[B of A Check ▼]	Next payment date:*	[7/9/2004 ▼]
Payment method:*	[Write Check ▼]	Frequency:*	[Monthly ▼]
Amount:*	[1,544.23]	[This is a fixed amount ▼]	
Category:	[Salary ▼]	[Split]	
Properties:	[▼]		
Memo:	[ ]		

☐ Automatically enter transaction into my register the following number of days before the payment date: [3 ▲▼]

☑ This series will end at some point in time

Number of transactions remaining: [50]   Date of final transaction: [▼]

[OK] [Cancel]   * required

Figure 12-4:
In this
window,
describe bill
payments
and
scheduled
deposits
that you
intend to
make.

3. Answer the questions in the Create a Recurring Bill window, and click OK.

And no peeking over the shoulder of the next guy to see how he answered these questions.

Questions with an asterisk (*) in the window must be answered. Here is the lowdown on scheduling a bill or deposit:

- **Pay To/Receive From:** Choose the person or business that you will pay or is paying you. These names come from the Payee list.

- **Pay From/Deposit To:** Choose the bank account that you will pay the bill from or enter the deposit in. The Bills Summary (refer to Figure 12-3) has a button called Enter in Register. By clicking that button, you can enter the transaction without having to visit the account register.

- **Next Payment Date:** Enter the date when the next bill is due or the next deposit is to be made.

- **Payment Method:** In the case of a bill, tell how the payment will be made. Choose Print This Transaction if you print checks; choose Write Check if you will write the check by hand. In the case of a deposit, choose Manual Deposit if you make the deposit yourself; choose Direct Deposit if your employer deposits checks directly into your bank account.

- **Frequency:** Choose the option that describes how often the bill falls due or the deposit is made.

- **Amount:** Enter the amount, and then click the down arrow to open the pop-up menu and describe the amount:

  - **This Is a Fixed Amount:** The amount never changes and is the same from time period to time period. Choose this option to describe a bill or salary that is the same each month.

  - **Estimate Because the Amount Varies:** You estimate the amount. Choose this option to describe an amount that changes from period to period. Money uses your estimates in cash-flow forecasts and budgets.

  - **Estimate Based on the Last Number of Instances:** If you have used Money for a while, choose this option as well as a number from the Time Period submenu, and Money enters the average amount of the payment or deposit for you.

- **Category:** Choose a category or subcategory for the payment or deposit.

- **Automatically Enter Transaction:** Rather than click the Enter in Register button in the Bills Summary window (refer to Figure 12-3) to enter a transaction, you can have Money enter it for you if you choose this option. (This option isn't available with essential bills.)

✔ **This Series Will End:** Choose this option if you know that the bill will stop falling due or that the deposit will stop being made at a certain time in the future. Either enter the number of transactions that remain or enter an ending date in the text boxes. (This option isn't available with essential bills.)

The following are listed in the Bills Summary window: the payee, the amount, the due date, the frequency of the payment or deposit, and the payment method.

To get a very good look at when bills are due or deposits are supposed to be made, click the Bill Calendar button in the Bills Summary window (you can find it below the Bills tab). Instead of the baby bear calendar at the bottom of the window, you see a papa bear calendar in a new window called View Bills and Deposits on the Calendar.

How Money tells you to pay bills

After a bill or deposit is scheduled, Money gives you ten days' warning to pay it. In other words, you get ten days to get out of Dodge, and if you don't heed the warning but stick around and gamble at the saloon, Wyatt Earp and Doc Holiday ride you out of town on a rail (whatever that means).

Ten days before a bill is due, Money reminds you to pay it in these locations:

✔ **The Bills Summary window:** This window lists upcoming bills and deposits (refer to Figure 12-3). Bills that are overdue are shown in red.

✔ **Home Page:** If you so choose, you can make the Bills & Deposits list appear on the Home Page. (Refer to Figure 12-2, and see Chapter 2 to find out how to make the list appear.) Clicking a bill or deposit takes you to the Bills Summary window.

If ten days isn't enough time, or if you don't want the Money Express icon to crowd your taskbar, follow these steps to tell Money precisely how to handle upcoming bills and deposits:

1. **Choose Tools⇨Settings, and click the Bills Settings link in the Settings window.**

   You can also click the Change Bill Settings link in the Bills Summary window. You see the Bills and Deposits tab of the Options dialog box.

2. **In the Remind Me text box, enter how many days ahead of their due dates you want to be reminded that bills and deposits are due.**

   While you're there, notice the Count Only Business Days check box. Select it to exclude weekends and holidays from the countdown.

3. **Click the OK button.**

Recording a paycheck deposit automatically

If you schedule advanced bills, the pop-up menu that appears when you click the New button in the Bills Summary window offers an option called Paycheck for recording paycheck deposits. Don't bother choosing this option button unless you want to keep track of how much of your gross income is devoted to taxes, Social Security, employee-sponsored IRA accounts, health plans, and so on. In other words, don't choose the Paycheck option unless you are a stickler for keeping records.

If your employer is worth anything, he or she keeps these records for you. You can consult your employer to get the numbers. If your employer contributes to an IRA account, record that contribution as a scheduled deposit in the IRA, not as a paycheck deposit in which part of your income is diverted to the IRA. The Paycheck option is really for people who want to track small business activity in Money.

Scheduling deposits, transfers, and investment purchases

People who opted for advanced bills (not essential bills) can schedule transfers and investment purchases in the Bills Summary window as well as bill payments. Schedule a transfer if, for example, you always transfer part of your paycheck to a savings account. You can also schedule an investment purchase if you regularly buy shares of a security.

In the case of transfers and investment purchases, the steps for scheduling the transaction are nearly identical to those for scheduling a bill payment: Starting from the Bills Summary window, click the New button, choose an option from the pop-up menu, and answer the questions in the dialog boxes. (See the section "Scheduling a bill payment or deposit," earlier in this chapter, if you need help).

Recording a scheduled transaction in a register

Terrible, isn't it, when a bunch of bills raise their ugly heads in the Bills Summary window or the Bills & Deposits list in the Home Page window. How can you remove all those notices and start from a clean slate? I'm afraid you have to pay the bills (or else skip or cancel them, which is the subject of the next section in this chapter).

Many a Money user has recorded a bill that is due in the Bills Summary window but then forgotten to actually pay the bill. I don't know why that is. Having gone to the trouble of recording a bill payment, it seems that many people think that the bill is really paid. It's not paid. No, You still have to get out the old checkbook and mail the check.

Follow these steps to pay bills and make other transactions that you scheduled:

1. **Click the Bills tab.**

   You go to the Bills Summary window (refer to Figure 12-3). You can also get to this window by clicking the Record or Pay Bills link in an Account Register window.

2. **Double-click the transaction that needs recording.**

   You can also select a transaction and then click the Enter into Register button or right-click the transaction and choose Enter into Register. As shown in Figure 12-5, you see the Record dialog box. Looks like a transaction form, doesn't it? And look — it's already filled out. (Well, it's mostly filled out, anyway.)

Figure 12-5: Recording scheduled transactions is pretty simple — most of the boxes in the Record dialog box are already filled in.

3. **If necessary, fill in the Number box.**

   You can either enter a check number or click the arrow for a drop-down list of options. Select Print This Transaction to print the check on your printer.

4. **If you are paying a bill or recording a transaction whose amount changes from month to month, enter the correct amount in the Amount text box.**

5. **Click the Record Payment button or press Enter.**

To visit the account register where the scheduled transaction was recorded (and see what the new account balance is), right-click the transaction in the Bills Summary window and choose Go to Account from the shortcut menu.

Click the View History link in the Bills Summary window if you have second thoughts about whether a bill needs paying. After you click the link, you see a list of the scheduled transactions that you recorded in the last 60 days. The list tells you plain and simple which bills were paid and which may need to be paid again.

Skipping a scheduled transaction

Suppose that you want to skip a scheduled transaction this month, perhaps because you already recorded it in a register. Follow these steps:

1. **Click the Bills tab to go to the Bills Summary window (refer to Figure 12-3).**

2. **Find the transaction that you want to skip, and click it.**

3. **Click the Skip This Occurrence button.**

   The Skip Scheduled Transaction dialog box asks whether you want to skip it this time around, skip all overdue occurrences, or drop the transaction from the list of scheduled transactions.

4. **Choose an option, and click the OK button.**

Changing a scheduled transaction

If you need to alter a scheduled transaction, select it in the Bills Summary window, click the Edit button, and choose one of these options from the button's pop-up menu:

✔ **Edit Series:** Takes you to an Edit window that looks and operates just like the Create a Recurring Deposit or the Create a Recurring Bill window (refer to Figure 12-4) so that you can change the scheduled transaction.

✔ **Edit a Single Occurrence:** Takes you to a window where you can choose the date of the scheduled transaction that you want to change and then change the transaction.

Canceling a scheduled transaction

You've been a loyal subscriber to the by-mail bodybuilding course, and you're as scrawny as ever, so you decide to quit making the monthly payments that you scheduled in the Bills Summary window. Follow these steps to cancel a scheduled transaction and remove it forever from the window:

1. **Click the Bills tab to go to the Bills Summary window (refer to Figure 12-3).**

2. **Select the scheduled transaction that you want to abandon, and click the Delete button.**

3. **Click the Yes button when Money asks whether you really want to delete the transaction.**

Budgeting with Money

Except for getting a higher-paying or second job, begging, borrowing, or stealing, the only way to save more money is to put yourself on a budget. A *budget* is a plan for keeping spending down in different areas, the idea being to make more money available for the things that you want to do — go to college, go to Greece, pay off a credit card debt, and so on.

If you've ever tried to draft a budget on paper, you'll be delighted with the Money budgeting features. As long as you categorize expense transactions when you record them in registers (see Chapter 5), half the work of drafting your budget is already done. You already know how much you spend on groceries, clothing, and dining, for example. Now all you have to do is get Money's help to target the categories where you spend too much. In other words, all you have to do now is to set budget goals for yourself.

This section of the chapter explains how to draft a budget with Money, including how to set budget goals and, just as important, how to generate graphs and reports that tell you whether you've met your budget.

I strongly recommend waiting at least three months before formulating a budget. Here's the reason: Money gathers data about your spending habits from the transactions that you enter in registers. You can save a good deal of time by using this data for budget projections. To use the data, however, you must have been recording transactions in Money for at least three months.

You formulate a budget in Money through the Budget windows, where you tell Money the following things:

- ✔ What you expect your income to be
- ✔ How much you propose to set aside for savings and reducing debt

✔ How much you want to set aside for retirement

✔ How much you prefer to spend in different expense categories

After making these determinations, you can find out how much money will be left for spending or saving if you meet your budget. You also can generate reports and charts to see whether you've met your budget in each spending category.

Before you visit the Budget windows, however, I suggest taking these two steps:

✔ **Prepare your budget estimates.** The mechanics of drawing up a budget with Money are pretty simple, but creating an actual budget is not. Before you start formulating your budget, create and print a Monthly Cash Flow report, which can help you decide how much to spend each month in different categories. Chapter 15 explains how to create and print reports.

✔ **Gather the necessary documents.** Figures from paycheck stubs and bills come in handy when budgeting with Money.

Choosing between advanced and essential budgets

To make budgeting a little simpler, Money offers what it calls *essential budgeting* and *advanced budgeting*. Essential budgets don't permit you to examine your income and spending in as much detail, but they are easier to set up. Advanced budgets permit you to peer into all the little details of your spending and income, but they require more thought on your part. In a nutshell, here are the differences between essential and advanced budgets:

✔ In an essential budget, you track your spending in three categories that you deem your "favorites," but in an advanced budget, you can track your income and spending in every category and subcategory.

✔ You can formulate only one essential budget, but you can formulate as many advanced budgets as you need.

✔ You can enter only savings goals in an advanced budget. Savings goals represent a way to track the money that you save by budgeting.

✔ You can account for variations in your income with an advanced budget but not with an essential one.

✔ You can figure one-time expenses, such as car purchases and vacations, into an advanced budget but not into an essential budget.

Some gratuitous budgeting advice

Budgeting is like dieting: It requires discipline. When you are on a diet, your stomach rumbles. You feel hungry all the time. At dinner parties, you have to say "Just a sliver, please," no matter how delicious the cake looks. The only pleasures in going on a diet are noticing how well your clothes fit and seeing the needle on the bathroom scale point to new, uncharted regions.

Similarly, the only pleasure in living with a budget is seeing the balances in your savings and checking accounts rise to new, uncharted heights. Having to compare prices in the supermarket and

go without fancy new duds is hard. Postponing a vacation is hard. Eating meat loaf at home when you could be enjoying *oie rotie aux pruneaux* (roast goose with prune stuffing) in a swanky restaurant is hard.

To make living with a budget easier, try to set realistic goals for yourself. Don't set yourself up for failure by making your budget too strict. Draft a budget that you can live with. Challenge yourself, but don't go overboard. That way, disciplining yourself is easier, more likely to be successful, and much more rewarding.

Essential budgets are useful if you have a regular monthly income and you are only concerned with how you spend in a handful of categories. They take but a few minutes to set up. Follow these steps to declare whether you want to create an essential or an advanced budget:

1. **Choose Tools⇨Settings.**

2. **Click the Budget Settings link.**

   You see the Budget Settings window.

   When you switch from advanced budgeting to essential budgeting, the advanced budget that you already created (if you created one) is stripped down to the, well, the bare essentials. And if you created more than one budget, all except the first one is deleted from your Money file.

3. **Click the Switch from the Essential Budget to the Advanced Budget link or the Switch from the Advanced Budget to the Essential Budget link.**

   The Budget Settings dialog box appears.

4. **Click the Use Essential Budget or the Use Advanced Budget button.**

   If you opted for essential budgets, Money opens the Welcome to Budget window. (For details, see the section "Formulating an essential budget," later in this chapter.) Money opens the Create a Budget window if you opted for advanced budgets. (Click the Create a Budget link, and skip to Step 3 in the next section of this chapter.)

Getting started with an advanced budget

The next four sections explain how to formulate an advanced budget. (Later in this chapter, "Formulating an essential budget" explains how to handle essential budgets.) You can start formulating an advanced budget by following these steps:

1. **Click the Budget tab.**

   If this is your first stab at creating a budget (and you told Money to create advanced budgets), you see the Create a Budget window. If you've already created one budget, you see the Budget Summary window.

2. **Click the Next button if this is your first budget; click the Create a New Budget link to start a new advanced budget.**

   You come to the Set Up a Budget window. It outlines what budgeting entails.

   If the Enter Income window appears instead of the Set Up a Budget window, Money thinks that you want to create an essential budget, not an advanced one. See the previous section in this chapter to find out the difference between the two kinds of budgets.

   To formulate a budget, you give Money information about your income, your expenses, your savings goals, and how much you want to spend in each category. To get from window to window, click the Next button (or the Previous button). These buttons are located at the bottom of windows.

3. **Click the Next button to go to the Enter Your Income window.**

   This window is shown in Figure 12-6. If you've scheduled any deposits in the Bills Summary window (see "Scheduling Bills So That They Are Paid on Time," earlier in this chapter), the monthly amounts of those deposits already appear in the window and are marked by an icon. Your next task is to enter your monthly income (and perhaps your spouse's monthly income as well) in this window. After you are finished, the Total Monthly Income figure should describe your household's monthly income. Better keep reading.

Enter your income: Telling Money about your income

To stay within the budget that you create, your spending cannot exceed your income. Unless your income varies wildly from month to month, you don't have to be a rocket scientist to complete this part of the budget. You can simply tell Money to get your average monthly income and enter it in the window. However, if you are self-employed or if you use Money to track a business, your income probably varies from month to month, and estimating your monthly income is not as easy.

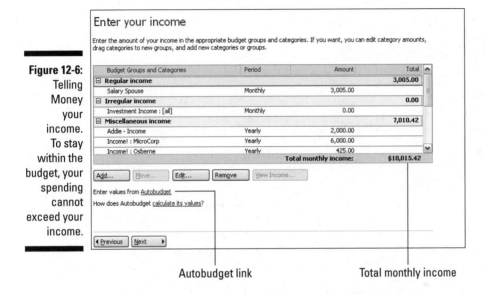

Figure 12-6: Telling Money your income. To stay within the budget, your spending cannot exceed your income.

Autobudget link

Total monthly income

Follow these steps to report your income to the Budget Planner if you haven't scheduled any deposits or if you earn income beyond what you're scheduled to receive:

1. **Click the Add button.**

   You see the Budget Group Name dialog box.

2. **Select the second option button, Add a Category to a Budget from the List Below, and choose Budget Group from the drop-down list; then click the Next button.**

   The budget groups are Regular Income, Irregular Income, and Miscellaneous Income. After you add an income category from the Categories list in the next step, the category's name appears under a budget group in the Enter Your Income window.

   The Choose Categories dialog box, shown in Figure 12-7, appears after you click the Next button. Do these categories look familiar? They are the income categories in the Categories list.

3. **Select income categories and subcategories by clicking the check boxes next to their names.**

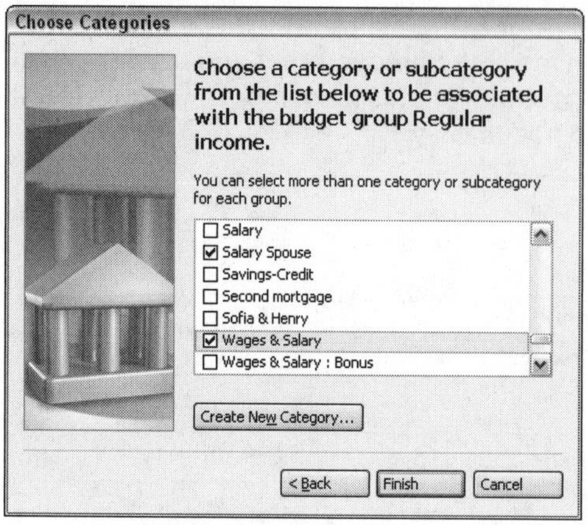

Figure 12-7:
Choosing
budget
categories
and sub-
categories.

4. Click the Finish button to include each category's subcategories in the budget estimate.

You return to the Enter Your Income window.

Based on the transactions that you have entered in your account registers, Money enters an average monthly income figure in the Amount column. But what if the figure doesn't truly represent your monthly income in the category? Either double-click the category, or select it and click the Edit button. You see the Edit dialog box, as shown in Figure 12-8. Describe your monthly income as follows:

✔ **Recurring:** Select the Recurring option. From the Period drop-down list, select the option that describes how often you receive income in the category. Enter the amount in the Amount text box.

✔ **Different each month:** Select the Custom option. In the month text boxes, enter roughly how much you earn each month in the category.

The Enter Your Income window also offers techniques for doing these chores:

✔ **Moving a category to a different budget group:** Click the Move button, and choose the group in the Move dialog box.

✔ **Creating a new budget group:** Click the Add button, and in the Choose Categories dialog box (refer to Figure 12-7), select the first option button and enter a name for the group in the first text box. Then click the Next button and choose categories and subcategories for the group.

✔ **Removing categories:** Click a category name, and then click the Remove button.

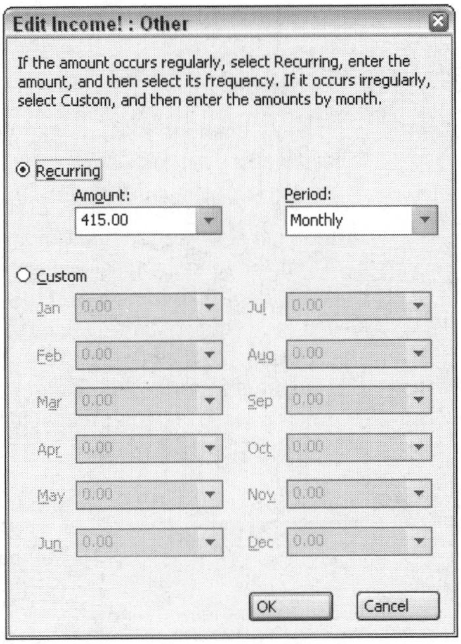

Edit Income! : Other

If the amount occurs regularly, select Recurring, enter the amount, and then select its frequency. If it occurs irregularly, select Custom, and then enter the amounts by month.

⦿ Recurring

Amount: Period:
415.00   Monthly

○ Custom

Jan 0.00   Jul 0.00
Feb 0.00   Aug 0.00
Mar 0.00   Sep 0.00
Apr 0.00   Oct 0.00
May 0.00   Nov 0.00
Jun 0.00   Dec 0.00

OK   Cancel

Figure 12-8: Describe your income here if Money didn't estimate it correctly.

Enter your expenses: Budgeting your monthly expenses

Now comes the hard but interesting part — the Enter Your Expenses window, which is shown in Figure 12-9. Your task now, if you choose to accept it, is to enter category-by-category budget goals and tell Money how much you intend to spend in each category. In this window, you look long and hard at your spending habits to find out where you spend and how you can rein in your spending. If you've scheduled any bills in the Bills Summary window (see "Scheduling Bills So That They Are Paid on Time," earlier in this chapter), the monthly amounts of those bills are already listed in the window and are marked by an icon.

The buttons along the bottom of the window — Add, Move, Edit, Remove, and View Spending — work the same way in this window as they do in the Enter Your Income window. Click the Add button to add a category or subcategory to the list of budget categories. Select a category and click the Edit button to open the Edit dialog box (refer to Figure 12-8) and declare how much you spend monthly in a category. Tinker with the numbers until you formulate a budget that challenges you to spend more wisely.

Autobudgeting with Money

One way to take some of the tedium out of setting budget goals is to click the Autobudget link in the Enter Your Income window (refer to Figure 12-6) and the Enter Your Expenses window. An Autobudget is a bit like the 1040EZ tax form: It does the job as long as your finances are not particularly complicated and you don't have a lot of categories to budget for.

When you click the Autobudget link, you see the Autobudget dialog box (see the following figure). The dialog box analyzes your past spending (yeah, right) and lists the amounts that it thinks

you should spend in most of your categories. Autobudget doesn't work, however, if you haven't entered at least a month's worth of transactions.

To enter new budget goals quickly, get the numbers from the Autobudget dialog box. To do that, click the Clear All button, select the check box next to each category and subcategory that you want to enter in your budget, and then click OK. The numbers from the Autobudget dialog box are transferred to the Enter Your Income and the Enter Your Expenses windows.

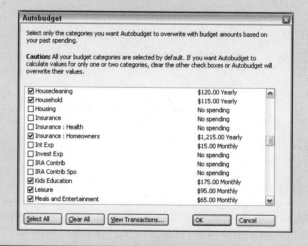

Entering category-by-category spending goals can be a tedious activity. Fortunately, Money offers a shortcut for doing the job a little faster — the Autobudget. Read the sidebar "Autobudgeting with Money" to find out how you can enter starting-point numbers for spending goals.

Savings goals: Declaring what to do with extra money

The Savings Goals window is for declaring what you will do with the money that you save by budgeting. Click the Spend All Excess Income option button if you want to spend it, but if you are looking ahead to a vacation, a new car, or something else you want to save for, you can put its name in the Savings Goals window. In Budget reports, Money lists these goals and shows you in monetary terms how close or far away you are from attaining them.

Click the Add Another Goal button, enter a name for the goal, declare the date by which you hope to achieve it, and enter the amount that you hope to save.

Budget summary and status

After you fill in the Savings Goals window, you come to the first Budget Summary window. Scroll through the window, admire the pie charts, and marvel at how much you will save by sticking to your budget. Then click the Finish button.

The final window, Budget Summary, is shown in Figure 12-10. It tells you whether you are meeting your budget goals this month. By choosing an option from the Change Time Period drop-down list, you can see whether your weekly or yearly income covers your budget expenses. Scroll down the list. Overbudgeted items are listed at the top.

Click the Done button to go to the Budget Summary tab.

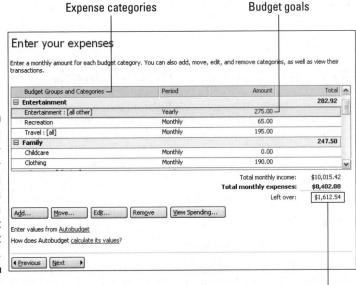

Expense categories   Budget goals

Figure 12-9:
The Enter
Your
Expenses
window is
where you
hammer out
your budget
goals.

What you can save by budgeting

The Budget Summary window offers a couple of buttons for tinkering with the budget. Click the Reallocate Funds button if you have exceeded your spending limit in one category and you want to "borrow" money from another category to cover the overrun. Click the Add a One-Time Item button to enter a one-time expense, such as a major car repair, into the budget. Personally, I think these buttons are silly. The purpose of a budget is not to track your spending more closely. The purpose is to get a better sense of where you spend and how you can spend more wisely. These buttons are meant to help you force your budget to balance, but is that really necessary?

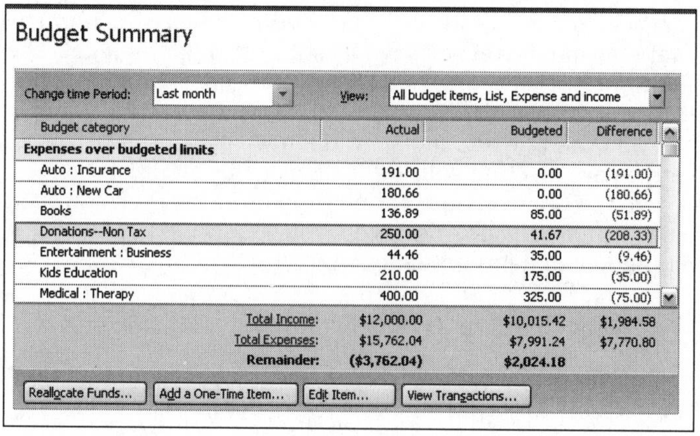

Figure 12-10:
The Budget Summary window shows whether your average monthly income can cover the average monthly expenses that you list.

Formulating an essential budget

Earlier in this chapter, the section "Choosing between advanced and essential budgets" explained the difference between the two budgets. Follow these steps to formulate a budget if you chose essential budgets over advanced ones:

1. **Click the Budget tab.**

   You see the Create a Budget window.

2. **Click the Next button.**

   The Enter Income window appears.

3. **Describe your income in this window by entering a figure in the middle text box and, from the drop-down menu, describing how often you are paid; then click the Next button.**

For example, if you are paid $1,500 twice monthly, enter 1500 and choose Twice a Month from the drop-down menu. Money uses the figure that you enter to see whether your spending exceeds your income.

4. **In the Select Budget Categories window, select the name of each spending category that you want to track in your budget; then click the Next button.**

   Money compares your monthly spending in these categories to your monthly income.

5. **In the Enter Expenses window, enter how much you want to spend monthly in each category that you select in Step 4; then click the Next button.**

   The total of your expenses appears in the upper-right corner of the screen, as shown in Figure 12-11. Make sure that the expense total doesn't exceed your monthly income total.

6. **In the Select Favorite Categories window, select the three favorite categories that you want to track closely; then click the Finish button.**

   Graphs showing your spending in these three categories appear in the Budget Summary window so that you can track your spending more carefully.

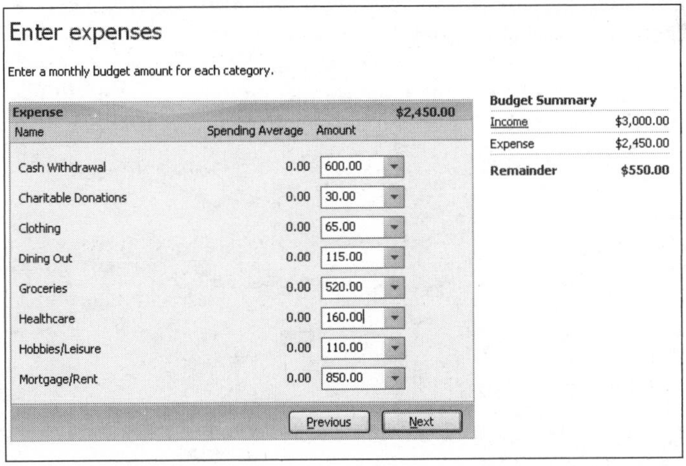

Enter expenses

Enter a monthly budget amount for each category.

Expense			$2,450.00
Name	Spending Average	Amount	
Cash Withdrawal	0.00	600.00	
Charitable Donations	0.00	30.00	
Clothing	0.00	65.00	
Dining Out	0.00	115.00	
Groceries	0.00	520.00	
Healthcare	0.00	160.00	
Hobbies/Leisure	0.00	110.00	
Mortgage/Rent	0.00	850.00	

Budget Summary

Income	$3,000.00
Expense	$2,450.00
Remainder	$550.00

[Previous]   [Next]

Figure 12-11: Formulating an essential budget.

Seeing whether you met your budget goals

You've drawn up a budget and carefully recorded your income and expenses for a month or more, and now the moment of truth has arrived. It's time to see whether you've met your budget. The envelope, please . . . . Follow these steps to create a budget report or graph and find out how well you did:

Reports

1. **Click the Reports tab.**

   The Reports Home window appears.

2. **Click the Monthly Budget or the Annual Budget link to create a monthly or annual budget report.**

   You can find these links in the Income and Expenses report category.

   You see a Budget report, as shown in Figure 12-12. It shows how your budget projections compare to your actual spending. Look in the Difference column to see whether you overspent or underspent your budget projections. Where you overspent, you see a red, negative number in parentheses.

   Care to see the report in chart form?

3. **Under Common Tasks, click the Change View link and then choose Bar Chart from the submenu.**

   A pair of bars corresponds to each category and subcategory in your budget. Gently slide the mouse pointer over the bars to read the category names and spending amounts. The Actual bar on the left shows what you spent, and the Budgeted bar on the right shows how much the budget called for you to spend. The Difference bar shows by how much the Actual and Budgeted figures differ.

You can customize the Home Page to make it show a small budget summary report (see Chapter 2).

Monthly Budget
6/1/2004 through 6/30/2004

Categories	Actual	Budgeted	Difference
Other expenses			
Auto : New Car	180.66	0.00	(180.66)
Auto : Registration fee	0.00	20.00	20.00
Auto : Repair	0.00	135.00	135.00
Backpacking Equipment	0.00	77.92	77.92
Books	136.89	85.00	(51.89)
Donations	110.89	260.00	149.11
Donations--Non Tax	250.00	41.67	(208.33)
Education : Addies Loan	0.00	100.00	100.00
Entertainment : Business	44.46	35.00	(9.46)
Fees : [all]	0.00	25.00	25.00
Gardening	0.00	35.00	35.00
Gifts	107.42	210.00	102.58
Hair	0.00	10.83	10.83
Home Repair	0.00	70.00	70.00
Housecleaning	0.00	10.00	10.00
Insurance : Homeowners	0.00	101.25	101.25
Kids Education	210.00	175.00	(35.00)
Leisure	0.00	95.00	95.00
Meals and Entertainment	0.00	65.00	65.00
Medical : Dental	0.00	10.83	10.83
Medical : Optometry	0.00	29.17	29.17

Figure 12-12:
Look in the Difference column to see whether you met your budget.

Working with more than one budget . . .

You can formulate more than one budget. Some people formulate a pessimistic and an optimistic budget. Some formulate a gloomy and a hopeful budget. In any case, if you have already fashioned a budget and you want to fashion a second one, click the Budget tab to go to the Budget Summary window and then click the Create a New Budget link. You see the Set Up a Budget window. Take it from there.

To open and examine different budgets, click the Budget tab and then click the Save or Open a New Budget link. You see the Save or Open a Budget dialog box, as shown in Figure 12-13. Select the budget that you want, and click the Load Budget button.

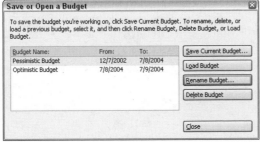

Figure 12-13:
Choosing
which
budget to
tinker with.

Tracking Your Frequent Flyer Miles

Some credit card companies entice their customers with frequent flyer miles or frequent flyer points. For every dollar that you charge to your credit card, you are awarded miles or points to be redeemed at an airline ticket counter. These programs are a wonderful way to fly for free, and to make sure that you are being credited properly, you can track miles or points in a Frequent Flyer account.

Follow these steps to set up an account for tracking frequent flyer miles or points:

1. **Click the Banking tab to go to the Account List window.**

2. **Click the Add a Frequent Flyer Plan link.**

   You can find this link under Common Tasks. After you click it, you see the New Frequent Flyer dialog box.

3. **For tracking purposes, enter a name for the program and click the Next button.**

4. **Choose Track Miles or Track Points to describe how miles are earned; then click the Next button.**

5. **Enter how many miles or points you have already earned, if any; then click the Next button.**

6. **Declare how and when the program expires, and click the Next button.**

7. **Click the Yes button to link the program to a Money credit card account, and then choose the name of the account from the Account drop-down list.**

The name for the frequent flyer program that you entered in Step 1 is added to the Account List window. (If you don't see a name, select the Show Frequent Flyer Programs check box.) To see how many miles or points you have earned, add more miles or points, or deduct miles or points, select the name of the account in the Account List window. You see a Frequent Flyer screen like the one shown in Figure 12-14. From here, you can keep careful tabs on your miles or points and make sure that you get that trip to Hawaii.

Figure 12-14:
Tracking
frequent
flyer miles.

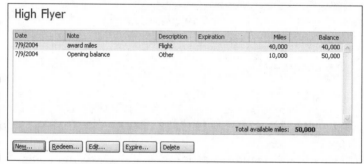

Chapter 13

Planning for the Years Ahead

● ●

In This Chapter

▶ Being alerted to important financial events

▶ Projecting your cash flow

▶ Projecting your financial future with the Lifetime Planner

▶ Devising a plan to get out of debt

● ●

Most people don't like focusing on the future, and who can blame them? Retirement, children's college expenses, next year's taxes — who wants to think about that? Maybe it's better to live fast, die young, and leave a beautiful memory.

Actually, you would do well to plan ahead for, or at least give a moment's consideration to, your financial future. This chapter explains how to enlist Money's help in planning for your retirement and other long-term objectives. You also discover how to use Money as your executive secretary and have Money remind you when you need to make important financial decisions and considerations. This chapter even shows you how to use Money to gaze into the future and predict how full or empty your checking and savings accounts will be.

 FYI Alerts, the Lifetime Planner, and the Debt Reduction Planner are not available in the Standard edition of Money. The Introduction of this book explains the differences between the Standard, Deluxe, Premium, and Small Business editions of the program.

Being Alerted to Important Events

Who doesn't need a wake-up call now and then? To keep from slumbering, you can make what Money calls *Advisor FYI alerts* appear on the Home Page and in Monthly reports (if you generate Monthly reports). Clicking an alert takes you to the Review the Advisor FYI Details window, where you can find out why you are being alerted. Alerts are notices about upcoming financial events and dates. As part of the Advisor FYI feature, you can also get financial advice. Figure 13-1 shows an alert in the Review the Advisor FYI Details window.

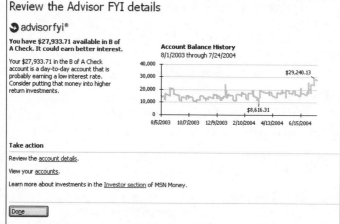

Figure 13-1:
Advisor FYI alerts tell you when something important needs to be done.

To tell Money that you want to be alerted and what you want to be alerted about, choose Tools⇨Alerts Center and click the Customize Your Advisor FYI alerts link in the Alerts Center window. You see the Advisor FYI Options dialog box, as shown in Figure 13-2.

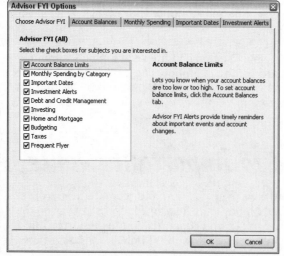

Figure 13-2:
In the Advisor FYI Options dialog box, tell Money how to alert you.

Select check boxes beside the subjects that you deem important enough to be alerted about. If you have questions about a subject, read its description on the right side of the dialog box.

Notice that the first four alert check boxes on the Choose Advisor FYI tab also happen to be similar to the names of tabs in the Advisor FYI Options dialog box. If you selected one of the first four check boxes, visit its tab to tell Money precisely how to alert you:

- ✔ **Account Balances:** Choose an account and use the text boxes to tell Money to alert you when the balance rises above or falls below a certain level.

- ✔ **Monthly Spending:** Choose an expense category and enter an amount so that Money can warn you when you go over the amount. (Chapter 12 explains this one in detail.)

- ✔ **Important Dates:** Enter and describe a date. Money alerts you to important tax-filing dates. Click the New button and enter a date that means something to you — a birthday, for example.

- ✔ **Investment Alerts:** Have Money alert you when a security reaches a certain high or low level. (Chapter 9 explains this one in detail.)

The last six check boxes on the Choose Advisor FYI tab are for getting articles and advice about debt reduction, investing, mortgages, budgeting, taxes, and your frequent flyer program, if you are enrolled in one (Chapter 12 explains that one).

Projecting Your Cash Flow

Cash flow is a business term that describes how much day-to-day money will be on hand in the future. Cash flow is a measure of a business's health. Thanks to the miracle of computing, you can look ahead to what your cash flow will be — sort of. Money permits you to peek into the future with the Cash Flow Review command, but for the command to do its job, you must have been using Money for a while and have a regular income. The Cash Flow Review command works best for people who make a monthly salary or earn roughly the same amount of money each month.

To make cash-flow projections, Money takes into account your present account balances, postdated transactions in account registers, average increases and decreases in your primary checking and savings accounts, scheduled transactions (if you've scheduled any), and your budget (if you formulated a budget).

Scheduling transactions, a subject of Chapter 12, does wonders for cash-flow projections because it gives Money more data to work with. Money offers one or two ways to tinker with projections to make them more accurate.

Bills

Click the Bills tab and, in the Bills Summary window, click the Forecast Cash Flow link (you can find it under Common Tasks). You see the Forecast Your Cash Flow window, as shown in Figure 13-3. I hope the lines on your cash-flow chart are rising gloriously, not steeply falling. By choosing accounts from the Account drop-down list and different time periods from the Time Period drop-down list, you can peer into different time frames. How do you like this crystal ball?

Choose an account.　　　Choose a time period.

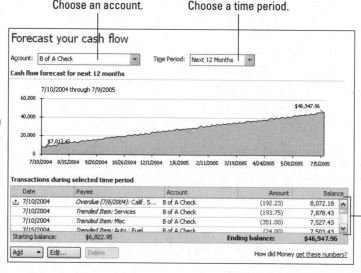

Figure 13-3:
Looking ahead to how much day-to-day cash you will have on hand.

Schedule and add transactions.

If the cash-flow projections aren't reported correctly, try adding transactions to the list at the bottom of the window to describe your financial activity. Choose an option from the Time Period drop-down list to describe how often the activity takes places, click the Add button at the bottom of the window, and choose Withdrawal, Deposit, or Transfer from the pop-up menu. You'll see the Edit Transaction window, which looks and works like a transaction form. Enter a transaction, and click OK. The transaction is entered on the list in the window. Scheduled transactions, if you've made any, already appear on the list. Choose the One-Time Item option from the pop-up menu to find out how one-time expenses or earnings — the purchase of a boat, a cash gift from Aunt Enid — affect your cash flow.

Under Common Tasks on the left side of the window, Money offers techniques for adjusting cash-flow projections and playing what-if games. Check out these options to read the future more accurately:

- **Try Cash Flow Scenarios:** Takes you to the Play What-If Cash Flow window, where you can see what happens to projections if you spend or earn more

- **Add an Item:** Offers the same options as the Add button

- **Read Cash Flow Tips:** Takes you to a window where you can read tips for cash flow optimization, courtesy of American Express

- **Change Cash Flow Settings:** Takes you to the Change Cash Flow Settings window, where you can tell Money whether to include data from your budget (if you've formulated one) and your scheduled transactions (if you've scheduled any)

Introducing the Lifetime Planner

I call the Lifetime Planner a "monster" because if you want to — and if you have *a lot* of spare time on your hands — you can use it to map out your hopes and dreams for the future and find out whether your income will support your hopes and dreams. The Lifetime Planner is a sort of financial counselor in a can. Rather than visiting the offices of a financial counselor (and be charged accordingly), you can try your hand with the Lifetime Planner.

Planning

To check out the Lifetime Planner, click the Planning tab, and in the Planning window, click the Lifetime Planner link. You land in the Lifetime Planner window. Notice the links on the left side — About You, Income, Taxes & Inflation, and so on. By clicking those links and entering information in different windows, you tell Money how long you expect to live, what you expect your income to be, how you think taxes and inflation will affect your income, how much you expect your savings and investments to grow, what your assets are, how much debt you have, and what your living expenses are. (I show you how to do all these things shortly.)

When you finish prognosticating, you can go to the Summary window and generate a Bottom Line chart like the one displayed in Figure 13-4, which shows how much money you will have when you retire. To generate the chart, Money looks at the balances in your accounts, makes projections about your future income, and compares your future income to how much you expect your living expenses and financial obligations to cost in the future.

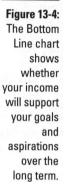

Figure 13-4:
The Bottom
Line chart
shows
whether
your income
will support
your goals
and
aspirations
over the
long term.

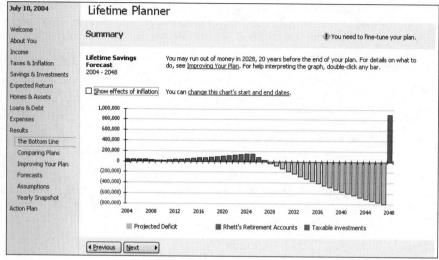

The fellow whose chart is shown in Figure 13-4 will retire in 2027 with an accumulated wealth of about $75,000, start drawing on his savings and retirement income, fall deeply into debt, die in the year 2047, and leave behind approximately $750,000 in debt. The message You need to fine-tune your plan appears at the top of the chart. Most people have to fine-tune their plan, but that is the purpose of the Lifetime Planner — to make you think long and hard about the future.

Besides the Bottom Line chart, you can generate many other charts when you finish formulating your lifetime plan. The chart in Figure 13-5, for example, shows how a couple's combined salaries will grow over time. To forecast the future in a chart, select a question from the Pick a Question drop-down list.

Figure 13-5:
Select
questions
from the
Pick a
Question
drop-down
list on the
Forecasts
screen to
learn more
about your
lifetime
plan.

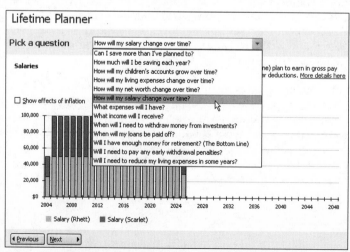

The Lifetime Planner makes its projections in today's dollars, not the inflated dollars of tomorrow. Most of the Lifetime Planner screens, however, have check boxes called Show Effects of Inflation that you can check to change the dollar figures to tomorrow's dollars.

About you: Telling Money about yourself and your dependents

The first step in using the Lifetime Planner is to click the Lifetime Planner link to get to the Lifetime Planner window, and then click the Get Going on Your Plan link or the About You link. You land in the Tell Us about Yourself window, as shown in Figure 13-6. Money uses the data you enter here to make long-term projections. For example, between your retirement age and your life expectancy age (read "the age you want to die"), you will draw from the money that you saved for retirement. Money uses that data to determine how much you need to save for retirement.

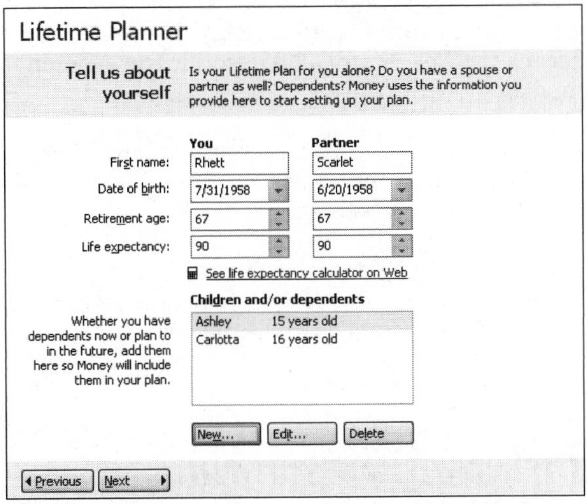

Lifetime Planner

Tell us about yourself — Is your Lifetime Plan for you alone? Do you have a spouse or partner as well? Dependents? Money uses the information you provide here to start setting up your plan.

	You	**Partner**
First name:	Rhett	Scarlet
Date of birth:	7/31/1958	6/20/1958
Retirement age:	67	67
Life expectancy:	90	90

☐ See life expectancy calculator on Web

Children and/or dependents

Whether you have dependents now or plan to in the future, add them here so Money will include them in your plan.

| Ashley | 15 years old |
| Carlotta | 16 years old |

[New...] [Edit...] [Delete]

◀ Previous   ◀ Next ▶

Figure 13-6: Describing yourself.

If you have dependents or a spouse, enter their data as well in the bottom half of the window. Click the New button and fill in the Add Person dialog box to describe a dependent. Money needs information about dependents because, with you as their sole support, they draw upon your income now and in the future. Click the Edit button to change the information about a dependent or the Delete button to delete a dependent from the list.

Income: Describing your present and future income

The next step is to click the Income link (or click Next) and tell the planner what your income is and how you expect it to increase (I certainly hope it increases) over time. The Lifetime Planner needs to know this information so that it can determine whether you will have enough income to meet your goals.

In the Career window, enter your gross annual salary or wage income (what you make before taxes) in the Annual Gross Salary text box. Notice the following gizmos on this screen that you can use to help describe your future income:

- ✔ **Annual Raises button:** Money assumes that your salary or wage income will increase by 3 percent each year until age 50, at which time society will cruelly stop giving you pay raises. To change these assumptions, click the Annual Raises button and make entries in the Annual Raises dialog box.

- ✔ **What Events will affect your salary?:** Click the New button to describe an event — a life change that affects your income, such as changing jobs, taking time off, or working fewer hours. If an event is looming in your future, click the New button and describe the event in the New Career Event dialog boxes.

If you have a spouse or partner and you are tracking his or her income in Money, fill in the second Career screen as well. Then click the Other Income button to go to the Other Income screen.

On the Other Income screen, you describe income from pensions, Social Security, inheritances, alimony, and other such income sources. Click the New Income button, and make choices in the dialog boxes to describe this extra income.

Taxes & Inflation: Describing the tax and inflation rate

When you click the Taxes & Inflation link (or click Next), you come to a window for describing the two things that eat away at your income: taxes and inflation. Tell Money what the tax rate in your state is and what you think the annual inflation rate will be:

- ✔ **Tax rate:** Select your home state from the Enter Your State drop-down list to let Money determine the tax rate. You can also select the Adjust the Effective Tax Rate Myself option button and then drag the slider option to the rate that you think is correct.

✔ **Inflation rate:** Money assumes that the inflation rate will be 3 percent, but if you disagree, click the Change Inflation Rate button and enter a different rate.

Savings & Investments: Describing your retirement savings

The next step is to click the Savings & Investments link in the Lifetime Planner window and tell Money which of your accounts are meant for retirement savings. When you click this link, you see the window that's shown in Figure 13-7. The amounts in the Account Value column come directly from your account registers.

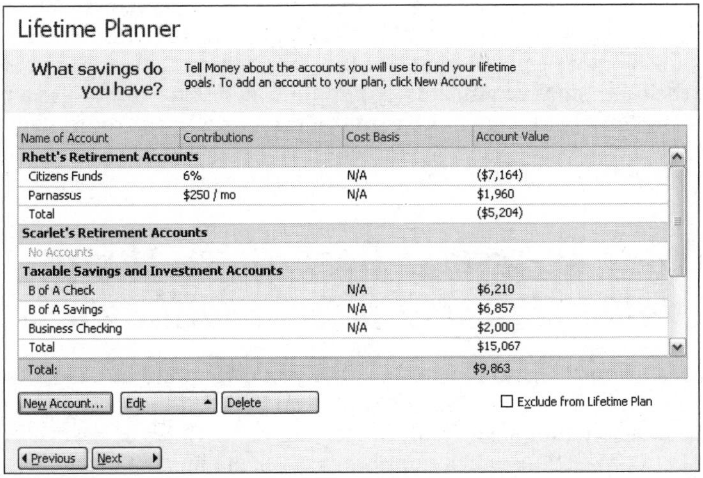

Figure 13-7: In the Savings & Investments windows, tell Money which of your accounts are for putting away money for retirement.

Lifetime Planner

What savings do you have?   Tell Money about the accounts you will use to fund your lifetime goals. To add an account to your plan, click New Account.

Name of Account	Contributions	Cost Basis	Account Value
Rhett's Retirement Accounts			
Citizens Funds	6%	N/A	($7,164)
Parnassus	$250 / mo	N/A	$1,960
Total			($5,204)
Scarlet's Retirement Accounts			
No Accounts			
Taxable Savings and Investment Accounts			
B of A Check		N/A	$6,210
B of A Savings		N/A	$6,857
Business Checking		N/A	$2,000
Total			$15,067
Total:			$9,863

New Account...   Edit   ▲   Delete   ☐ Exclude from Lifetime Plan

◄ Previous   Next ►

In this and the other two Savings & Investments windows, you tell Money whether to include an account in future projections, how much you will contribute to these accounts in the years ahead, and by what rate you expect the accounts to grow:

✔ **Accounts window:** Checking and savings accounts for day-to-day expenses do not belong in projections. To exclude an account, click its name and then select the Exclude from Lifetime Plan check box (you can find it in the lower-right corner of the window). Click the New Account button to describe an account that isn't on the list.

✔ **Savings Contributions window:** Click the New Contribution button and fill in the dialog boxes to describe how much you will contribute to your retirement, savings, and investment accounts over the years. When you click a contribution on the Contribution Name list, its particulars appear in the bottom part of the window. To change a particular, click a link on the bottom of the screen and fill in the dialog box that appears.

✔ **Life Insurance window:** Click the Add Policy button and describe any life insurance policies that you and your partner have (if you have a partner) in the dialog boxes. The Lifetime Planner uses the value of the policy as a means of calculating future income.

Expected Return: Describing how your money will grow

Click the Expected Return link to describe how you expect your savings and investments to grow until you retire and after you retire. Money has preconceived (and rather liberal) ideas about how much accounts will grow in value (by 9 percent before retirement and by 7 percent after retirement). If you don't care for Money's estimates, select the Use Custom Rate option button or the Use the Rate Money Estimates option button. If you want to use a custom rate, click the Simple Change link to enter a rate for all your retirement accounts, or click the Details Change link to enter rates for each account.

Homes & Assets: Describing things of value that you own or will own

Houses, property, and businesses that you own count as assets that will grow in value over the years. As such, they can be included in wealth projections. You can also count jewelry, antiques, and collectibles as assets. To include assets in projections, click the Homes & Assets link.

To tell Money about an asset, click the Add Asset button and fill in the dialog boxes. Assets appear on the Name of Asset or Asset Account list. To change the particulars of an asset — its value, appreciation rate, and so on — click the asset on the list and then click a link at the bottom of the screen. You see a dialog box for changing the particulars.

Do not count things that *depreciate* (decrease in value over the years), such as equipment or cars, as assets.

Loans & Debt: Describing current and future loans

No projection can be accurate unless it includes information about loans and debts. Click the Loans & Debt link to describe the money that you owe and will owe for future debts, loans, and mortgages.

Loan and mortgage accounts that you set up already (see Chapter 16) appear in the Loans & Debt window, as do the projections of your debt reduction plan if you make one. (See the section "Planning to Get Out of Debt," later in this chapter.)

To describe a future debt or loan, click the New Loan button and fill in the dialog boxes. Be sure to select the No, I Plan to Open This Loan in the Future option button — if you don't, you go to the Loan Wizard, where you set up a new Loan account.

To change the particulars of a loan or debt on this screen, select the name of the loan or debt, click the Edit button, and then change the particulars in the Edit Loan dialog boxes.

Expenses: Describing the cost of living

When you click the Expenses link, you see the Living Expenses screen, as shown in Figure 13-8. Here you describe how much it costs for you and anyone you support to live. The names of people on this list come from the About You screen.

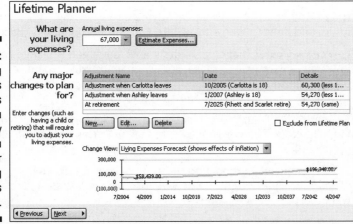

Figure 13-8:
The Living Expenses screen is where you tell Money what you expect your annual living expenses to be.

Money gets the annual living expenses figure at the top of the screen by deducting taxes, savings contributions, and loan payments from your annual income. If you want to get the figure from your budget (if you created a budget), click the Estimate Expenses button and, in the dialog box that appears, select the Use the Annual Budget Estimate check box to get the number from your budget. (Chapter 12 describes budgeting.)

Adjustments to your living expenses — for example, caring for an elderly person or having a child — appear on the list. Click the New button and fill in the New Living Expense Adjustment dialog box if an event in your future will affect your living expenses. Similarly, you can select an adjustment on the list and click the Edit button to adjust its cost or duration.

The College & Other window is for taking account of college expenses, trips to Madagascar, and other expensive interludes. Click the New Expense button and fill in the dialog boxes to describe these expenses.

Results: Reading your financial future

At last, you can click the Results link in the Lifetime Planner window and examine your plan to see whether you will be financially sound in the years to come. You can discover the following about your future by clicking these links:

- **The Bottom Line:** A chart that shows how much wealth you will have in the years to come and how well your savings will support you in retirement (refer to Figure 13-4).

- **Comparing Plans:** A chart showing different lifetime plans. If you click the Improving Your Plan link and tinker with your plan, the results of the new plan show on this screen in comparison to the baseline plan, the plan that you started with.

- **Improving Your Plan:** Practical advice for improving your financial future and links to Web sites where you can get financial advice.

- **Forecasts:** Charts that clearly show how much you will save each year, how your salary will increase, and when loans will be paid off, among other things. Choose a question from the Pick a Question drop-down list to generate a new chart. (Refer to Figure 13-5.)

- **Assumptions:** A summary of all the choices and entries that you made in the Lifetime Planner windows. Money uses this data for its financial projections.

- **Yearly Snapshot:** A report on the state of your future finances. Drag the Pick a Year slider or enter a new year to see what your financial picture will be in the years to come.

Action Plan: What you should do next

Click the Action Plan link to receive a ream of advice about improving your financial position. You can find advice about saving, choosing profitable investments, and choosing the right life insurance policy, among other things.

Playing "what if" with your future

After you have gone to the significant trouble of formulating a lifetime plan, you can use the plan as a means of playing "what if" with your future. What if you retire early — how well would your retirement savings and investments support you? Suppose that you decide to take a sabbatical from work — can you afford it? You can ask questions like these and see what happens to your lifetime plan. Figure 13-9 answers the question "What would happen to my retirement savings and investments if the stock market fell, *gulp!,* by 50 percent?"

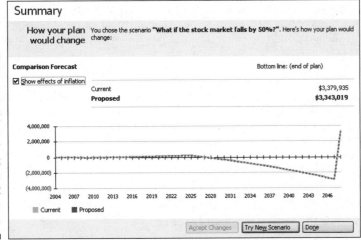

Figure 13-9:
Use the Financial Event Modeler to find out how different events would affect your lifetime plan.

Follow these steps to test different scenarios on your lifetime plan:

1. **Click the Planning tab to go to the Planning window.**

2. **Click the Financial Events Modeler link.**

   After you click this link, you see the Welcome to the Financial Event Modeler window.

3. **Click the Start Exploring link.**

4. **In the Goal window, choose a question from the Scenario drop-down list, and enter other information as necessary.**

   Depending on the question that you pose, you are asked for different types of information.

5. **Click the Compare My Plan button.**

   A chart shows how your lifetime plan is altered by the what-if scenario that you chose.

Click the Try New Scenario button to return to the Goal window and test another scenario. To make the scenario a part of your lifetime plan, click the Accept Changes button.

Planning to Get Out of Debt

Paying off your credit card debt may be the single most important step you can take to improve your financial picture. Credit card issuers charge outrageous rates of interest, and you have to pay these interest charges every month if you don't pay off, or at least pay down, the balance that you owe on your credit cards.

To help you get the discipline to pay off credit card debt, Money offers the Debt Reduction Planner. With this gizmo, you decide how much you can devote to reducing debt each month, and then you schedule an extra payment to help ensure that the debts are paid each month. (Chapter 12 explains scheduling payments.)

Follow these steps to devise a debt-reduction plan:

1. **Click the Planning tab to go to the Planning window.**

2. **Click the Debt Reduction Planner link.**

   You go to the Debt Reduction Planner window.

3. **Click the Continue button.**

   You see the Include Debt Accounts in Your Plan window, which lists all the credit card, liability, line of credit, loan, and mortgage accounts you set up with Money (Chapter 16 explains loan and mortgage accounts), as well as how much you owe on each account, the interest rate, and other information.

Your next step is to tell Money which accounts you want to pay off, but you shouldn't include loan and mortgage accounts in the plan. The interest rates on these types of accounts are not high, or they are at least reasonable, and the interest on some of them is tax deductible as well. To reduce your debt, your first job is to pay down credit card and line-of-credit debt.

4. **Tell Money which accounts to include in your plan by selecting an account and clicking the Move Up or the Move Down button.**

   Clicking this button moves the plan under Account in Debt Plan or Debt Accounts Not in Debt Plan.

5. **Select an account and click the Edit Debt Info button to describe the account to Money.**

   You must fill in dialog boxes to describe how much you owe and how much you have to pay each month on the debt, as well as describe the interest rate, payment frequency, and other particulars of the plan.

6. **Click the Next button to move to the Define Your Payment Plan window.**

   Under Status, in the lower-left corner of the window, you see how much you owe, how much you spend to service your debts, and when you will be out of debt at the rate that you are paying now, as shown in Figure 13-10.

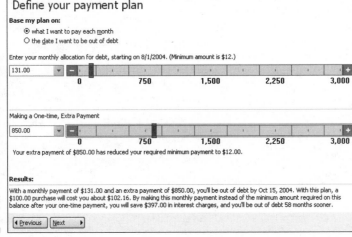

Figure 13-10:
Telling
Money
when you
want to pay
off your
high-
interest
debts.

7. **Do one of the following:**

   - Click the What I Want to Pay Each Month option button, and enter how much extra money you want to pay each month to get out of debt in the text box.

   - Click the The Date I Want to Be Out of Debt option button, and drag the slider to choose a new target date.

   - Click the Next button. You see the View Your Debt Plan graph, which shows how your debt is reduced over time.

8. **Click the Next button.**

   You see the Take Action and Reduce Your Debt window. It offers some gratuitous advice about reducing debt. If you want to schedule debt payments, click an item in the box and see Chapter 12 to see how scheduling works.

9. **Click the Finish button.**

   You land on the Home Page.

Chapter 14

Preparing for Tax Time

• •

In This Chapter

▶ Tagging categories for tax-reporting purposes

▶ Seeing line-item income and expenses

▶ Generating tax reports

▶ Estimating how much you will owe in taxes

▶ Scheduling tax dates

▶ Discovering tax-deductible expenses

▶ Calculating how much to withhold for taxes

▶ Estimating capital gains taxes

▶ Exporting Money data to a tax-preparation software package

• •

*B*enjamin Franklin wrote, "In this world, nothing is certain but death and taxes." This chapter explains how to do your best by one of these certainties. As for the other, all you can do about it is to eat right, get enough sleep and exercise, and hope for the best.

In this chapter, you discover how to estimate your next tax bill, get Money's help finding tax-deductible expenses, and determine how much to withhold from your paycheck for taxes. You also find out how to determine capital gains taxes on the sale of a security, generate tax reports, and prepare Money data so that you can use it in a tax-preparation software package.

Tagging Categories for Tax-Reporting Purposes

Especially if you are self-employed, one of the most important things you will ever do in Money is to tag categories that pertain to income taxes. By doing that, you can generate tax reports that tell you how much you spent in tax-deductible categories such as Office Supplies or Business Travel. Accountants charge a small fortune to review registers and find tax-deductible expenses, and if you do your own taxes, searching for and tabulating tax-deductible expenses can take hours. Knowing what your income is can also be a chore if you are self-employed and you have to tabulate your income and determine precisely where all that money came from. However, if you tag tax-related categories, Money can tabulate your tax deductions and income in a matter of seconds. You can take the numbers that money generates in tax reports and plug them into your tax return or give them to your accountant.

Money offers a special window for tagging tax-related categories and subcategories. In the window, you can select a check box to make sure that a category is figured into the tax reports you can generate with Money. And you can also assign a category or subcategory to a line item on a tax form.

Follow these steps to give an existing category or subcategory tax-related status so that it is figured into tax reports and, if possible, assign tax forms and line items to a category or subcategory:

Banking

1. **Click the Banking tab.**

2. **Click the Account Tools button and choose Categories & Payees from the drop-down menu.**

   The Set Up Your Categories window opens.

3. **Click the Set Up Tax Categories link.**

   You can find this link on the left side of the window under Common Tasks. After you click the link, you see the Categories window, only this time, drop-down lists appear in the lower-right corner so that you can mark categories for tax reports and assign categories to line items on tax forms, as shown in Figure 14-1.

   Where possible, the generic categories and subcategories that Money creates automatically are assigned tax forms and form lines. You can see them by scrolling down the list. Tax-related categories show an X in the Tax column. In the Tax Form and Form Line columns, you can see where tax forms and lines have been assigned to categories and subcategories.

4. **Scroll down the list until you find a category or subcategory whose tax status needs changing; then click the category or subcategory to select it.**

5. **Select the Include on Tax Reports check box.**

6. **Click the down arrow on the Tax Form drop-down list, and select a tax form.**

   Being able to tag categories and subcategories to tax forms (such as a W-2, Schedule B, or Form 1040) is a neat idea, but you have to know the tax forms well to pull it off. You have to know, for example, that tax-exempt interest is reported on the Interest Income line of Schedule B. Who besides a tax accountant knows that?

If you want to be able to run Tax Software Reports, study your income tax returns from past years to see which forms and form lines to assign to the categories and subcategories that you use. You can also speak to an accountant. Be aware that tax forms change yearly, so what goes on one line one year may go somewhere else the next.

7. **Click the down arrow on the Form Line drop-down list, and select the form line on which the income or expense is to be reported.**

8. **If you use multiple forms (more than one W-2, for example) to report your income, enter the number of forms that you use in the Form Copy text box.**

9. **Continue scrolling in the window until you have marked all the tax-related categories appropriately.**

In the section "Generating Tax Reports," later in this chapter, I explain how to generate reports that tell you precisely how much you spent or paid in tax-related categories and subcategories.

Choose a category.

Click to include it on tax reports.

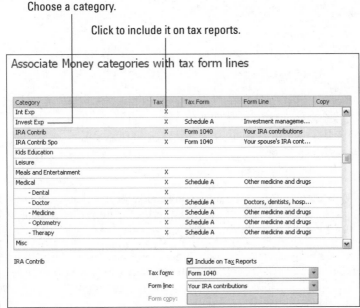

Figure 14-1:
Assigning a
tax form and
line to a
category.

Looking at Line-Item Income and Expenses

Taxes

As long as you went to the trouble to assign line items to different categories (see the previous section in this chapter), you can find out very quickly what your tax-related income and expenses are as reported on tax forms. Click the Taxes tab, and in the Taxes window, click the Tax Tools button and choose Tax Line Manager from the drop-down menu. You see the Review Your Tax-Related Income and Expenses window, as shown in Figure 14-2. If you have the wherewithal to do your own taxes, you can plug these numbers right into your tax return. In fact, this window is modeled after a tax form to make plugging in the numbers easier.

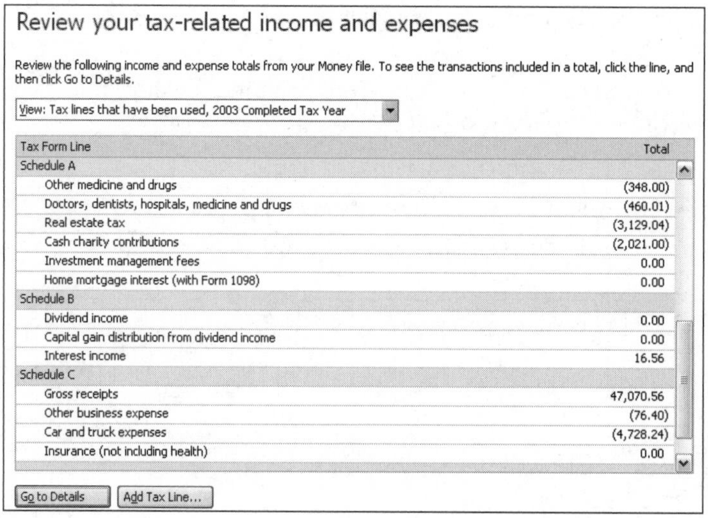

Figure 14-2:
You can plug these numbers straight into a tax form.

Review your tax-related income and expenses

Review the following income and expense totals from your Money file. To see the transactions included in a total, click the line, and then click Go to Details.

View: Tax lines that have been used, 2003 Completed Tax Year

Tax Form Line	Total
Schedule A	
Other medicine and drugs	(348.00)
Doctors, dentists, hospitals, medicine and drugs	(460.01)
Real estate tax	(3,129.04)
Cash charity contributions	(2,021.00)
Investment management fees	0.00
Home mortgage interest (with Form 1098)	0.00
Schedule B	
Dividend income	0.00
Capital gain distribution from dividend income	0.00
Interest income	16.56
Schedule C	
Gross receipts	47,070.56
Other business expense	(76.40)
Car and truck expenses	(4,728.24)
Insurance (not including health)	0.00

Go to Details   Add Tax Line...

The View menu offers some nifty commands for examining tax lines. Choose Tax Lines That Have Been Used to see only the lines that pertain to your income and expenses in the window.

To remove a line item from the window or change a line item, select the line item and click the Go to Details button. You land in a window for deleting line items (click the Remove button) and changing income and expense figures (click the Edit button).

Generating Tax Reports

Money tax reports are very convenient indeed. Instead of scouring an account register for tax-related income and expenses, you can simply generate a report. You know right away what your income is and how many adjustments and deductions you can make.

Reports

The fastest way to generate a tax report is to click the Reports tab. You land in the Reports Home window, where you can generate one of these reports:

- ✔ **Tax-Related Transactions:** Shows category by category what your income and expenses are in tax-related categories. Use this report to calculate income and tax-deductible expenses for tax returns.

- ✔ **Capital Gains:** Shows capital gains and losses for the securities that you sold or purchased this year. Use this report to calculate and tabulate capital gains and losses.

- ✔ **Loan Interest:** Shows how much of your loan payments went to servicing interest. Use this report to calculate tax-deductible interest payments. You must have set up a loan account to generate this report. (See Chapter 16.)

- ✔ **Tax Software Report:** Shows your total income and expenses as they are to be reported on tax lines on various tax forms. Use this report to gather data for tax-software programs.

Chapter 15 explains reports and charts in detail, including how to customize them and change their reporting dates.

Estimating Your Tax Bill

Knowing what you will owe in taxes next year never hurts, especially if you don't like surprises. Money offers the Tax Estimator to help you estimate what you owe for last year and what you will owe for this year. Notice, however, that the thing is called the Tax Estimator, not the Tax Accountant. The Tax Estimator can give you a rough idea of what you owe or will owe the IRS, but it can't take the place of a tax accountant and do your income taxes for you.

Taxes

To find out what your tax bill is for last year or maybe for the coming year, click the Taxes tab to go to the Tax window, and then click the Tax Estimator link. You land in the Welcome to the Tax Estimator window. Clicking the Next button as you go along, you answer Money's survey questions about you, your income, adjustments to your income, deductions, and tax credits. These questions are the very same ones that tax accountants ask when they determine how to lower your taxes. By the time you reach the Summary window, Money has prepared an estimated tax return for you, like the one shown in Figure 14-3. Either click the Next button or click the Tax Estimator Steps links on the left side of the Money screen to get from window to window.

Click to go from window to window.

July 10, 2004	Estimated tax summary			
Tax Estimator steps				
Welcome		**Completed Tax Year 2003**		**Current Tax Year 2004**
Getting started				
Income	Filing status:	Married filing jointly	Filing status:	Married filing jointly
	Marginal tax rate:	10.0	Marginal tax rate:	10.0
Adjustments				
Deductions	Wages & salary:	$35,686.42	Wages & salary:	$32,268.64
	Capital gains & losses:	$0.00	Capital gains & losses:	$0.00
Credits	Interest / dividend income:	$16.56	Interest / dividend income:	$9.93
Summary	Other income:	$0.00	Other income:	$0.00
	Total income:	$35,702.98	Total income:	$32,278.57
	Total adjustments:	$3,000.00	Total adjustments:	$3,000.00
Common tasks	Adjusted gross income:	$32,702.98	Adjusted gross income:	$29,278.57
Create a tax payment				
Print analysis and sum...	Deductions:	$9,500.00	Deductions:	$9,700.00
Find possible deductions				
Associate categories w...	Nonrefundable credits:	$3,200.00	Nonrefundable credits:	$3,200.00
Use Tax Withholding E...	Refundable credits:	$800.00	Refundable credits:	$800.00
Estimate capital gains tax				
Capital gains tracking f...	Total exemptions:	$12,200.00	Total exemptions:	$12,400.00
	Taxable income:	$11,002.98	Taxable income:	$7,178.57
	Estimated taxes:	$300.30	Estimated taxes:	$0.00
	◀ Previous Done			

Figure 14-3: Answer the questions, and get a mini tax return.

Here's some good news: Some of the information is already entered in these windows because Money grabbed it from the data file. If you enter your own numbers and regret doing so, you can get the numbers from Money by clicking the Reset Value button along the bottom of a window and choosing an option from the pop-up menu that describes how you want Money to plug in its numbers.

Describe your tax situation in these six windows:

✔ **Getting Started:** Enter your personal information. In the first window, declare your filing status, number of dependents, and whether you are blind and over age 65. Question 5, Estimated Taxes Paid and Withheld, should already be entered. Money gets this information from Tax categories. It is very likely quite correct, but you can enter your own numbers if you want.

✔ **Income:** Enter your income. Describe your income from salaries, wages, alimony, unemployment, and so on. Once again, many of these values come straight from the data file. Do your best to estimate these numbers.

Finding out the tax rates

Built into the Money 2005 Tax Estimator are accurate tax rates for 2004. But suppose that you are trying to estimate your income taxes for 2006 or 2007. How can you obtain the correct tax rates for those years?

Follow these steps to download the latest tax rates from Microsoft:

1. **Choose Tools⇨Settings to go to the Settings window.**

2. **Click the Tax Settings link.**

   You land in the Set Up Your File for Tax Tracking window.

3. **Click the Set Your Filing Status and View Tax Rates by Income Bracket link.**

   A window appears and shows you the latest tax rates.

4. **Click the Update Internet Info link.**

5. **Click the Update button in the Update Online Information dialog box.**

   Your machine connects to the Internet, and the latest tax rates are downloaded to your computer.

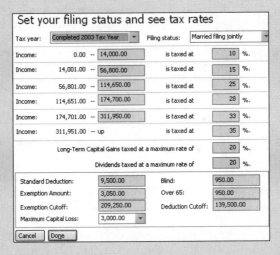

Set your filing status and see tax rates

Tax year:	Completed 2003 Tax Year	Filing status:	Married filing jointly

Income:	0.00 -- 14,000.00	is taxed at 10 %.
Income:	14,001.00 -- 56,800.00	is taxed at 15 %.
Income:	56,801.00 -- 114,650.00	is taxed at 25 %.
Income:	114,651.00 -- 174,700.00	is taxed at 28 %.
Income:	174,701.00 -- 311,950.00	is taxed at 33 %.
Income:	311,951.00 -- up	is taxed at 35 %.

Long-Term Capital Gains taxed at a maximum rate of 20 %.
Dividends taxed at a maximum rate of 20 %.

Standard Deduction:	9,500.00	Blind:	950.00
Exemption Amount:	3,050.00	Over 65:	950.00
Exemption Cutoff:	209,250.00	Deduction Cutoff:	139,500.00
Maximum Capital Loss:	3,000.00		

Cancel   Done

✔ **Adjustments:** Enter your adjustments to income. Describe adjustments to your income — contributions to IRAs and SEPs, health insurance payments, and so on. The numbers that you enter here lower your tax bill.

✔ **Deductions:** Enter your itemized deductions. Describe the payments that you made that can be deducted from your gross income — payments for medical and dental work, taxes, mortgage interest, charitable contributions, and so on.

  ✔ **Credits:** Enter your tax credit information. Describe credits for child-care, education, and so on. Click the Detail links in this window to find out whether you are eligible for any of these credits.

  ✔ **Summary:** This is an estimated tax summary. There it is — a mini tax return that shows your taxable income and roughly what you will owe in taxes (refer to Figure 14-3). If a number needs adjusting, click a link to return to the window where the number came from and make an adjustment.

Scheduling Important Tax Dates

Especially if you are self-employed and you pay quarterly tax estimates, certain dates are sacrosanct. Quarterly tax estimates are due on June 15, September 15, January 15, and April 15. Miss those dates at your peril!

As Chapter 13 explains in detail, you can use the Advisor FYI feature to help you remember these dates. Choose Tools➪Alert Center, and click the Customize Your Advisor FYI Alerts link to view the Advisor FYI Options dialog box; then click the Important Dates tab. Make sure that the quarterly esti-mated tax payment check boxes on the tab are selected. This way, the dates will appear on the Home Page to remind you when the IRS needs feeding.

Getting Help for Lowering Your Tax Bill

If you itemize deductions on income tax reports or you use Money to track business expenses, you owe it to yourself to find every tax-deductible expense that you can claim on income tax forms. Money offers a way to do that.

Taxes

To get Money's help to locate tax-deductible expenses, click the Taxes tab and then click the Deduction Finder link (or click the Tax Tools button and choose Deduction Finder from the drop-down menu). In the What Deductions Are You Eligible For window, click the Next button. Very shortly, you land in the Tax Deduction Finder form, a questionnaire that you fill out. Keep answer-ing the questions and clicking the Continue button. These questions are the very same ones that tax accountants ask when they determine how to lower your taxes. When you're done, the Deductions You May Qualify For window explains in detail all the different deductions for which you are eligible, as shown in Figure 14-4.

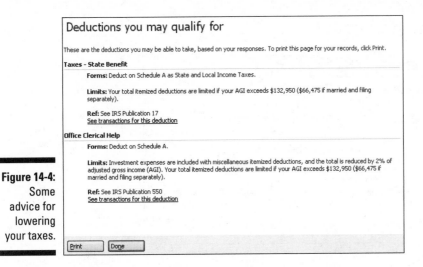

Deductions you may qualify for

These are the deductions you may be able to take, based on your responses. To print this page for your records, click Print.

Taxes - State Benefit

Forms: Deduct on Schedule A as State and Local Income Taxes.

Limits: Your total itemized deductions are limited if your AGI exceeds $132,950 ($66,475 if married and filing separately).

Ref: See IRS Publication 17
See transactions for this deduction

Office Clerical Help

Forms: Deduct on Schedule A.

Limits: Investment expenses are included with miscellaneous itemized deductions, and the total is reduced by 2% of adjusted gross income (AGI). Your total itemized deductions are limited if your AGI exceeds $132,950 ($66,475 if married and filing separately).

Ref: See IRS Publication 550
See transactions for this deduction

Print   Done

Figure 14-4:
Some
advice for
lowering
your taxes.

Determining How Much to Withhold

How much should you withhold from your paycheck for taxes? This question has puzzled philosophers for centuries. Being told on April 15 that you didn't withhold enough and that you owe taxes is very unpleasant. Most people like to be told that they are due a refund because they withheld too much in taxes from their paycheck. To help you determine how much to withhold, Money offers the Tax Withholding Estimator. With this gizmo, you declare your income, state whether you want a tax refund, and find out precisely how much to withhold.

You must have used the Tax Estimator to estimate what you owe in taxes before you can take the Tax Withholding Estimator for a spin. Money uses information you entered in the Tax Estimator to determine how much to withhold. See "Estimating Your Tax Bill," earlier in this chapter.

Taxes

To get Money's help to locate tax-deductible expenses, click the Taxes tab and then click the Withholding Estimator link (or click the Tax Tools button and choose Withholding Estimator from the drop-down menu). You see the Estimate My Withholding window shown in Figure 14-5. Answer the questions in this and the subsequent window. When you are done, Money tells you the total amount to withhold per paycheck to reach your refund goal.

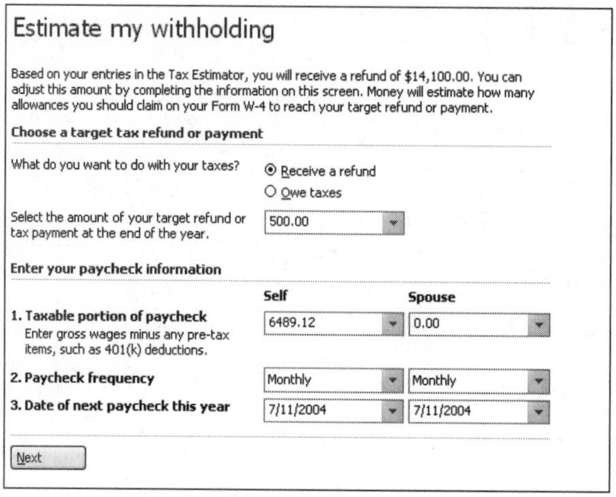

Estimate my withholding

Based on your entries in the Tax Estimator, you will receive a refund of $14,100.00. You can adjust this amount by completing the information on this screen. Money will estimate how many allowances you should claim on your Form W-4 to reach your target refund or payment.

Choose a target tax refund or payment

What do you want to do with your taxes?   ⦿ Receive a refund
                                           ◯ Owe taxes

Select the amount of your target refund or   [500.00   ▾]
tax payment at the end of the year.

Enter your paycheck information

	Self	Spouse
1. Taxable portion of paycheck Enter gross wages minus any pre-tax items, such as 401(k) deductions.	[6489.12 ▾]	[0.00 ▾]
2. Paycheck frequency	[Monthly ▾]	[Monthly ▾]
3. Date of next paycheck this year	[7/11/2004 ▾]	[7/11/2004 ▾]

[Next]

Figure 14-5:
To get a tax refund, how much should you withhold?

Estimating Capital Gains Taxes

Estimating the capital gains taxes on the sale of a security can be difficult, so Money offers the Capital Gains Estimator. In the Capital Gains Estimator, you tell Money the rate at which you are taxed, select one of the securities that you own, enter how much you propose to sell your shares for, and find out how much you stand to profit and how much capital gains tax you have to pay on your profits.

Use the Capital Gains Estimator before you sell a security to see whether selling it is worthwhile, given the taxes you have to pay on the profits. In order to use the Estimator, you must have set up an investment account and recorded the purchase of the security in the account. (See Chapter 8.)

Taxes

To estimate capital gains taxes, click the Taxes tab and then click the Capital Gains Estimator link. (You can also find this link on the Investing tab.) You land in the Welcome to the Capital Gains Estimator window. Click the Get Started button, and provide information about your tax situation and the security in these four windows:

  ✔ **Set Tax Rates:** Describe your filing status, your income bracket, and whether you want to estimate state as well as federal capital gains taxes. The Capital Loss Carryover input boxes are for declaring a capital loss from the previous year that you have carried into the current year. You can deduct up to $1,500 per year per taxpayer and per spouse in capital losses.

  ✔ **Select Accounts:** Choose the name of the investment account where you track the security.

✔ **Estimate Capital Gains Tax:** Select the security that you propose to sell and update its price by clicking the Update Prices button under Common Tasks. Then enter the sale price and the quantity of shares you want to sell, as shown in Figure 14-6.

If you bought the security in more than one lot, choose an option from the Distribution Method drop-down list to describe which shares you want to sell. A *lot* is a group of securities purchased at the same time and at the same price. FIFO means "first in, first out," and LIFO is "last in, first out." Choosing FIFO sells the oldest shares, no matter which lot they belong to; LIFO sells the newest shares. Choosing Max Gain or Min Gain tells Money to sell shares from whichever lot will earn the most or the least money. Choose Custom to pick and choose shares from different lots.

✔ **View Action Plan:** Read the summary information about how much you stand to lose or gain by selling the security.

After you go to the trouble to investigate the capital gains implications of selling a security, you can save the information that you entered in a *scenario*. To examine the sale later on, you can simply call up its scenario without going to the trouble of entering the stock sale information again. To save a scenario, click the Scenarios button under Common Tasks, choose Save This Scenario, and enter a name in the Save This Capital Gains Scenario text box. To call up the scenario, click the Scenarios button and choose its name from the submenu that appears.

Enter the sale price and quantity.

Plan sales of investments

Enter the date you plan to sell investments. For each security, enter the expected sale price and the quantity you plan to sell, and then press Enter. To see lots, click the plus (+) beside a security name.

Date of sale: 7/11/2004   **Distribution method:** FIFO

Accounts and Securities	Holdings	Cost Basis	Unrealized Gain	Sale Price	Qty to Sell	Gain/Loss
⊟ **Fidelity Investments Investment**						
⊞ Tibo	10.000	10.00	15.00	11.5	10	15.00

Figure 14-6: Seeing how much in capital gains taxes you must pay when you sell a security.

Results of proposed sales

	Gross Proceeds	Carryovers	Gain/Loss	Federal Tax	State Tax	Net Proceeds
Short-term	115.00	0.00	15.00	3.75	0.00	111.25
Long-term	0.00	0.00	0.00	0.00	0.00	0.00
Total	**115.00**	**0.00**	**15.00**	**3.75**	**0.00**	**111.25**

< Previous   Next >

Proceeds from sale

Tax

Exporting Money Data to a Tax-Preparation Program

The TaxCut Deluxe tax-preparation program (produced by H&R Block) accepts data from Money files. In other words, you can draw on data from Money as you prepare your taxes with TaxCut. To provide tax information to TaxCut, you save your Money data in a TXF file, open TaxCut, and import the TXF file into the tax-preparation program. Money has a special command for saving data in a TXF file. Before you create the TXF file, however, you need to tell Money which accounts to include in the file.

Follow these steps to tell Money which accounts hold tax data:

1. **Choose Tools⇨Settings.**

   You go to the Settings window.

2. **Click the Tax Settings link.**

   The Set Up Your File for Tax Tracking window appears.

3. **Click the Choose Accounts to Include in Tax Return Information link.**

   The Choose Accounts for Tax Preparation dialog box appears.

4. **Select the names of accounts where you keep tax data and click OK.**

   I find it easiest to click the Clear All button to deselect all the check boxes and then check off the handful of accounts where tax data is kept.

Now you're ready to create the TXF file for the TaxCut tax-preparation package. Go to it:

1. **Choose File⇨Export to Tax Software.**

   You land in the Prepare to Export Tax Information window.

2. **Choose a year from the Review Taxes For drop-down list.**

3. **Click the Continue button.**

   As shown in Figure 14-7, the next window asks which line items to include in the file.

4. **Go down the list and check off line items that pertain to your tax situation; then click the Continue button.**

   Very likely, the line items that pertain to you are the ones with monetary figures in them.

   After you click the Continue button, you come to the Prepare Your Taxes Using Software window.

Select the items you want to include in your tax reports for 2004

Schedule A

☑ Other medicine and drugs	(650.00)
☑ Doctors, dentists, hospitals, medicine and drugs	(40.24)
☑ Real estate tax	0.00
☑ Cash charity contributions	(910.89)
☑ Investment management fees	0.00
☐ Home mortgage interest (with Form 1098)	0.00

Schedule B

Dividend income	
Capital gain distribution from dividend income	
Interest income	
☐ B of A Check	3.25
☐ B of A Savings	6.68

Schedule C

☑ Gross receipts	34,000.00
Other business expense	
☑ Bank Chrg	(18.00)
☑ Copying	(21.78)
☑ Car and truck expenses	(1,967.21)

Figure 14-7: Choosing line items for a TXF tax-preparation file.

5. **Choose Export Your Tax Information as a Data File link.**

   The Export Tax dialog box appears.

6. **Name and save the file.**

   Don't forget what you named the file and where you saved it. TaxCut or the other tax-preparation software that you use will ask you where to get this file.

As I write this, only TaxCut accepts TXF files from Money, but if your taxes aren't complicated, you can use other programs for tax reporting by generating a Tax Software report and entering the numbers by hand in the tax-preparation program. The previous section in this chapter explains how to generate a Tax Software report. Table 14-1 describes the leading tax-preparation software packages.

Table 14-1	Tax-Preparation Software Packages	
Program	**Cost***	**Imports Directly from Money?**
TaxAct Deluxe	$29.95	No
TaxCut Deluxe	$39.95	Yes
TurboTax Deluxe	$39.95	No

*Prices listed here are current as of July 2004.

For reviews and information about software, including tax-preparation programs, go to www.cnet.com, type **tax** in the Search box, and click the Go button. Cnet.com offers detailed information about software, and you can purchase software from Cnet.com as well.

Getting Tax Help on the Internet

The MoneyCentral Web site (www.moneycentral.com) offers advice about tax planning and preparation. Here are a handful of other Web sites that are useful to taxpayers:

- **The Digital Daily:** The Digital Daily is the official home page of the Internal Revenue Service. The site offers tax information as well as a means of downloading any tax form (click the Forms & Pubs hyperlink). Address: www.irs.gov

- **Federal forms and publications:** Save yourself a trip to the post office by going to this Web site. From here, you can download tax-reporting forms, schedules, and publications. Address: www.irs.gov/formspubs/index.html

- **State forms and publications:** From here, you can click a link, go to your state's tax Web site, and download forms, schedules, and publications for reporting state income taxes. Address: www.taxadmin.org/fta/forms.ssi

- **Yahoo! Finance Tax Center:** Offers tax tips as well as information about estimating and lowering tax bills. Address: http://taxes.yahoo.com

Part V
Improving Your Financial Picture

The 5th Wave By Rich Tennant

"Face it Vinnie — you're gonna have a hard time getting people to subscribe online with a credit card to a newsletter called 'Felons Interactive!'"

In this part . . .

1s your financial picture out of focus? Can't tell how much you're earning or where you're spending all that money? Can't see what your financial future looks like?

Part V explains how to create reports and charts that show in no uncertain terms where you stand financially. You also find advice here for tracking loans, mortgages, and other assets, as well as liabilities. In Part V, you find out what your net worth as a financial entity is. What is your net worth as a human being? That's for you to decide.

Chapter 15

Reports and Charts for Seeing Where You Stand Financially

· ·

· ·

*R*eports and charts are two of my favorite things in Money 2005. Reports and charts determine right away what your financial standing is. Until I discovered the Tax-Related Transactions report, I used to spend hours and hours on April 14 tabulating tax-deductible expenses for my income tax report. Until I discovered the Spending by Category chart, I had no idea where I spent all that money. Until I spent a night in the Sierra Mountains, I didn't know that the sky has so many stars, but that's another story.

Maybe you want to create a report or chart to prove to a loan officer how creditworthy you are. Maybe you want to find out how much it cost to drive your car last year. Maybe you want to see how a stock price fluctuated to find out whether the price fluctuation really resembled a roller coaster ride. Whatever you need, Money can help.

This chapter tells you about the 39 types of reports and two dozen kinds of charts that you can create with Money; how to customize a report or chart so that it yields precisely the information that you want it to yield; how to print reports and charts; and how to export the reports to other computer programs.

A Look at the Reports Home Window

Reports

To create a report or chart, you start from the Reports Home window, as shown in Figure 15-1. Click the Reports tab to get to the Reports Home window. (If you chose essential reports over advanced reports, your window will look somewhat different from the one in the figure. The sidebar "Advanced and essential reports" explains the differences between the two kinds of reports.)

All you have to do to generate a report or chart is click a link in the Reports Home window. By now you must be wondering, "But how can I tell which of these names are reports and which are charts?" Good question. The answer is that you can make a report or a chart from almost every name in the Reports Home window. For example, Figure 15-2 shows both the report and the chart that you can create with the Spending by Category option in the Income and Expenses category. On the left side of Figure 15-2 is a Spending by Category report; on the right side is a Spending by Category pie chart. To change a report into a chart or vice versa, click the Change Views link and then choose Report or a chart option on the drop-down menu.

Figure 15-1:
The Reports
Home
window is
the starting
point for
creating a
report or
chart.

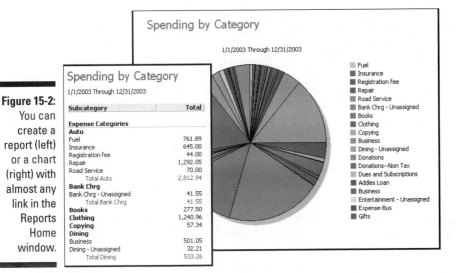

Figure 15-2:
You can
create a
report (left)
or a chart
(right) with
almost any
link in the
Reports
Home
window.

Advanced and essential reports

For people who abide by the "keep it simple" philosophy, Money gives you the opportunity to see fewer charts and reports in the Reports Home window. If you opt for essential reports rather than advanced reports, you get 8 reports rather than 39, which makes it easier to find your way around the Reports Home window.

Follow these steps to tell Money whether you want advanced or essential reports:

1. **On the Reports tab, click the Change Report Settings link to go to the Report Settings window.**

2. **Click the Switch from Advanced Reports to Essential Reports link or the Switch from Essential Reports to Advanced Reports link.**

3. **In the Report Settings dialog box, click the Use Essential Reports or the Use Advanced Reports button.**

This illustration shows which reports are available in the Reports Home window if you opt for essential reports.

Reports

- Spending by Category
- Spending by Payee
- Spending by Category Comparison
- Monthly Budget
- Net Worth
- Credit Card Debt
- Portfolio Value by Investment Type
- Monthly reports

Looking at the Different Reports

Money offers no fewer than 39 types of reports (8 if you opted for essential reports). As fast as I can — because I know that you're in a hurry — I briefly tell you in the following sections what the different reports and charts are. Turn to these pages when you are looking for a report or chart to illuminate your financial picture.

Income and Expenses

You can create these reports and charts (in Table 15-1) in the Income category. Reports marked with an asterisk are the only ones available if you asked for essential reports, not advanced reports.

Table 15-1	Income and Expenses Reports	
Report	*What It Tells You*	*Use*
*Spending by Category	How much you spend by category, ranked from largest expense to smallest (refer to Figure 15-2).	To find out your biggest expenses.
*Spending by Payee	The names of payees to whom you paid money, and the amounts you paid.	To find out where you shop most often and perhaps where you should stop shopping so often.
*Monthly Budget	Your monthly budget goals.	To help find out whether you met your budget.
Monthly Income and Expenses	How much you spent and how much you earned in the past three months, by category, in your bank and credit card accounts.	To find out what your expenses and sources of income were.
Transactions by Category	A report that lists, under each expense category, the spending transactions you entered so far this year.	To examine your spending habits.

Report	What It Tells You	Use
Transactions by Payee	A report that lists, under each category, who you paid money to or received money from.	To examine sources of income and expenses.
Account Transactions	A report that lists all the transactions in an account by month, or a line chart that shows a running account balance of the history of the account.	To find transactions in an account or to list and print part of an account register.
Income and Spending	Your expenses by category and your income by category.	To compare your income to your expenses and find out how much you are saving or going into the red.
Income and Spending Over Time	Your income and expenses on a timeline.	To see how your income and spending change in relation to one another over time.
Annual Budget	Your annual budget goals.	To help you find out whether you met your budget.

Investment

The Investments category in the Reports Home window offers these reports and charts (as shown in Table 15-2) for finding out how skilled an investor you are. Reports marked with an asterisk are the only ones available if you asked for essential reports, not advanced reports.

Table 15-2	Investments Reports	
Report	What It Tells You	Use
*Portfolio Value by Investment Type	What percentage of your investments are in mutual funds, stocks, and so on.	To find out how diversified your investments are.

(continued)

Table 15-2 *(continued)*

Report	*What It Tells You*	*Use*
Portfolio Value by Investment Account	The value of each of your investment accounts, as well as each security in the accounts.	To see changes in the monetary value of your securities.
Performance by Investment Account	The gain or loss in monetary terms and the gain or loss as a percentage of the security's total value in the past year of each security you own.	To compare investments to determine which is performing the best.
Performance by Investment Type	The gain or loss in monetary terms and by percentage for each of your securities, with securities grouped by investment type.	To compare types of investments — stocks, mutual funds, and so on — to see which type performs best.
Price History	The up-and-down performance of individual stocks and other securities this year so far, as shown in Figure 15-3. Choose a type of investment from the Investments drop-down list.	To exercise your eyeballs and make them move up and down.
Investment Transactions	The investment transactions you entered in investment registers.	To review activity in investment accounts.
Asset Allocation	How diversified your investment portfolio is.	To find out whether all your eggs are in one basket.
Bond Summary	The value and latest price, as well as other details, of the bonds you own.	To examine your bond investments.
Bond Performance	Performance data concerning the bonds you own, including the percentage price gain and annual return.	To see how well your bond investments are performing.

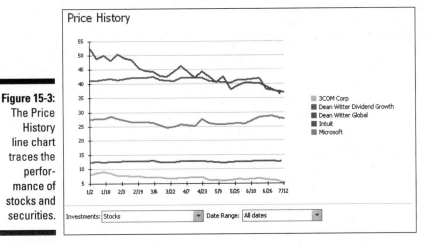

Figure 15-3:
The Price
History
line chart
traces the
perfor-
mance of
stocks and
securities.

Assets and Liabilities

The following reports and charts (Table 15-3) fall under the Assets and Liabilities category. Reports marked with an asterisk are the only ones available if you asked for essential reports, not advanced reports.

Table 15-3	Assets and Liabilities Reports	
Report	*What It Tells You*	*Use*
*Net Worth	How the values of your assets and liabilities compare to one another.	To find out your net worth.
*Credit Card Debt	Your total credit card debt.	To suffer despair over credit card debt and see which one you owe the most on.
Net Worth Less Capital Gains Tax	How the value of your assets and liabilities is affected by capital gains taxes.	To get a better look at your net worth.

(continued)

Table 15-3 *(continued)*

Report	*What It Tells You*	*Use*
Net Worth Over Time	How the values of your assets and liabilities compare over a certain time period. (Use the Date Range drop-down list to select a time period.)	To examine your net worth over time.
Net Worth Over Time Less Capital Gains Tax	How the values of your assets and liabilities, affected by capital gains taxes, change over time.	To get a focused picture of your net worth.
Account Balances	How much money is in your bank and other kinds of accounts at present.	To find out how much money is on hand.
Account Balance History	How the balance and value of all your accounts have changed over time. (Choose an option from the Accounts drop-down list if you want to select a single account.) Figure 15-4 shows an Account Balance History chart.	To see how fickle time, fate, and one's spending habits are.
Account Balances with Details	The information about your accounts that is kept in the Account Details window — the account number, opening balance, and so on.	To quickly look up account numbers and other information.
Asset Allocation	A description of how diversified your investments are.	To see whether all your eggs are in one basket.
Frequent Flyer Miles	Information about the frequent flyer points or miles you've earned.	To see whether you have enough miles or points for a vacation you've been planning.
Scheduled Bills	Which bills you have scheduled in the Bills Summary window.	To find out which bills are due or nearly due.
Upcoming Bills and Deposits	Which bills and deposits in the Bills Summary window are due this month.	To compare your income to your expenses so that you can decide which bills to pay.

Report	What It Tells You	Use
Loan Terms	The information about your loans that is kept in the Payment Terms window — the loan amount, remaining balance, interest rate, and so on.	Print this report if you apply for a new loan so that you can give the lender details about your other loans.
Loan Amortization	How much of each loan payment goes toward servicing interest, how much goes toward reducing the principal, and a running balance of how much you owe. (You must have set up a loan account in Money, as described in Chapter 16, to run this report.) Select a new loan or mortgage from the Accounts drop-down list.	To see how principal and interest payments on a loan break down.

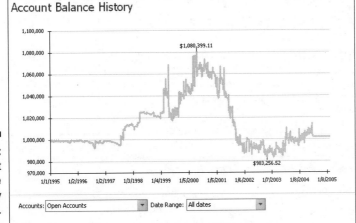

Figure 15-4:
An Account
Balance
History
chart.

Taxes

As tax time draws nigh, go to the Taxes category in the Reports Home window and create a handful of these reports (in Table 15-4). These reports are not available if you opted for essential, not advanced, reports.

Table 15-4	Taxes Reports	
Report	**What It Tells You**	**Use**
Tax-Related Transactions	Category by category, your total income and expenses in tax-related categories.	For calculating income and tax-deductible expenses on tax returns.
Capital Gains	Capital gains and losses for each security you own or owned.	For calculating capital gains and losses.
Loan Interest	How much of your loan payments go each month and year toward servicing interest.	For determining what your loan interest payments were. Some loan interest payments are tax deductible.
Tax Software Report	Your total income and expenses as can be reported on the tax lines on various tax forms.	For gathering data so that you can plug it into tax-preparation software programs.

Comparison Reports: For comparing the past with the present

Are you better off than you were four years ago? You can find out very quickly by generating a report in the Comparison Reports category. Reports in Table 15-5 marked with an asterisk are the only ones available if you asked for essential reports, not advanced reports:

Table 15-5	Comparison Reports	
Report	**What It Tells You**	**Use**
*Spending by Category Comparison	How you spent in different categories in two different time periods. Choose time periods from the drop-down lists.	For understanding your spending habits better.
Spending by Payee Comparison	Your income in two different time periods. Choose time periods from the drop-down lists.	For comparing your earnings from year to year.

Report	What It Tells You	Use
Income and Spending Comparison	Your expenses *and* earnings presented by category in different time periods.	For comparing what was with what is.

Monthly Reports

Money creates monthly reports automatically. The reports show where you spent money and your net worth, among other things. To see a report from your economic past, click a monthly report link in the Reports Home window.

My Favorites

The My Favorites category in the Reports Home window is for you and you alone. The "Adding a Customized Report or Chart to the Favorites Menu" section, later in this chapter, explains how you can keep your own customized reports in the My Favorites category and draw upon them whenever you please.

Creating a Report or Chart

To create a report or chart, you need to be familiar with the different types that Money offers. (Refer to the section "A Look at the Reports Home Window," earlier in this chapter.) You may be interested to know that you can usually turn a report into a chart and a chart into a report. Too bad life isn't always that easy.

Generating the report or chart

Follow these steps to create a report or chart:

Reports

1. **Click the Reports tab.**

   The Reports Home window appears (refer to Figure 15-1).

2. **Click a report or chart name in the Reports Home window.**

   Depending on the report or chart you select, a drop-down list or two appear along the bottom of the window.

3. **Make a selection from a drop-down list to make your report or chart show exactly what you want it to show.**

What you see next depends on which report or chart you created. Sometimes you get a chart and sometimes you get a report. Sometimes the report or chart covers the right time period; sometimes it doesn't. Read on to find out how to turn a report into a chart or a chart into a report. Later in this chapter, the "Customizing Reports and Charts" section explains how to change the appearance and parameters of a report or chart.

To create a report or chart in one mighty stroke, click the View Reports link, select a report category from the drop-down list, and then select a report/chart name, as shown in Figure 15-5.

Figure 15-5:
The speedy
way to
create a
report or
chart.

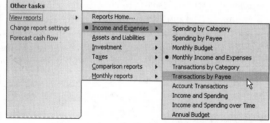

After you add a report to your Favorite Reports list, you can generate it by choosing Favorites➪Favorite Reports and clicking the report's name on the submenu. See the section "Adding a Customized Report or Chart to the Favorites Menu," later in this chapter.

Turning reports into charts and charts into reports

When you create a report or chart from the Reports Home window, Money does its best to give you the report or chart you want, but sometimes it makes the wrong choice. Frequently, the program gives you a chart when you wanted a report or a report when you wanted a chart. And sometimes the program gives you the wrong kind of chart.

You can sometimes fix that dilemma by clicking the Change View link, the first link under Common Tasks, and choosing an option from the submenu. To turn a report into a chart, for example, choose Bar Chart or Line Chart from the submenu.

Investigating the figures from which a chart or report is constructed

The figures on reports and the lines on charts are constructed from numbers that you entered in your account registers. Suppose that you get curious about a number on a report or pie slice in a pie chart. Maybe you want to know why a number is so high or a pie slice is so fat. Maybe you can't believe that you spent so much or profited so little. You can move the mouse pointer over the number or pie slice and do some investigating.

In Figure 15-6, a pie slice on the right side of the chart is awfully large. Suppose that you want to know why it's so large. As the figure shows, you can move the pointer over part of a chart and see a box with a figure that shows you what the chart segment represents in monetary terms. In the figure, you can see that this person spent a whopping $18,692.34 on home repairs. That must have been a big hailstorm.

Figure 15-6:
Move the pointer over part of a chart to see what it represents.

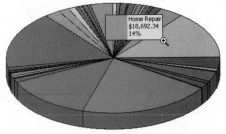

Home Repair
$18,692.34
14%

In reports and charts, the pointer turns into a magnifying glass when you move it over a summary figure, pie slice, bar, or whatnot. It does that, I should say, if you can double-click to see the figures from which the chart was constructed. By double-clicking when the pointer looks like a magnifying glass, you can see the account transactions from which the part of the chart or report was constructed.

Miscellaneous reports and charts

The Reports Home window isn't the only place where you can get a report or chart that describes your financial picture. You can also get reports and charts from the following places:

✔ **Home Page:** If you so choose, you can make a Spending by Category chart appear on the Home Page. This chart shows, for the past month, in which categories you spent your hard-earned money. See Chapter 2 for details.

✔ **A register:** While you are staring at an account register, click the Analyze Spending link and choose an option from the menu to generate a report or chart that illuminates activity in the account.

✔ **Set Up Your Categories window:** Click a category name in the Set Up Your Categories window and click the Go to Category button

to see a chart that shows how much you spent in the category in each of the past six months. Click a Payee name in the Payees window and click the Go to Payee button to see a miniregister that shows what you paid the payee.

✔ **Bills Summary window:** Click the Forecast Cash Flow link to see a chart that shows how the bills you have scheduled affect account balances.

✔ **Find and Replace dialog box:** On the Search Results screen of the Find and Replace dialog box is a button called Create Report. Click it and you get an Account Transactions report that shows when and where the transactions you were looking for were entered.

Customizing Reports and Charts

Chances are, the report or chart you created doesn't meet your high expectations. Perhaps it doesn't look right or it covers the wrong time period. Perhaps you want to remove data from one or two accounts in a report to keep the report's figures from being skewed. Maybe you want to change a chart's title.

When you want to change anything about a report or chart, click the Customize link (you can find it under Common Tasks on the left side of the window). Whether you are dealing with a report or a chart, you see the Customize Report dialog box, as shown in Figure 15-7.

This dialog box offers a number of tabs for tinkering with the contents of a report or chart. Experiment freely, but don't forget the rules of engagement (the buttons) that apply to the Customize Report dialog box:

✔ **Apply:** Applies the changes you've made but does not close the dialog box. Click the Apply button after you make a change but you aren't sure whether you want it to be permanent. After your improvements have been applied, drag the Customize Report dialog box to a corner of the screen and look at the damage you did. If you don't like what you see, select different options in the dialog box.

✔ **Reset:** Unravels all the work you did to the report or chart and applies the default settings that you had to begin with.

✔ **Cancel:** Closes the dialog box. Click this button if you decide not to customize.

Maybe the biggest change you want to make to a chart or report is to its title. Change it by typing a new name in the Title box. Beyond that, read on to find out how to customize charts and reports with the 11 tabs in the Customize Report dialog box.

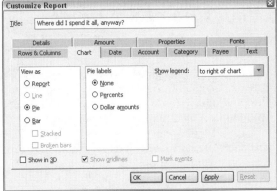

Figure 15-7: Customize charts and reports in the Customize Report dialog box.

Rows & Columns tab: Changing the rows and columns

The Rows & Columns tab in the Customize Report dialog box is for changing the rows (legend items, if you are customizing a chart) and columns (labels, if you are dealing with a chart):

✔ **Rows:** The Rows drop-down list is for selecting how items on the report or chart are grouped. In the case of reports, you specify which items appear as row headings along the left side. In the case of charts, you decide which items comprise the bars, pie slices, or Y-axis values in a line chart.

✔ **Columns:** The Columns drop-down list offers a number of different choices. For reports, select the items that are to appear along the top of the report as column headings. For charts, select the X-axis values.

✔ **Combine All Values Under % of Total:** Rather than include every scrap of data in a report or chart, you can bundle the smaller amounts into a single row, pie slice, or whatever. Enter a percentage in this box to tell Money where to draw the line between amounts that get bundled and items that don't get bundled. This option cleans up pie charts and makes them look much better.

✔ **Sort By:** Usually, items are sorted by amount from highest to lowest, but you can arrange items in different ways from this drop-down list.

✔ **Include Abbreviations:** If you entered abbreviations for categories in the Details window, selecting this check box makes abbreviations as well as category names appear on reports and charts.

Chart tab: Choosing chart types and other chart options

The options on the Chart tab for changing the look of a chart are self-explanatory, I think. True, it's difficult to figure out what the bar chart's Stacked option is, but all you have to do to find out is click one of the options, click the Apply button, and peek at your bar chart.

On the other hand, in case you really need an explanation, here are descriptions of the options for changing the look of a chart:

✔ **View As:** Select the appropriate radio button to change the chart to a bar chart, a line chart, or a pie chart, or to turn a chart into a report.

✔ **Stacked option:** When you are working with a bar chart, select Stacked to put the bars one on top of the other and show total amounts.

✔ **Broken bars:** Select this option to make breaks appear in bars when they have reached important thresholds.

✔ **Pie labels:** Select None to keep labels off the chart, Percents to display a percentage figure that shows how fat each pie slice is, or Dollar amounts to list dollar figures rather than percentage figures next to each pie slice.

✔ **Show in 3D:** Select this option to give the chart a third dimension. Line charts look especially good in three dimensions. Three-dimensional charts look great (refer to Figure 15-6).

✔ **Show Gridlines:** Select this option to draw or removes *gridlines* — the lines on bar and line charts that show roughly how big or small a value is — on the chart.

✔ **Show Legend:** Select this option to tell Money where to place the *legend*, the key that tells what the pie slices, bars, or lines mean, and whether to show the option at all.

✔ **Mark Events:** Select this option to mark highs and lows on line charts.

Date tab: Changing the date range

To change the time period that the report or chart covers, select an option from the Range drop-down list or enter a beginning and ending date of your own in the From and To text boxes.

Account tab: Choosing accounts for the report or chart

To start with, your report or chart gathers data from all your accounts, but perhaps you want it to focus on two, three, or four. To decide which accounts get covered, click the Clear All button on the Account tab and then click each account whose data you want to include in the report or chart. You can also click the All Open Accounts button to gather data only from accounts that are open.

Category tab: Excluding categories from reports and charts

To begin with, reports and charts gather data from all categories and subcategories, but you can exclude categories by way of the Category tab. Click a button to generate a report solely with Income, Expense, or Tax-related categories, or else click the Clear All button and select each category on the list from which the report is to draw data. Deselect the Show Subcatgories check box to keep subcategories from appearing on reports and charts.

Payee tab: Excluding payees and income sources

If you want to get really picky, you can even exclude certain payees and sources of income from reports and charts. Perhaps including a certain payee or income source would skew a report or chart and render it invalid. In that case, go to the Payee tab and click to remove the check mark beside the name of the payee or income source.

Text tab: Using text criteria to gather data

This odd tab is for gathering data on the basis of the words in transactions. For example, entering **Bills** in the text box results in having data gathered only from transactions in which the word *Bills* appears, be it in the Payee field, the Category field, or the Memo field.

Be sure to click the Apply button if you use this tab. Gathering data this way can have weird consequences.

Details tab: Gathering data on the basis of type and status

Use the Type drop-down list on the Details tab to generate reports about payments, deposits, unprinted checks, online bill payments that were not sent, or transfers, and whether or not these transaction types have been reconciled. You can also generate reports around check numbers from this tab.

Amount tab: Querying by amount

On the Amount tab, you can fish in your records for certain amounts or within a certain range.

Classification tab: Including classes and subclasses in reports

If you track your spending and income with classes as well as categories, your Customize Report dialog box includes a Classification tab (it is named after the classification you created). From this tab, you can exclude classes and subclasses from reports and charts.

Fonts tab: Changing how reports and charts look

To change the way the letters look on reports and graphs, go to the Fonts tab and choose a new font and type size. You can also make columns on reports wider or narrower from this tab, but be sure to click the Apply button first. Changing fonts and especially font sizes has a way of throwing everything out of whack on a report or chart. You can always click the Reset button if you create too much chaos.

Adding a Customized Report or Chart to the Favorites Menu

After you go to the trouble of customizing a report or chart, you may as well put it in the My Favorites category of the Reports Home window. That way, you can generate it again without having to tinker with the settings in the Customize Report dialog box.

Follow these steps to add a report or chart to the My Favorites category:

1. **Create and customize the report or chart.**

2. **Click the Add to My Favorite Reports link.**

   You see the Add to Favorites dialog box.

3. **Enter a descriptive name in the Report Name text box.**

4. **Click OK.**

Besides landing in the My Favorites category of the Reports Home window, the name of your customized report or chart also appears on the Favorites➪Favorite Reports menu. You can select it there, too.

To remove a customized report from the Reports Home window, choose Favorites➪Organize Favorites➪Reports. You land in the Modify Favorite Reports window. Select the name of the report or chart, click the Delete button along the bottom of the window, and click Yes in the confirmation box.

Printing Reports and Charts

Before you print a report or chart, I strongly recommend visiting the Report and Chart Setup dialog box, where you tell Money what kind of printer you use and whether you want to print in portrait or landscape style. The following pages reveal intimate secrets that I got from a tabloid about the Report and Chart Setup dialog box. They also tell you how to print a report or chart.

Getting ready to print a report or chart

Follow these steps to tell Money how you want to print your report or chart:

1. **Choose File➪Print Setup➪Report and Chart Setup.**

   You see the Report and Chart Setup dialog box.

2. **From the Printer drop-down list, select the name of the printer with which you will print, if you print on more than one printer.**

3. **Under Orientation, select the Landscape option if you want to print lengthwise on the paper.**

Wide reports and charts fit on the page better when they are printed in landscape fashion. With the Landscape option, the page is turned on its side and it is longer on the top and bottom, like a landscape painting.

4. **Click OK.**

If you are printing a detailed chart and you want it to look especially good, click the Options button in the Report and Chart Setup dialog box. The Option button opens the Printer Properties dialog box, where you can choose options for changing the resolution of your printer, if your printer permits resolution options to be changed.

Printing the report or chart

To make a hard copy of your report or chart so that you can send it to the hard-hitting *Hard Copy* television show, follow these steps:

1. **Put the report or chart on your computer screen.**

2. **Press Ctrl+P or choose File⇨Print.**

You see the Print Report or Print Chart dialog box.

3. **In the Copies box, enter the number of copies you want, if you want more than one copy.**

4. **Click OK.**

Exporting a Report or Chart

The wonderful report or chart that you created is not trapped inside the Money program. No indeed. You can export it to other programs so that you can include it in an annual report or a slide presentation, for example. Follow these steps to export a report and help improve the trade deficit:

1. **With the report or chart on-screen, choose Edit⇨Copy (or press Ctrl+C).**

Doing so copies the report or chart to the Windows Clipboard.

2. **Move to the program to which you want to make the copy and choose Edit⇨Paste (or press Ctrl+V).**

After a chart is pasted, it lands in the other program in the form of a vector graphic. You can change the shape of a vector graphic by pulling and tugging at its perimeters.

After a report is pasted, it lands in the other program in the form of a *tab-delimited text file,* a list in which each component is separated from the next by a tab space. That's no big deal, however, because most spreadsheet and word processing programs can handle tab-delimited text files. The only thing you have to worry about is reformatting your report after it lands in the other program.

To format a report in Microsoft Word, remove all empty rows from the report and then select the table part of the file — that is, select everything except the title, date, and so on. To do that, click to the left of the first row in the report (the row with the column headings), hold down the mouse button, and drag down the screen until the last row is selected. Then choose Table⇨Convert Text to Table and click OK in the Convert Text to Table dialog box. If you need help formatting the table, get a good book on Word. May I suggest *Word 2002 For Windows For Dummies Quick Reference,* by Peter Weverka (Wiley)? It's a classic.

Exporting a report to an Excel worksheet

Fans of Microsoft Excel will be glad to know that Money offers a special command for turning a Money report into an Excel worksheet. For that matter, you can use a Money report in any program that can handle comma-separated value (CSV) files (these files are sometimes called "flat files").

Follow these steps to transplant a Money report in an Excel worksheet:

1. **Generate the report and click the Export to Microsoft Excel link under Common Tasks.**

   You see the Export Report dialog box.

2. **Enter a name for the report and click OK.**

   The Excel program opens, if it isn't open already, so you can open and see your report in a worksheet.

Chapter 16

Tracking Assets, Liabilities, Loans, and Mortgages

*A*nything of value that you own or that adds to your net worth can be counted as an *asset* — jewelry, stock, the equity in a house, a vintage baseball card autographed by the great Willie Mays. The money in your checking and savings account is an asset. So is money that is owed to you.

A *liability*, on the other hand, counts against net worth. A debt that you owe is considered a liability. Credit card debt is a liability, as are taxes owed to the IRS, a mortgage, a student loan, and a car loan.

If you want a clear picture of your net worth or the net worth of your business, you need to identify your assets and liabilities. Fortunately, Money offers account types to track not only assets and liabilities but also loans and mortgages — two other critical elements in the net-worth equation. In this chapter, you discover how and why to set up and use these kinds of accounts. You also find out how to fine-tune them so that they track exactly what you want them to track.

Understanding How to Track Assets, Liabilities, Loans, and Mortgages with Money

If you think about it, all the accounts you can set up in Money fall either into the asset or liability category. The money in savings and checking accounts is an asset. Debt that you track in a credit card account is a liability. However, Money offers the following special account types for keeping a close tab on assets and liabilities:

- ✔ **Asset account:** For tracking the value of personal property, such as art collections, coin collections, and other valuables. If you use Money to track a business, you can create asset accounts for office equipment, tools, machinery, or anything else that adds to the worth of the business or can be used as collateral.

- ✔ **Car or Other Vehicle account:** For tracking the value of a car or boat. Even if you own a car, don't bother tracking its value unless you want to put it up as collateral for a loan or figure its value into your net worth.

- ✔ **Cash account:** For tracking cash on hand for business expenses. This very simple kind of account is for businesses that want to track petty-cash spending.

- ✔ **Home account:** For tracking how much equity is in a house. *Equity* is a house's market value, minus the amount that is owed on the house. For example, if $100,000 is owed on the house and its market value is $150,000, the owner has $50,000 equity in the house. Each time you make a mortgage payment, you can transfer the principal part of the payment to a house account and thereby track how much equity is in the house. A house account is a specific type of asset account.

- ✔ **Liability account:** For tracking no-interest debt, such as quarterly tax payments that you owe the IRS, property taxes, insurance premiums, or money you owe a friend. This account is for tracking business expenses.

- ✔ **Loan account:** For tracking loans on which you have to pay interest, such as student loans and car loans. Loans on which you pay interest are called *amortized loans*. With an amortized loan, part of each payment goes toward paying interest on the debt and part goes toward reducing the principal (the amount you borrowed). A loan account is a type of liability account.

- ✔ **Mortgage account:** Similar to a loan account, a mortgage account is for tracking a mortgage. A mortgage is also an amortized loan. And a mortgage counts, of course, as a liability.

Tracking the Value of a House or Other Asset

Ask most homeowners what their most valuable asset is, and they'll say their house. But ask them how much equity they have in that house, and you usually get a much less definitive answer — if you get an answer at all. And you would probably get the same response if you ask about other tangible assets, such as art collections, baseball cards, or office equipment. Money can help you peg the value of your assets.

Read on to find out how to track the equity in a house or the value of tangible assets, such as art collections, baseball cards, office equipment, and other property that you can sell.

Setting up an asset or house account

A Money house account and a Money asset account work exactly the same way. Setting them up is easy. You can find more specific instructions for setting up accounts in Chapter 3 (where I show you how to set up checking and savings accounts), but for now, follow these steps to set up a house or asset account:

Banking

1. **Click the Banking tab to go to the Account List window and click the Add a New Account link under Common Tasks.**

2. **In the Choose an Account Type window, select the Other option button; then click Next.**

   You see the first of several windows for setting up new accounts.

3. **Select the Asset or Home option and click Next.**

   You see the Choose Level of Detail window.

4. **Tell Money whether you want to simply track the value of the property or asset, or you want to associate the account with a loan or mortgage you are tracking with Money.**

   If all you want to do is record how the value of the property or asset fluctuates over time, choose the first option; if you want to associate the account with a home or mortgage account so that the principal portion of loan payments counts toward the value of the property or asset, choose the second option.

- **Tracking the value of the property or asset value:** Click the Just Track the Total Value option, enter a name for the Account in the Account Name text box, enter the value of the property or asset, and click the Finish button. For the value, enter its value as of today if you just acquired it or if you don't want to track its growth since the time you acquired it. If you want to track how the asset or property has grown or shrunk in value since you acquired it, enter **0**. Later, you can go into the account register and enter dates and values to show how the value of the property or asset has increased or decreased over time.

- **Associating the property or asset with a mortgage or loan:** Click the Track Transactions and Other Details option, and click the Next button. In the ensuing dialog boxes, you are asked to name the account, enter the value of the property or asset, and declare whether you want to associate a loan or mortgage with the property or asset. As the "Tracking Loans and Mortgages" section explains, later in this chapter, you can transfer the principal portion of a loan or mortgage payment to an asset or house account. By doing so, you can track how much the value of the asset or the equity in the house increases each time you make a loan or mortgage payment.

  To track value or equity increases this way, click the Yes button when Money asks whether you would like to associate a loan account with the asset or house. When you click the Next button, you see a dialog box for selecting loan accounts. From the drop-down list, select the loan account from which you will transfer the principal portion of the loan payments.

Home equity loans should be associated with a house. When you take out a home equity loan, you use your house as collateral. Even if you use the money from the loan to buy a car or boat, for example, associate the home equity loan with your house, not with the asset you purchased with money from the loan.

What's your most valuable asset?

Did you know that your most valuable asset is not your car or truck, your most profitable investment, or even your house? No, your most valuable asset is you — your abilities and talents. They are the qualities employers value you for. And they can't be measured by any computer program.

Recording changes in the value of an asset or house

After you set up the asset or house account, you can record changes in its value simply by opening the account register and entering amounts in the Decrease or Increase column. However, if you associated the asset or house account with a loan or mortgage account, changes in value are recorded automatically each time you make a loan payment. Follow these steps to record a change in value by hand:

1. **Open the register of the house or asset account.**

   Figure 16-1 shows an asset account for tracking the value of a Ming vase collection.

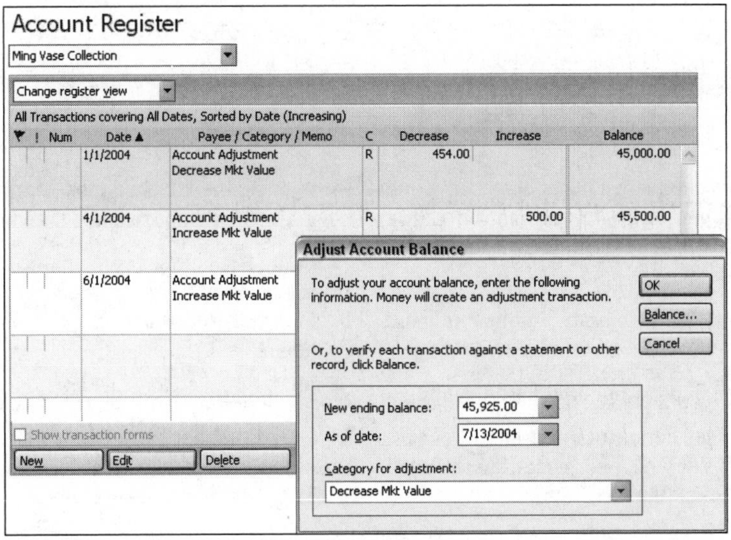

Figure 16-1: To track the value of an asset, enter its current value.

2. **Click the New button or the Update Current Value link.**

   You see the Adjust Account Balance dialog box, shown in Figure 16-1.

3. **In the New Ending Balance text box, enter what the value of the asset or home is as of the date you will enter in the next step.**

4. **Enter the date of the change in value in the As of Date text box.**

5. **Categorize the change in value in the Category for Adjustment drop-down list.**

For example, I suggest creating an income category called Increase Mkt Value (Increase Market Value) to record an increase in value, or a category called Decrease Mkt Value (Decrease Market Value) to record a decrease in value. Chapter 5 explains how to create new categories.

6. **Click OK.**

In the Decrease or Increase columns of the account register, Money enters the amount by which the asset or home increased or decreased in value.

As you can see, the value of the Ming Vase Collection asset account in Figure 16-1 has been fluctuating, but the collection nevertheless is slowly increasing in value. Let's hope none of the vases gets broken.

Another way to associate an asset account with a loan account

Suppose that you set up an asset or home account but you forgot to associate it with a loan or mortgage account, and now you want to do that. Here's how:

1. **Open the asset account or house account register.**

2. **Click the Change Account Settings link.**

3. **Scroll to the bottom of the Change Account Settings window, and, under "Associated Loans," click the Add button.**

4. **In the Line of Credit or Mortgage Loan dialog box, choose Loan; then click Next.**

5. **In the Associate Loans dialog box, select the name of the loan or mortgage that you took out in order to pay for the asset or house.**

6. **Click OK in the Associate Loans dialog box.**

The Details window also has a Remove button. Click the button to sever the link between a loan or mortgage account and an asset or home account.

Associated Loans

Loan	Balance	
2418 23rd Street.	198,525.86	Add...
		Remove
		Go to Account
Total Outstanding Liability	$198,525.86	

Tracking Your Liabilities

Set up a liability account to track loans on which you don't have to pay interest, such as income tax payments. This is not the place for debts that fall in the credit card, line of credit, mortgage, or other interest-paying loan category, but it is the place to include anything else that counts against your net worth, such as insurance premiums.

It's hard to imagine anything easier than creating a liability account in Money. Follow these steps:

1. **Go to the Account List window, and click the Add a New Account link.**

2. **Click the Other option; then click the Next button.**

3. **In the Choose an Account Type window, select Liability and click the Next button.**

    You land in the Choose Level of Detail window.

4. **Select the Just Track the Total Value option.**

5. **Enter a name for the liability account in the Account Name text box.**

6. **In the Total Value text box, enter what you owe for the liability.**

    Enter what you owe as of today if you just started owing or if you don't care to track how your liability has shrunk or grown since the time you started owing. If you want to track how the liability has grown or shrunk since the time you acquired it, enter **0**.

7. **Click the Finish button.**

To record transactions in a liability account, click the Update Amount Owed link in the account register window. Then, in the Adjust Account Balance dialog box, enter a date and the amount you owe as of that date. Money will calculate increases or decreases for you in the register.

Tracking Loans and Mortgages

The following sections explain how to set up a loan or mortgage account for tracking amortized loan payments and mortgage payments. An *amortized loan* is a loan for which you make regular payments of the same amount. Part of each payment goes toward paying interest on the loan and part goes toward reducing the principal (the amount you borrowed).

Is creating a loan or mortgage account worthwhile?

Before you go to the considerable trouble of creating a loan or mortgage account, you should know that you may not have to create one to track mortgage or loan payments.

As long as the lender tells you how much you owe after each payment and how much you are paying in interest, you really don't need to track the loan. You can simply get the numbers from the lender and record the interest portion of the payment as a decrease in a liability account and the principal part of the payment under Loan: Loan Interest or a similar category. In other words, when you record the check you used to make a loan or mortgage payment, split

the payment so that the principal portion is recorded as a transfer to the liability account and the interest portion is recorded in the Loan: Loan Interest category.

In the case of mortgages, business loans, and investment loans, the lender should send you a 1098 tax form at the end of the year that explains how much of your payments went toward interest. That is the amount you need to know for income tax purposes. To save time and heartache, you may as well let the lender do the work and get the numbers from the lender rather than track the loan yourself.

After you find out how to set up a loan account, I show you how to stand on your head and sing *Dixie*. Actually, I do no such thing. I show you how to record loan payments in loan account registers, handle irregular loan payments that involve escrow accounts, and record a payment above and beyond the amount you are expected to pay.

Setting up a loan or mortgage account

When you set up a loan or mortgage account, Money asks you all kinds of questions and uses the information to break down the loan payments into interest charges and principal reductions. With each payment you make on the loan or mortgage, Money reduces the amount you owe in the loan or mortgage register and records how much of the payment did not lower the total debt but went only toward servicing the interest in a mortgage or loan category.

Gather all the papers that pertain to the loan or mortgage and then follow these steps to set up a loan or mortgage account for tracking the payments:

1. **Go the Account List window, and click the Add a New Account link.**

   You go to the Choose an Account Type window.

2. **Click the Other Account Type option; then click the Next button.**

3. **In the next window, which asks what kind of account you want to set up, select Loan or Mortgage; then click the Next button.**

4. **Click the Track Transactions and Other Details option; then click Next.**

   You see the New Loan Wizard dialog box.

5. **Speed-read the "You are about to enter the Twilight Zone" message box and click the Next button.**

   No, it doesn't really say that you are about to enter the Twilight Zone. It just tells you what the dialog boxes in the New Loan Account Wizard are about to ask you.

6. **Speed-read the next message, which explains the three types of general information that will be needed, and click the Next button.**

7. **You're borrowing money, and the Borrowing Money option is already selected, so click the Next button.**

8. **Enter a name in the Loan Name text box and choose to whom the payments will be made by entering a name in the Make Payments To box or by selecting a name from the drop-down list; then click the Next button.**

   The name you enter will appear in the Account List window when you finish setting up the loan or mortgage account.

9. **Select Adjustable Rate Loan (ARM) or Fixed Rate Loan and click the Next button.**

   The interest rate remains the same in a fixed-rate loan or mortgage. In an adjustable-rate loan or mortgage, the rate of interest is subject to change.

   Which dialog box you see next depends on the option you choose in this step.

10. **If you selected Fixed Rate Loan in Step 9, click the Yes or No option to say whether payments have been made on the loan; if you selected Adjustable Rate Loan, enter the date that the first interest rate adjustment is to be made and enter the number of years or months between adjustments.**

    If you are setting up a fixed-rate loan or mortgage and you select the Yes, Payments Have Been Made option, you see an additional dialog box that asks whether to schedule all the payments made on the loan or mortgage since you began paying it. Money needs this information to create a loan payment schedule. Money can gather information for scheduling no matter how you answer this question.

    Click the Next button, of course, after you're done.

11. **Enter the due date of the first payment on the loan or mortgage.**

    Be sure to enter the due date of the first payment, not the next payment. Money needs the first due date to create the amortization schedule.

12. **Speed-read the next dialog box, which tells you how far you've come, and click the Next button.**

13. **From the Paid How Often drop-down list, select the option that describes how often payments are due (probably Monthly) and click the Next button.**

14. **Select the option that describes how the loan is calculated and click the Next button.**

    Home mortgages are usually calculated based on the date the payment is due; consumer loans (such as car loans) are based on the date the lender receives payment. However, you may have to dig into the paperwork that came with your loan or call the lender to find out how interest is calculated.

15. **In the following five dialog boxes, enter the amount of the loan, the interest rate, the loan length, the principal and interest, and the balloon payment, if there is one.**

    Keep clicking the Next button after you make each entry. After you are done, your dialog box looks something like Figure 16-2. Click the Back button if you need to go back and change an entry.

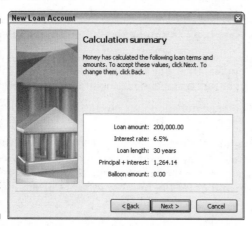

Figure 16-2:
Calculating
the
particulars
of the loan.
If you leave
one of the
entries
blank,
Money
calculates it
for you.

> **New Loan Account**
>
> **Calculation summary**
>
> Money has calculated the following loan terms and amounts. To accept these values, click Next. To change them, click Back.
>
> Loan amount: 200,000.00
> Interest rate: 6.5%
> Loan length: 30 years
> Principal + interest: 1,264.14
> Balloon amount: 0.00
>
> < Back   Next >   Cancel

The Principal + Interest entry is a little confusing. What Money is really asking for is the amount of your monthly payment (or weekly payment or whatever). If you don't know the amount offhand, leave the box blank. Money can calculate payment amounts for you as long as you can provide information in the other four boxes.

When you enter the interest rate, be sure to enter the loan interest rate, not the compounded interest rate. The two are different.

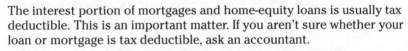

16. **Speed-read the dialog box, which tells you how far you have come, and click the Next button.**

    It's not as though you have any choice in the matter, is it?

17. **Type in category names or select the names from the drop-down lists; then click the Next button.**

    When you make a loan or mortgage payment, the portion of the payment that goes toward interest is categorized under the category choice you make in this step. The portion that goes toward reducing the debt is recorded in the loan account register as a decrease in the amount you owe.

    You can create a new category and subcategory if you want. If you enter names that Money doesn't know, you see the New Category dialog box. Fill in the dialog boxes (and click the Next or Finish button) to create your new category.

18. **Click the Yes or the No button to tell Money whether or not interest on the loan or mortgage is tax deductible; then click the Next button.**

    The interest portion of mortgages and home-equity loans is usually tax deductible. This is an important matter. If you aren't sure whether your loan or mortgage is tax deductible, ask an accountant.

19. **If part of your payment goes toward fees such as escrow accounts, click the Other Fees button; otherwise, click the Next button.**

    This dialog box asks whether you must pay fees on top of the principal and interest payments that are due. Chiefly, this dialog box is for people who pay into escrow accounts when they make their mortgage payments. An *escrow account* is an account that a mortgage company takes out on behalf of a borrower to make sure that property taxes and property insurance get paid.

    If you click the Other Fees button, you see the Other Fees dialog box, as shown in Figure 16-3. This box works exactly like the Transaction with Multiple Categories dialog box I describe in Chapter 4. Use the Other Fees dialog box to categorize the fees you have to pay; then click the Done button.

20. **If you want to schedule a payment in the Bills Summary window so that you are reminded when payments are due, click the Yes, Remind Me check box, fill in the dialog box, and click the Next button; otherwise, click the No, Do Not Remind Me check box and then click the Next button.**

    Chapter 12 explains how the Bills Summary window works. I strongly recommend scheduling the loan or mortgage payment. Lenders charge hefty fees for late payments. By scheduling your loan or mortgage payment, you increase your chances of paying it on time.

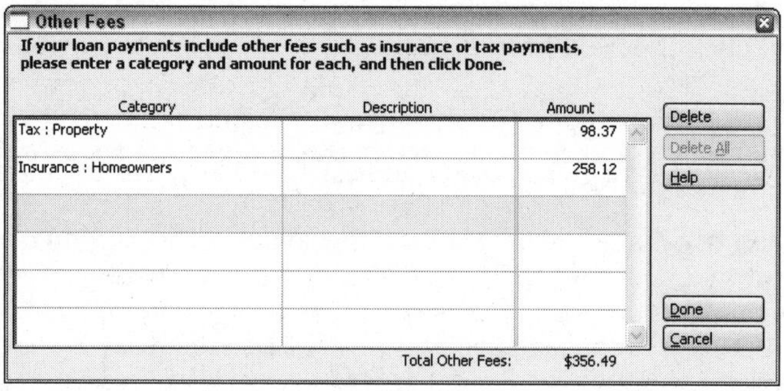

Figure 16-3:
Describing
the part of a
monthly
payment
that goes
toward
escrow
fees.

Other Fees

If your loan payments include other fees such as insurance or tax payments, please enter a category and amount for each, and then click Done.

Category	Description	Amount
Tax : Property		98.37
Insurance : Homeowners		258.12

Delete
Delete All
Help

Done
Cancel

Total Other Fees: $356.49

21. **Study the Summary Information dialog box and then click the Next button.**

    As shown in Figure 16-4, the next dialog box you see provides a rundown of all the information you gave Money in the last *(whew!)* 20 steps. Study this dialog box for a moment, and if anything is wrong, start clicking the Back button like crazy until you reach the dialog box where you can correct the error.

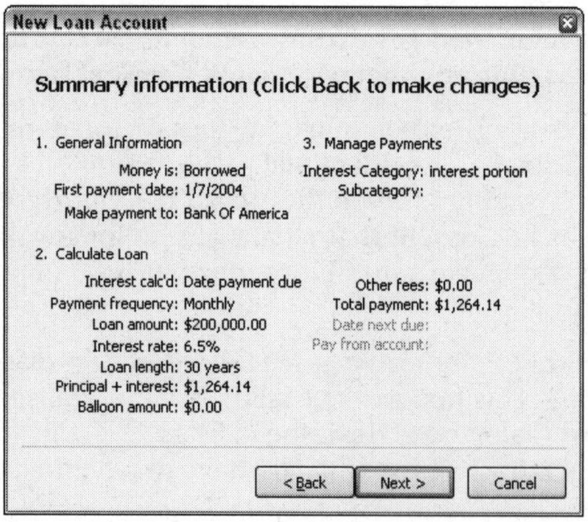

Figure 16-4:
The
Summary
Information
dialog box
sums up
all the
information
you gave
Money.

New Loan Account

Summary information (click Back to make changes)

1. General Information

   Money is: Borrowed
   First payment date: 1/7/2004
   Make payment to: Bank Of America

3. Manage Payments

   Interest Category: interest portion
   Subcategory:

2. Calculate Loan

   Interest calc'd: Date payment due
   Payment frequency: Monthly
   Loan amount: $200,000.00
   Interest rate: 6.5%
   Loan length: 30 years
   Principal + interest: $1,264.14
   Balloon amount: $0.00

   Other fees: $0.00
   Total payment: $1,264.14
   Date next due:
   Pay from account:

< Back   Next >   Cancel

22. **If you want to associate your new mortgage or loan account with a house or asset account, click the Yes button, click the Next button, and select the asset or house account from the dialog box; otherwise, click the No button and then click the Finish button.**

    The dialog box you see if you click Yes asks whether you want to associate an asset account with this loan account. Choose the account from the drop-down list and then click the Next button.

If you already created a house account for tracking the equity in a house, or if you already created an asset account for tracking the value of a car or other asset, you can associate your house or asset account with the loan account you are almost finished setting up.

You can always go back later and associate an asset or house account with your new loan account (see the sidebar "Another way to associate an asset account with a loan account," earlier in this chapter).

Fixing loan or mortgage account errors

Suppose that you make an error when you set up a loan or mortgage account. One little mistake — an incorrect due date, for example — can throw everything out of whack. To fix mistakes you made when you set up a loan or mortgage account, open the account register, click the Change Account Settings link, and click the Change Loan Terms button. You can find this button on the right side of the window (you might have to scroll to find it). Money opens the Change Loan dialog box. Answer the dialog box's questions and keep clicking the Next button until you correct your error.

See how much you're paying in interest

Are you curious about how much you spend in interest payments over the life of a loan? Want to know how much the total payments on a loan are?

To find out, open the account register where you track the loan or mortgage, click the Analyze Loan link, and choose View Loan Amortization Schedule. You see a Loan Amortization report.

The report shows, over time, how much of each payment is devoted to paying interest and how much is devoted to reducing the principal. Scroll to the bottom of the report and you see the total payments and total interest payments. The report in the figure shows that, on a $198,525.86 mortgage, $246,451.38 is devoted to servicing interest and the total payments equal $444,977.24.

Date	Payment Number	Payment Amount	Principal	Interest	Principal Balance
3/7/2033	351	1,264.14	1,197.66	66.48	11,075.11
4/7/2033	352	1,264.14	1,204.15	59.99	9,870.96
5/7/2033	353	1,264.14	1,210.67	53.47	8,660.29
6/7/2033	354	1,264.14	1,217.23	46.91	7,443.06
7/7/2033	355	1,264.14	1,223.82	40.32	6,219.24
8/7/2033	356	1,264.14	1,230.45	33.69	4,988.79
9/7/2033	357	1,264.14	1,237.12	27.02	3,751.67
10/7/2033	358	1,264.14	1,243.82	20.32	2,507.85
11/7/2033	359	1,264.14	1,250.56	13.58	1,257.29
12/7/2033	360	1,264.10	1,257.29	6.81	0.00
Grand Total		444,977.24	198,525.86	246,451.38	0.00

Recording loan and mortgage payments

If you are not tracking the principal portion of loan or mortgage payments in a loan or mortgage account, simply write a check to the bank or lender from whom you received the loan or mortgage and be done with it. But if you linked your loan or mortgage account to a checking account so that you can track how the amount you owe decreases with each payment, follow these steps to record it:

1. **Open the loan or mortgage account register with which you track the loan or mortgage.**

2. **Click the New button in the transaction tab.**

   A dialog box asks, "What do you want to do?"

3. **Select the Make a Regular Loan Payment option and click OK.**

   You see the Edit Transaction dialog box, as shown in Figure 16-5. The amount of your monthly (or weekly or yearly) payment already appears in the Amount box.

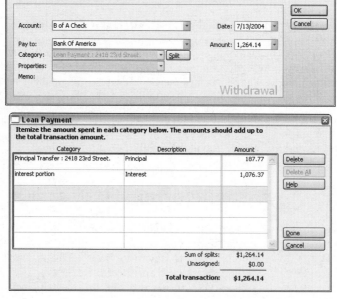

Figure 16-5: Click the Split button in the Edit transaction dialog box to see how much of a payment goes toward paying interest and reducing the principal.

4. **In the Account drop-down list, choose the account from which you will make the payment.**

   Your choice is probably a checking account.

   Try clicking the Split button to see how much of your payment is devoted to reducing the principal and how much is devoted to servicing interest. In Figure 16-5, part of the payment is a transfer to a House account to show how the principal of the loan is reduced; part is categorized as Loan: Mortgage Interest. At tax time, you could run a report and see in the Loan: Mortgage Interest category how much you paid for the year in tax-deductible interest payments.

5. **Enter the name of the bank or lender to whom you will write the check in the Pay To box.**

6. **Click OK.**

   In the loan account register, the balance is reduced by the amount of the payment that is devoted to reducing the principal of the loan.

   The transaction is entered in both the loan or mortgage account register and the checking account register from which the payment was made. To go to the checking account in which the payment was made, right-click the transaction and choose Go to Account.

When you record a mortgage or loan payment, the payment is divided:

✔ The portion that goes toward reducing the principal (your debt) is recorded as a transfer to the loan or mortgage account. In the loan or mortgage account register, the balance is reduced accordingly.

✔ The portion that goes toward paying the interest is categorized as mortgage interest (or another category, depending on which category you selected when you set up the account).

✔ If you have to pay fees, the payment is divided even further.

Paying early and often

The faster you pay off an amortized loan or mortgage, the less you have to pay altogether, because much of the cost of an amortized loan goes toward paying interest. Suppose that you want to pay more than you are required to pay so that you can pay off the loan quicker and save on interest costs. How do you record a payment you've made above and beyond what the lender expects of you?

Follow these steps to record a larger-than-usual or extra loan or mortgage payment:

1. **Open the loan or mortgage account register.**

2. **Click the New button.**

   You see the dialog box that asks "What do you want to do?"

3. **Either make an extra payment or pay more on top of your usual payment:**

   - **Extra payment:** Select the Make an Extra Loan Payment option and click OK to go to the Edit Transaction dialog box (refer to Figure 16-5). Fill in this dialog box as you normally would, and enter the amount of the extra payment in the Amount box.

   - **Larger-than-usual payment:** Select the Make a Regular Loan Payment option and click OK. Fill in the Edit Transaction dialog box as you normally would, and then click the Split button. In the Loan Payment dialog box (refer to Figure 16-5), increase the amount on the Principal Transfer line by the additional amount you're paying. Next, click Done. You see the Adjust Loan Payment Amount dialog box, as shown in Figure 16-6. Select the third option, Change the Loan Payment Amount to Be the Sum of the Loan Split Amounts, and click OK.

   Amounts you pay above and beyond what the lender expects go toward reducing the principal of the loan — they go directly toward reducing the total amount you owe. Therefore, you have to add the extra amount to the amount already shown on the Principal Transfer line.

   For example, if the amount of principal you are scheduled to pay is $68.63 and you want to pay an extra $100 this time around, enter $168.63 on the Principal Transfer line.

4. **Click OK in the Edit Transaction dialog box.**

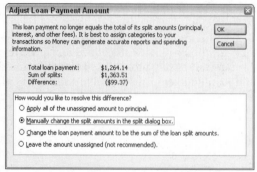

Figure 16-6:
Making
a larger-
than-usual
mortgage
or loan
payment.

TIP

You are hereby encouraged to make extra payments on a loan or mortgage when you can afford to. Not only do you increase the amount of equity you have in the thing you borrowed money to purchase, you also dramatically lower the interest amounts you have to pay to service the debt.

Adjusting loan account balances

Money does its best to calculate interest and principal payments, but computers are only human and sometimes they make mistakes. When you receive a statement from a lender, compare the balance on the statement to the balance in your loan or mortgage account, and if the balances are out of line with each other, follow these steps:

1. **Open the mortgage or loan account register.**

2. **Click the Update Amount Owed link.**

   You'll find the button under Common Tasks. You see the Adjust Loan Balances dialog box, shown in Figure 16-7.

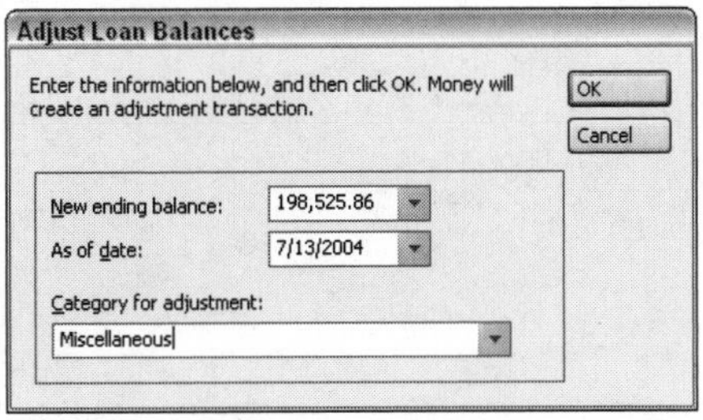

Figure 16-7:
Adjusting
the amount
you owe on
a loan.

> **Adjust Loan Balances**
>
> Enter the information below, and then click OK. Money will create an adjustment transaction.
>
> [OK]
> [Cancel]
>
> New ending balance: `198,525.86`
> As of date: `7/13/2004`
> Category for adjustment:
> `Miscellaneous`

3. **Enter the date shown on the statement in the As of Date text box.**

4. **Enter the ending balance shown on the statement in the New Ending Balance text box.**

5. **Use the Category for Adjustment box to describe the few cents' or few dollars' difference between your records and the lender's.**

   Select an expense category such as Miscellaneous if the lender's records show a higher amount than what your records show; select an income category such as Other Income if the lender's records show a lower amount.

6. **Click OK.**

   Money makes an account adjustment entry in the register and all's well that ends well, as Shakespeare used to say when he used Money version 1603.

Updating the interest rate on a loan or mortgage

Suppose that the interest rate on your loan or mortgage changes. If yours is an adjustable-rate mortgage (ARM), it's bound to happen sooner or later. When the interest rate changes, you have to burrow into your loan account and record the change.

To adjust the interest rate, open the loan or mortgage account register and click the Change Account Settings link. You land in the Change Accounts Settings window. Scroll toward the bottom of the window and click the Update Interest Rate button. Money presents you with a series of dialog boxes for changing the interest rate. Keep answering the questions and clicking the Next button until, gratefully, you finish.

Part VI
Going Online with Money

The 5th Wave   By Rich Tennant

"The new technology has really helped me get organized. I keep my project reports under the PC, budgets under my laptop and memos under my pager."

In this part . . .

Part VI is dedicated to Buck Rogers, that citizen of the future who banks online and pays all his bills in digital cash. You won't catch Buck Rogers standing in line at a bank or ATM. You won't see him reconciling his bank accounts from a measly paper statement.

If your computer is connected to the Internet, you're invited to go online and make like Buck Rogers. Here's your chance to take advantage of the Money program's many online features. This part of the book explains how.

Chapter 17

Getting Ready to Go Online

· ·

In This Chapter

▶ Exploring the online services that Money offers

▶ Getting the equipment and services you need to bank online

▶ Seeing whether your bank offers online services

▶ Setting up bank accounts to work online

▶ Canceling the online banking service

· ·

*T*he makers of Money are betting that people will soon rely on home computers to do their banking in the same way that people rely on ATMs to do most of their banking today. Not so long ago, ATMs were regarded with suspicion: "What if the machine shortchanges me?" However, most people don't think twice about using ATMs nowadays, and someday they probably won't think twice about banking online, either.

This chapter explains the steps you must take before you can start banking online. I describe the online services and equipment that you need, and show you how to find out whether your bank offers the services, how to sign up for them, and how to cancel them if it comes to that.

Reviewing the Online Services That Money Offers

The Money program's online services enable you to do everything from pay your bills to investigate potential investments. Table 17-1 describes the Money online services. If you have the Premium edition of the program, some of these services are free.

Table 17-1	The Online Services That Money Offers
Service	*What You Can Do*
Online banking	Download records from your bank or credit card company to find out which transactions have cleared the bank (and then balance the account, if you so choose). Money automatically enters records that you download in the account register, which saves you some of the trouble of entering the records yourself. You can also download brokerage statements. *Cost:* Depends on whether you download transaction records directly into Money or go to the bank's Web site first. Varies from institution to institution. Some banks charge nothing and some charge $3 to $5 per month.
Online bill payment	Pay bills online with MSN Bill Pay. You can use this service to pay anyone, even Uncle Ernie. If your bank doesn't permit you to pay bills online, you can still do it through these third-party corporations such as CheckFree. Cost: MSN Bill Pay charges $5.95 per month for the first 15 payments (the first three months of the service are free). After 15, payments cost 50 cents each.
Online stock and mutual funds	Download stock, bond, and mutual fund prices from the Internet. Money automatically enters the current prices of the stocks, bonds, and mutual funds in your portfolio in the Portfolio Manager window. By using this service, your portfolio is always up-to-date (see Chapter 9). *Cost:* Free.

Before you can start banking or paying bills online, you have to sign up with your bank. After you sign up, the bank assigns you a password or a PIN (personal identification number) similar to the PINs used in automatic teller machines. You have to supply the password or PIN whenever you engage in an online activity.

Not all banks and financial institutions offer online banking, but the ones that offer the service do so in one of these ways:

- **Direct services:** You send instructions from inside Money to download a bank statement or transfer funds between accounts, and the instruction is sent directly from your computer over the Internet to the bank's computers. Usually, banks charge for this service.

- **Web services:** You go to the bank's Web site, enter your password, and download a statement to Money. You can't transfer funds with this type of online account. All you can do is view and download bank statements. Usually, this service is free.

When you pay a bill online through your bank, the payment order is sent to a third party such as MSN Bill Pay or CheckFree. Its computers contact your bank's computers and withdraw the money necessary for the payment. The third party sends a paper check or an electronic funds transfer to the payee. Which company handles these money transfers depends on your bank. Banks contract bill-pay services to other companies.

Laying the Groundwork

I'm afraid that getting online isn't as easy as counting one, two, three. Before you can start exploring cyberspace, you have to complete two or three irksome little chores. Sorry about that.

The following sections explain what equipment you need to go online, how to establish a connection between your computer and the Internet, how to investigate whether your bank offers online services, how to sign up for the services, and how to set up an account so that you can go online with it.

The good news is that you have to complete these irksome little chores only once.

The equipment you need

Before you even think about going online with Money, make sure that your computer is capable of connecting to the Internet. You also need a browser, a computer program that connects to Web sites and displays Web pages (*browser* is not a contraction of the word *brown-noser,* by the way). When you installed Money, you also installed Internet Explorer, the browser made by the Microsoft Corporation, so a browser is already installed on your system.

You need a .NET passport!

Stop! Do not pass Go. Do not collect $200. Before you can use any of the online banking services, you need a .NET passport from Microsoft. You can obtain the passport at this Web address: `http://register.passport.com`. As Chapter 11 explains in excruciating detail, you have to enter your .NET passport when you start Money. You need the passport to bank online or record Money transactions online.

One more thing: You need an account with an Internet service provider (ISP). When you download stock quotes or bank online, Money runs piggyback on your ISP connection. Money can't establish or make the connection on its own.

Disabling call waiting

Call waiting is wonderful unless you connect to the Internet by modem. The noise that call waiting makes to tell you someone is trying to call disrupts Internet connections. You can, however, enter a prefix before you call to disable call waiting for the duration of a telephone call. When you connect to the Internet by modem, make sure that your modem dials the prefix as well as the telephone number of your Internet provider. Find out what the prefix is and then follow these instructions to disable call waiting when you connect to the Internet:

- ✓ **In Windows 95 and 98:** Go to the Control Panel and double-click the Modems icon. Select a modem on the list, if necessary, and click the Dialing Properties button. Select the To Disable Call Waiting Dial check box, enter the prefix, and click OK.

- ✓ **In Windows 2000, Me, and XP:** Go to the Control Panel and double-click the Phone and Modem Options icon. On the Dialing Rules tab, click the Edit button, select the To Disable Call Waiting Dial check box, enter the prefix, and click OK.

Signing Up with Your Bank

If the online banking services tickle your fancy, the next step is to get in touch with your bank and find out whether it offers online services and which services it offers. One way to do that is to visit the bank's Web site by following these steps:

Banking

1. **Click the Banking tab to go to the Account List window.**

2. **Click the name of the account with which you want to bank online.**

   You see the Account Register window.

3. **Click the Go to *Your Bank's Name* link or, if you can't find that link, click the Connect to Bank link.**

4. **On the submenu that appears, choose Go to *Your Bank's Name* Web Site.**

   If you selected a bank when you set up the account, Money opens to the bank's Web site, as shown in Figure 17-1.

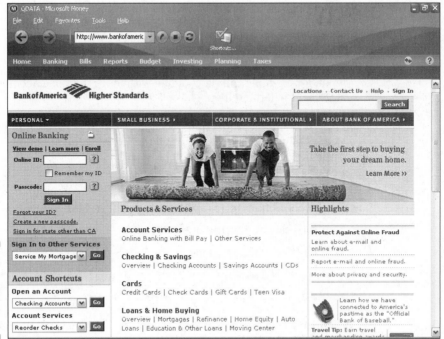

Figure 17-1:
Going to a
bank's Web
site in
Money.

If you didn't select a bank when you set up the account, click the Manage Online Services link in the Account List window. In the Manage Online Services window, click the Check for New Online Services link next to the bank's name. A series of windows appears so you can name the bank.

Whether you talk to a bank representative or look for information at your bank's Web site, be sure to get answers to these important questions before you decide whether to bank online:

✔ Can I download transactions directly into Money without visiting the bank's Web site? Probably the person on the other end of the line will be confused by this question. Explain that you want to know whether it is necessary to go to the bank's Web site to download a bank statement. Explain that some banks permit Money users to download the data right into their Money file without visiting a bank's Web site.

✔ How much do the services cost? How much for bill payment and banking online? Do you charge a flat rate or do you charge per transaction? Is there a trial period for using the services?

✔ Can I transfer money between accounts?

✔ Which accounts can be online accounts? (For example, banks as a rule do not allow IRA accounts to be online accounts.)

✔ If I decide to cancel the service, what is the quickest way to do so?

✔ How will I be billed? Will the charges show up on my monthly bank statement, for example? If I bank online with more than one account, which statement will the bill appear on?

If you like the replies and decide to sign up for online banking, the bank or credit card company needs some or all the following information, so be ready to provide it:

✔ Your address, home telephone number, and work telephone number

✔ Your account number(s) and perhaps your ATM card number

✔ Your birthday and birthplace

✔ Your mother's maiden name

✔ Your Social Security number

✔ Your e-mail address

What happens next depends on what kind of online services the bank offers. If the bank offers only Web services, you can get going very quickly. The bank will issue you a password. If you intend to bank online from inside Money, you usually have to wait a few days to receive a start-up kit in the mail. The kit includes the personal identification number (PIN) you need to access your accounts, as well as instructions for banking online.

Is online banking safe?

Occasionally, you read in the newspaper about an evil, twisted computer genius who crashes into others' computers and steals credit card numbers, account numbers, and the like. And stories like that make you wonder whether banking online is safe.

Banking online is safe. It's safe because banks and corporations such as Microsoft want it to be safe. Companies have poured millions of dollars into security measures to make banking on the Internet safe.

If you use an ATM card, you take a bigger risk than you do when you bank online. The odds that a thief will take your ATM card or demand your card's PIN are higher than the odds that an evil hacker will steal your bank account's PIN and use it to clean out your bank account.

Setting Up a Money Account So That It Works Online

After you find out your password or get your PIN from the start-up kit that the bank sends, your next step is to give the account you want to work with online status. In other words, you need to set up the account so that you can use it to bank online and perhaps pay bills online. Connect to the Internet and follow these steps:

Banking

1. **Click the Banking tab to go to the Account List window.**

2. **Click the Manage Online Services link.**

   You land in the Manage Online Services window, as shown in Figure 17-2. The names of banks and financial institutions where you have open accounts are listed in this window. If you can sign up for online banking with an institution, a Complete Setup for Online Services link appears beside its name. If an account has been set up for online services, the lightning bolt icon appears to the left of its name.

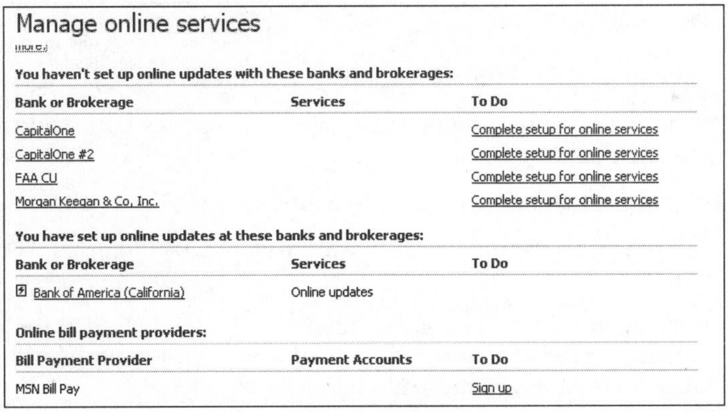

Figure 17-2: The Manage Online Services window.

> **Manage online services**
>
> You haven't set up online updates with these banks and brokerages:
>
> | Bank or Brokerage | Services | To Do |
> | --- | --- | --- |
> | CapitalOne | | Complete setup for online services |
> | CapitalOne #2 | | Complete setup for online services |
> | FAA CU | | Complete setup for online services |
> | Morgan Keegan & Co, Inc. | | Complete setup for online services |
>
> You have set up online updates at these banks and brokerages:
>
> | Bank or Brokerage | Services | To Do |
> | --- | --- | --- |
> | ⚡ Bank of America (California) | Online updates | |
>
> Online bill payment providers:
>
> | Bill Payment Provider | Payment Accounts | To Do |
> | --- | --- | --- |
> | MSN Bill Pay | | Sign up |

3. **Click the Complete Setup for Online Services link next to the name of the bank where you want to bank online.**

   You see the Select a Bank or Brokerage window.

4. **Make sure the correct bank or brokerage firm is selected, and click Next.**

   Probably the correct bank is already selected, but this is your chance to select the right name if you chose the wrong one when you set up the account.

5. **Click the Next button.**

   Money downloads information from the bank to your computer. What happens next depends on which bank you are dealing with and whether your bank offers Web services or direct services. Keep reading.

Setting up an account for Web services

If your bank offers Web services, you see windows for entering your online ID and password. Enter the information. Chapter 18 explains how to download a bank statement from your bank.

Setting up an account for direct services

If your bank offers direct services, including the ability to pay bills online, you see windows for entering particulars about your bank account. Starting here and clicking the Next button as you go along, provide the information that Money needs to bank and pay bills online. In the course of filling in these windows, your computer will download information from your bank. Provide this information:

- ✔ **User ID (Social Security Number):** You know what that is, I hope.

- ✔ **PIN:** The personal identification number that the bank supplied you in the start-up kit.

- ✔ **Account name:** The name of an account you want to bank online with.

- ✔ **Bill pay:** Declare whether you want to pay bills online as well as bank online.

- ✔ **Routing number:** The *routing number* (which you find in the start-up kit) consists of the first nine numbers in the lower-left corner of checks. On either side of the routing number is a colon (:).

Signing Up for MSN Bill Pay

Make sure you are signed into Money with a .NET passport, and then follow these steps to sign up for the MSN Bill Pay service.

1. **Click the Bills tab.**

2. **In the Bills Summary window, click the Go to MSN Bill Pay link.**

   You see an introductory window.

3. **Click the Sign Up for MSN Bill Pay button.**

4. **Follow the on-screen instructions for signing up.**

   You will be asked to for a security key (a four-character code you choose yourself), for your address, for your social security number, and for your banking account number and routing number on your check.

Changing Your Mind about the Online Banking Services

You tried. You tried your best and really put your heart into it, but banking online was not for you. It just didn't work out. You weren't ready for an online relationship.

Follow these steps to disable an online account:

Banking

1. **Click the Banking button to go to the Account List window.**

2. **Click the Manage Online Services link.**

   You see the Manage Online Services window.

3. **Click MSN Bill Pay.**

4. **Click the Stop Using Online Services link and follow the instructions on the screen.**

Chapter 18

Banking and Bill Paying Online

. . . .

In This Chapter

▶ Connecting to the Internet and your bank

▶ Downloading a bank statement and updating an account register

▶ Paying your bills online

▶ Transferring money between online accounts

. . . .

*B*anking online and paying bills online represent a brave new world. If you've made the arrangements with your bank and have prepared Money for online banking (see Chapter 17), you're ready to blast off for that world. You're going to do for the first time what many people will consider routine by 2007. You're about to enter the future. You're about to take your digital cash into cyberspace.

In this chapter, you find out how to pay bills electronically over the Internet and how to keep tabs on a bank account by banking online. Throughout this chapter, I show you how to record online transactions and online payments in account registers. So strap yourself in. Liftoff is approaching.

Sending Banking Instructions over the Internet

After you record online transactions and online payments (I show you how shortly), they appear in the Update Online Information dialog box, as shown in Figure 18-1. This dialog box also lists commands for downloading stock quotes and updating Money. The Update Online Information dialog box is where you tell Money which instructions to send to your bank, credit card company, or brokerage firm. Select each instruction you want to send and click the Update button to go onto the Internet and download information to your computer.

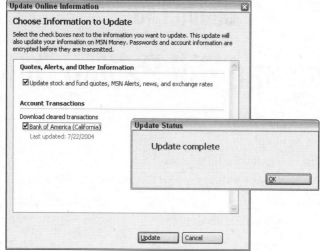

Money offers no less than four ways to open the Update Online Information dialog box:

- ✔ Click the down arrow on the Online Updates button, and choose Update Now. This button is located in the northeast corner of the screen, next to the Show Help Pane button (see Figure 18-2).

- ✔ Click an Update Now link in the Account List window.

- ✔ Click the Update icon in the Account List window. This icon appears beside the names of accounts.

- ✔ Choose Tools⇨Internet Updates⇨Update Now.

You hear your phone dialing (if you have a conventional modem rather than high-speed Internet service), and then you see the Update in Progress dialog box. If all goes well, the Update Status message box appears and tells you that the update is complete (refer to Figure 18-1).

As shown in Figure 18-2, the Tools⇨Internet Updates submenu and the drop-down menu on the Online Updates button offer commands for handling online transactions:

- ✔ **Update Now:** Displays the Update Online Information dialog box so that you can choose which online banking instructions to send.

- ✔ **Read Call Summary Messages:** Displays the Review Update Results window so that you can see the dates and times when instructions were last sent (refer to Figure 18-2).

- ✔ **View Electronic Transactions:** Displays the View All Electronic Payments and Transfers window so that you can see which online payments and money transfers need sending.

✔ **Customize Updates:** Displays the Customize Update Schedule window so that you can tell Money how often to send online transactions and receive online updates.

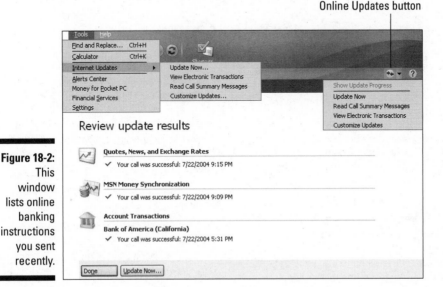

Figure 18-2:
This window lists online banking instructions you sent recently.

Banking Online

Remember the old movies and TV shows about Buck Rogers? Not one of them showed Buck banking online. Sure, you got to see Buck battle Ming the Merciless, but you never saw him battle his checkbook as he tried to balance it. Too bad Buck didn't have Money to download a bank statement and use it to update an account register, transfer money between online accounts, or send e-mail messages to a bank. (He could even have used e-mail to taunt Ming.)

Getting accurate, up-to-date account information

With the online banking service, you can find out how much money is in an account and which transactions have cleared the bank. After you get the information, you can compare it to the records in your account register and update the register with the downloaded information. You can even let Money do the work of recording transactions in registers. Instead of entering the transactions yourself, the bank "pours" them into the account register when you download.

Deciding how to download transactions

Be sure to visit the Online Services tab of the Options dialog box if you are serious about downloading transactions from banks. This tab gives you many opportunities to decide how you want to download stuff from the bank. Choose Tools⇨Settings and click the Online Services link in the Settings window. You see the Online Services tab of the Options dialog box. From top to bottom, here are the options on the Online Services tab:

✔ **Add a description to the Memo field:** Banks automatically enter descriptions in the Memo field for withdrawals, for example. Select this option to enter those descriptions in your account registers.

✔ **Match transactions:** When looking for matches, this option tells Money to search a certain number of days in the past. Sixty days is usually adequate because that represents about two statement periods.

✔ **Automatically accept all downloaded transactions:** I wouldn't touch this one with a ten-foot pole! I think you should review downloaded transactions before entering them in the register.

✔ **Overwrite transaction dates:** Instead of entering the date on which you made a transaction into the account register, Money enters the date on which the transaction cleared the bank.

✔ **Replace downloaded payee names with user-altered names:** Money offers a feature for filling in payee names for downloaded transactions. I don't cover it in this book because it doesn't work very well. You're welcome to try it, though, by selecting this option.

✔ **Automatically mark accepted transactions as Reconciled:** Select this option if you don't want to balance your bank account against the monthly statements that the bank sends in the mail and you prefer to balance the account on the basis of transactions that you download from the bank.

✔ **Show standardized payee names:** The payee name feature again!

✔ **Enter electronic payments in the register:** Instead of entering the date on which you made an electronic payment, Money enters into the register the date the payment clears the bank.

✔ **Automatically update accounts online when I start Money:** Gives the instruction to download bank statements each time you open the Money program.

✔ **After accepting a transaction:** What do you want to do after you click the Done button in the Change Transaction Matching window (refer to Figure 18-6)? Select an option from this drop-down list.

Unless you specify otherwise, you get months and months of information the first time you download a bank statement. You don't want that. You want about a month's worth of transactions.

How you download statements from a bank depends on whether you use direct services or Web services to bank online. Better read on.

Downloading a bank statement with Web services

To download a bank statement with Web services, start by going to your bank's Web site. You can get there in Money by using one of these techniques:

✔ Choose Favorites⇨Favorite Web Sites⇨Your Banks⇨*Name of Your Bank*⇨Home Page.

✔ In the Account Register window, click the Connect to Bank link, and choose Go To *Your Bank's Name* on the submenu.

On your bank's Home page, enter your Online ID and password. Then follow the instructions on the page for downloading a bank statement. Each bank's instructions are a little different. Select the name of your account, look for a Download to Microsoft Money button, and click the button.

After the account information is downloaded to your computer, you see the Online File Received screen, as shown in Figure 18-3. Follow these steps to download your bank statement:

1. **On the Money Accounts drop-down list, choose the name of the account where the transactions belong.**

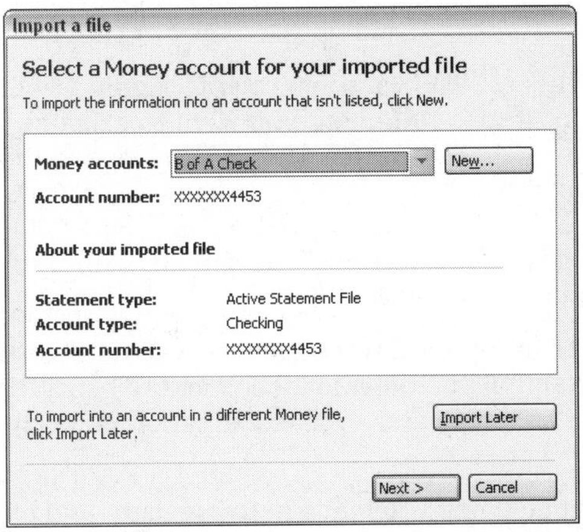

Figure 18-3:
Down-
loading
a bank
statement
with Web
services.

Import a file

Select a Money account for your imported file

To import the information into an account that isn't listed, click New.

Money accounts: B of A Check   ▼   New...

Account number: XXXXXXX4453

About your imported file

Statement type: Active Statement File
Account type: Checking
Account number: XXXXXXXX4453

To import into an account in a different Money file, click Import Later.   Import Later

Next >   Cancel

2. **Click Next.**

The You Have Statements to Read window, as shown in Figure 18-4, appears.

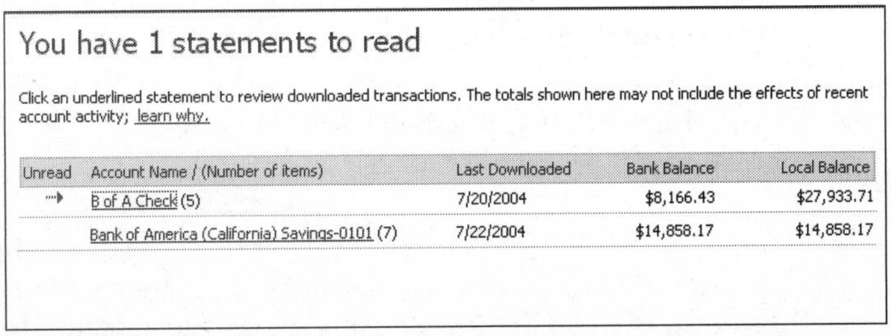

Figure 18-4:
The list of
downloaded
account
statements.

You have 1 statements to read

Click an underlined statement to review downloaded transactions. The totals shown here may not include the effects of recent account activity; learn why.

Unread	Account Name / (Number of items)	Last Downloaded	Bank Balance	Local Balance
→	B of A Check (5)	7/20/2004	$8,166.43	$27,933.71
	Bank of America (California) Savings-0101 (7)	7/22/2004	$14,858.17	$14,858.17

Downloading a bank statement with direct services

Options for getting bank statements appear automatically in the Update Online Information dialog box, the dialog box you see when you click the Online Updates button and choose Update Now. Money assumes that you want to download your bank statement whenever you connect to the Internet by way of Money. Enter your PIN, if necessary, and click the Update button. The You Have Statements to Read window (refer to Figure 18-3) lists the bank statements you downloaded.

Viewing and updating a register whose transactions you downloaded

After you've downloaded transactions from the bank, you can compare the bank's records to yours for the sake of accuracy. By doing so, you make sure that the amounts in your register match the amounts in the bank's records. If you find a discrepancy, Money gives you the chance to fix it.

In the You Have Statements to Read window (refer to Figure 18-4), click the name of the bank account whose statement you want to examine. You see an account register like the one in Figure 18-5. Here's how to read confusing registers like this one:

- Under "Downloaded" on the left side of the screen, Money tells you how many transactions need reviewing.

- Where Money thinks there is a discrepancy between a transaction you entered and a transaction you downloaded from the bank, the transaction appears in boldface type and a red exclamation point (!) appears in the ! column.

- If Money thinks that an entry you made in the register and one you downloaded may be different, the words Your Entry and Bank Entry appear in the register. As I explain shortly, you can fix these discrepancies by selecting the transaction and clicking the Accept or Change button.

- Where you entered a transaction in the register that is identical to a transaction you downloaded from the bank, the words Your Entry and Bank Entry *don't* appear in the register. These transactions are very likely accurate. You can simply click the Accept button to acknowledge them.

- If you downloaded a transaction but it is nowhere to be found in your register, the transaction appears in CAPITAL letters.

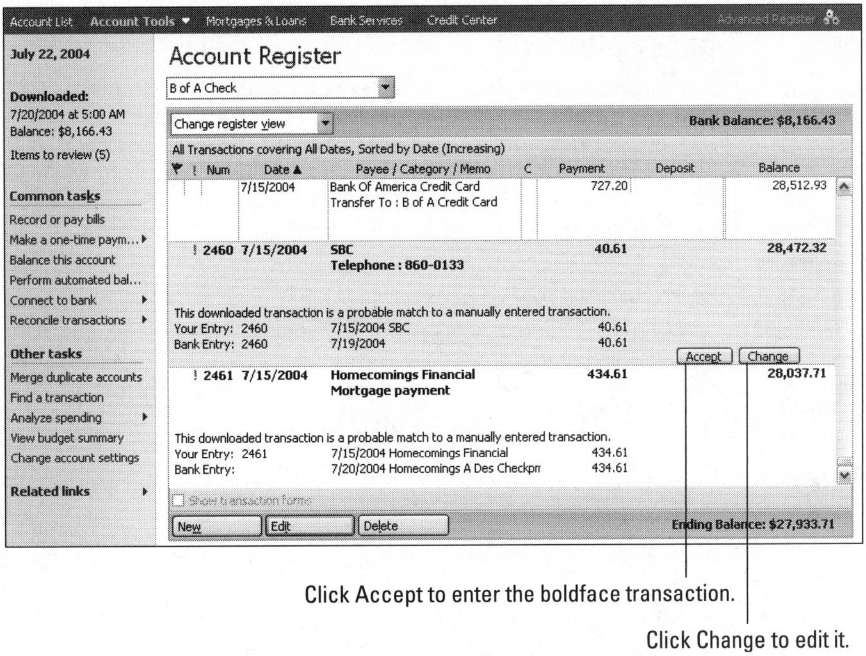

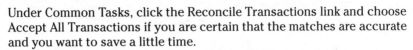

Figure 18-5:
Reviewing
transactions
downloaded
from the
bank.

Click Accept to enter the boldface transaction.

Click Change to edit it.

Your mission now, should you choose to accept it, is to examine the transactions, make sure they are accurate, and then accept or edit them as necessary. You don't have to clear all the transactions. You can always uncheck the mysterious ones and clear them later, when the paper statement arrives.

Click each boldface transaction that needs reviewing to select it; then do one of the following:

✔ **Accept it:** Click the Accept button. You hear a "beep," and that's the end of it. The transaction is officially entered in the register. Before you accept a transaction, make sure it is categorized correctly.

Under Common Tasks, click the Reconcile Transactions link and choose Accept All Transactions if you are certain that the matches are accurate and you want to save a little time.

✔ **Edit it:** Right-click the transaction and choose Edit. Then edit the transaction to make it accurate.

✔ **Change it:** Click the Change button if you want to match the transaction to one you already entered or create two separate transactions. You see the Change Transaction Matching window, as shown in Figure 18-6. This window gives you the chance to repair the little problem.

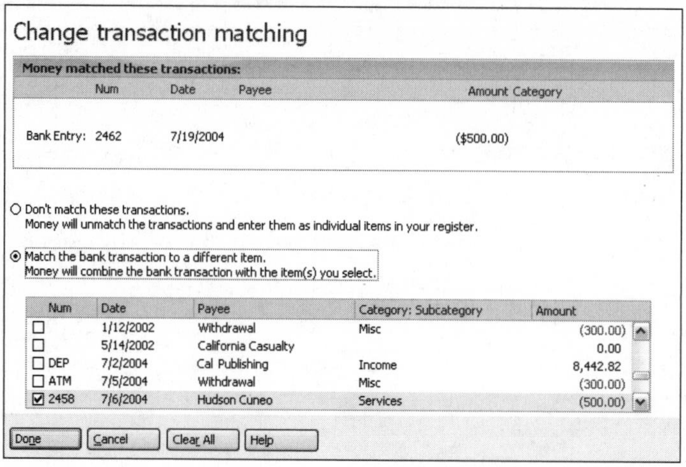

Change transaction matching

Money matched these transactions:

	Num	Date	Payee		Amount Category
Bank Entry:	2462	7/19/2004			($500.00)

○ Don't match these transactions.
　Money will unmatch the transactions and enter them as individual items in your register.

◉ Match the bank transaction to a different item.
　Money will combine the bank transaction with the item(s) you select.

Num	Date	Payee	Category: Subcategory	Amount
☐	1/12/2002	Withdrawal	Misc	(300.00)
☐	5/14/2002	California Casualty		0.00
☐ DEP	7/2/2004	Cal Publishing	Income	8,442.82
☐ ATM	7/5/2004	Withdrawal	Misc	(300.00)
☑ 2458	7/6/2004	Hudson Cuneo	Services	(500.00)

[Done] [Cancel] [Clear All] [Help]

Figure 18-6:
Changing transactions downloaded from the bank.

In the Change Transaction Matching window, do one of the following:

✔ **Enter two separate transactions:** Select the first option, Don't Match These Transactions. Then click the Done button.

✔ **Assign the transaction to another entry in your register:** Select the second option, Match the Bank Transaction to a Different Item. At the bottom of the screen, a list of unreconciled transactions in your account register appears. If the transaction is one you entered already, select its check box in the list and click the Done button.

Paying the Bills Online

Sure, paying bills online is disconcerting at first. That's your hard-earned money flying across cyberspace. Those coins that used to jangle in your pocket have been digitized and turned into bits and bytes — nothing you could feed a jukebox, for example.

On the other hand, you don't have to rummage through desk drawers to find stamps and envelopes when you pay bills online. As I note in Chapter 17, paying bills online is a little cheaper than paying bills by mail.

Money offers a shortcut to MSN Bill Pay. Click the Bills tab to go to the Bills Summary window. Then click the Go to MSN Bill Pay link. You'll find it under Common Tasks.

Recording the online payment

To record an online payment, follow these steps:

Banking

1. **Click the Banking tab.**

   You land in the Account List window.

2. **Click the name of the bank from which you will pay the bill.**

   You go to the Account Register window.

3. **Click the Make a One-Time Payment link and choose the Make an Electronic Payment option on the submenu.**

   The first time you record an online payment to a company or person and you click OK in the Edit Transaction dialog box, you see a dialog box for entering information about the company or person. Here you tell Money everything you know about the payee. Be sure to enter the information correctly.

   You have to fill out the Online Payee Details dialog box only once for each payee. After you make the first online payment, Money doesn't ask you for the payee's address and phone number again. If a payee's address or phone number changes, go to the Categories & Payees window and record the changes there (see Chapter 11).

   If you don't have an account number, enter your name in the Account Number text box.

4. **Click the Submit Payment button.**

   When you click the button, you see the Edit Transaction dialog box. Except for the Due Date text box and the Number box, which says Epay (for Electronic Payment), this dialog box works exactly like the Withdrawal transaction form I describe in Chapter 3.

What about check numbers for online payments?

When you record an online payment and send it across the Internet, Money assigns it a check number that is far, far removed from the numbers on the checks you enter by hand. The check number isn't assigned until the payment has been sent. Money even puts the online icon — an envelope being struck by lightning — next to the check number in the register so that you know that the payment was made online.

Stopping a payment after it's sent

What? You sent a payment over the Internet and now you regret doing so? If you sent the payment in the past four days, you can try to stop it by following these steps:

Bills

1. **Click the Bills tab to go to the Bills Summary window.**

2. **Click the View Electronic Transactions link.**

   The View All Electronic Payments and Transfers window appears. It lists all transactions you sent in the past 60 days.

3. **Select the electronic transaction you want to stop and click the Delete button.**

Transferring money between accounts

As long as both accounts are signed up for the online banking service and both accounts are at the same bank, you can transfer money between accounts. In fact, you can play digital Ping-Pong and send the money back and forth between accounts as many times as you wish. Sorry, you can't transfer money, for example, from a credit card account to a checking account. Also, you can't transfer money to someone else's bank account. Money laundering is not allowed.

Transfer funds between accounts the same way you record a normal money transfer in a register. However, choose Electronic Transfer (Xfer) in the Number box and click the Submit button to send the transfer across the Internet.

Part VII
The Part of Tens

The 5th Wave   By Rich Tennant

"I bought a software program that will help us control our spending habits, and 7 new games, 4 screen savers and this nifty mouse cozy."

In this part . . .

Each chapter in Part VII offers ten tidbits of good, rock-solid advice. With four chapters in this part, that makes — count 'em — 40 tidbits in all.

You'll find suggestions for staying on top of your finances, improving your financial health, using Money when you are self-employed, and converting from Quicken to Money.

Chapter 19

Ten Things You Should Do Periodically

*T*his little chapter explains ten things you should do from time to time with Money. Do these ten things and you will live happily ever after.

Back Up Your Data File

Whenever you shut down Money, the Back Up dialog box appears, and you get an opportunity to back up your data file. Seize this opportunity! Grab it by both ears and shout, "Yes, I want to back up my data file." If you don't back up your file and something bad happens to your computer, you may lose all the financial data you so carefully assembled.

Chapter 11 explains how to back up a file — and how to restore a file from its backup copy. Be sure to back up your file to a floppy disk, CD, or other removable device. The data needs to be outside your computer, preferably in a hidden place that is safe from hurricanes, tornadoes, and earthquakes.

Update Your Savings and Checking Account Registers

Breaking up may be hard to do, but falling behind is easy — especially when it comes to entering the checks you've written in a checking account and the transactions you've made in a savings account.

If you procrastinate, you fall further and further behind. Soon, updating your savings and checking accounts seems like a monumental task. You stop updating your accounts, and not long after that, you stop using Money.

Set aside ten minutes in the middle of the month and ten minutes at the end of the month to update your account registers. Twenty minutes a month isn't that bad, is it? Okay, you may miss a third of an "I Love Lucy" rerun each time, and that could be the death of you, but life isn't exciting unless you take a few risks.

Balance Your Accounts

Balance your bank accounts each month when the statements arrive. Balancing, also known as reconciling, is easy to put off until tomorrow. However, if you keep putting it off, you end up with a stack of unreconciled bank statements and a bad case of the blues.

In Chapter 6, I explain a few tricks for recognizing and fixing reconciliation problems. After a while, you get good at balancing your records with the bank's. Not that you enjoy it, but you do start to understand it. Eventually, a minute or two is all you need to reconcile. No kidding.

Balance Your Credit Card Accounts

Not only do you have to record credit card purchases from the statement if you don't record purchases throughout the month, but you also have to balance your credit card account when the statement arrives. Balancing a credit card statement, as with balancing a bank statement, is one of those monthly jobs that are easy to put off until next month. Try to do it each month. If you don't, you get behind, become discouraged, fall into a state of despair, stop grooming yourself, stare at the ground a lot, and wear a permanent grimace on your face.

Personalize the Home Page

The Home Page is the first thing you see when you start Money. You can always return to the Home Page by clicking the Home button. The Home Page is supposed to give you a quick overview of your finances — your changing finances, I should say. As your financial picture changes, as you buy and sell investments, or take on new debt, or win the lottery, or donate all you own to a worthy cause, periodically change what is shown on the Home Page so that you see precisely where you stand financially.

To change the Home Page, start by clicking the Customize Content or Layout link on the Home Page. Chapter 2 explains the Home Page in detail.

Generate a Monthly Income and Expenses Report

One of my favorite Money reports, and certainly one of the most revealing, is the Monthly Income and Expenses report. It shows in no uncertain terms where you spent all that money, how you earned it, and whether you earned more than you spent.

Chapter 15 explains how to generate and customize reports and charts. The Monthly Income and Expenses report shows spending and income in the past month, but you can customize the report to show what you did financially in the past year or the past six months, for example.

Print Your Account Registers

When you file your income tax return in April, print a copy of your account registers from the previous year and put them away with the rest of your income tax stuff — copies of your returns, receipts, and bank statements. I explain how to generate reports in Chapter 15.

By printing the past year's transactions, you leave behind a wide, easy-to-follow paper trail that the IRS posse can follow if it audits you.

Make an Archive File and Put It Away

Besides filing away a printed copy of your registers, make an archive file and put it away, too. An *archive file* is a file in which you store transactions from a certain time period. Make an archive file of transactions from the past year and file it away with copies of your tax returns and other important tax records. That way, you have a file of one year's records that auditors can examine at their leisure. Chapter 11 explains how to generate an archive file.

Prune Your Payee List

Once in a blue moon, go into the Payee list and remove the names of payees you no longer write checks to or receive money from. Money enters payee names automatically in the Payee text box on transaction forms. Type the first few letters, and Money immediately enters a name for you.

When the Payee list gets too long, however, Money throws outdated names in the Payee text box. To keep from seeing the names of people and companies you haven't dealt with for months or years, prune the Payee list. Chapter 11 explains how to do it.

Stop and Smell the Roses

I'm going to propose a radical idea: Computers aren't as wonderful as many people make them out to be. Even when you're surfing the Internet or exploring new cyberspace worlds, all you're really doing is staring into the glare of a monitor.

You can easily get carried away with all the features that Money has to offer. If you own stocks and track them with Money, you may be tempted to download stock quotes each day from the Internet. If you've read Chapter 13 of this book, you know how to forecast your future income, and you may be tempted to find out, for example, how rich you'll be in the year 2014.

Money is simply a tool to help keep your financial house in order. It simplifies the task of tracking your finances so that you can devote time to other things. So do those other things! Stop and smell the roses. Money shouldn't be another computer toy that distracts you from the rich and intriguing real world, the one that begins just outside your computer screen.

Chapter 20

Ten Ways to Good Health — Financially Speaking, That Is

- -

In This Chapter

▶ Record credit card transactions as you make them

▶ Pay off all your credit cards

▶ Leave your plastic at home

▶ Create a Spending by Category chart

▶ Create a Monthly Income and Expenses report

▶ Create a budget

▶ Plan ahead for your retirement

▶ Set aside money for a rainy day

▶ Make like a young dog — learn new tricks

▶ Take the day off

- -

*W*arning: The Surgeon General has determined that not being in good financial health causes undue stress and worry and can lead to other health complications. The ten tidbits of advice in this chapter are meant to improve your financial health.

Record Credit Card Transactions As You Make Them

You can very, very easily run up credit card debt. A purchase here and a purchase there, and pretty soon you owe $3,000, $4,000, or $5,000. Ouch!

To keep from spending so much with a credit card, record the transactions as you make them. After you buy the expensive piece of stereo equipment or the designer-label jacket, carry the credit card receipt home, lay it flat on your desk, and record the purchase in a credit card register. Watching the amount that you owe climb higher may discourage you from buying so many things with your credit card.

Pay Off All Your Credit Card Debt

Paying down or paying off a large credit card debt isn't easy, but it's worth it because credit card companies charge outrageous interest rates on credit card debt. Unless you pay off your credit card each month, you're paying extra for everything you buy with your credit card.

Look at it this way: If your credit card company charges 18 percent interest (the common rate in the United States) and you don't pay off your credit card debt over the course of a year, you pay an extra 18 percent with every purchase you make. The fancy handbag on sale for $180 doesn't really cost $180; it costs $212.40 after you add the 18 percent interest. The two tires don't really cost $112; they cost $132.16.

Leave Your Plastic at Home

Do you notice a theme developing in this chapter? Sorry for harping on credit card debt, but it is the single most daunting obstacle that comes between people and their financial well-being. If you have trouble keeping credit card spending in check, try leaving your credit card at home. Studies show that people are far more apt to spend with a credit card than they are to spend cash.

Create a Spending by Category Chart

I can't get enough of Money's Spending by Category chart. It's easy to generate, and it shows so plainly and nakedly where you spend money. The first time I saw the chart was a revelation. "Eureka!" I shouted. "So that's where all the money went — to ice cream!" Actually, my two biggest spending categories were Taxes and Home: Mortgage, which wasn't a very big surprise. It was surprising, however, to discover what a large chunk of my income I spent in those two categories.

Chapter 15 explains how to generate a Spending by Category chart. Money can generate many different revealing charts and reports.

Create a Monthly Income and Expenses Report

Another way to get a good look at your finances is to create a Monthly Income and Expenses report. The report shows how much you earned in the last six months and how you earned it. It also shows how much you spent in each category and subcategory. Chapter 15 explains how to generate reports.

Reading down the Expenses list, you may find a few surprises. You may discover one or two categories in which you spent much more than you thought. Next time you consider buying an item that falls into one of those categories, think twice.

Create a Budget

Chapter 12 explains how to formulate a budget with Money. Formulating a budget takes an entire evening, but if you have trouble keeping your spending in check, it is an evening well spent. Also, Money makes it very easy to find out whether you met your budget.

Plan Ahead for Your Retirement

For some people, retirement is a dirty word. They don't want to think that far ahead. But you really ought to plan for your retirement for two reasons. First, to spend your golden years comfortably, you have to start saving now. Second, setting aside money for retirement is the best way to lower your tax bill. With 401(k) plans, SEPs, and other tax-deferred investment plans, the federal government has made saving for retirement very practical.

Chapter 13 explains how to use Money to help plan for your retirement.

Set Aside Money for a Rainy Day

One of the first things that you realize when you read most financial self-help books is how important "rainy day" money is. Most authors recommend setting aside two month's income, the idea being that it usually takes two months to find a new job if you're bounced out of your present job.

Make Like a Young Dog — Learn New Tricks

In Chapter 16, which describes how to set up an asset account, I explain that assets are things that add to your net worth — the money in savings and checking accounts, an object of value that you own, the equity in a house. However, you can't record your most important asset in an account register: Your most important asset is *you*.

Your talents, your abilities, and your know-how are your most important assets. As such, you can make like a young dog and learn new tricks. Go back to school and acquire a few new skills. Or volunteer somewhere, gain new skills, and acquire new experiences. Doing so can make you a more valuable employee to others.

Take the Day Off

To use one of those man-as-machine metaphors, sometimes you have to relax and recharge your batteries. Take the day off. In fact (I'm writing this chapter late Friday afternoon), take the rest of the week off! You deserve it. The object of using Money is to get more free time to enjoy yourself.

Chapter 21

Ten Things to Do If You Are Self-Employed

As of the year 2005, I will have been self-employed for 15 years. Not bad for a country boy from Idyllwild, California!

Being self-employed isn't for everyone. You need the right temperament, and you have to be willing to suffer the risks as well as reap the rewards. The following pages offer a few suggestions for self-employed people who use Money.

Diligently Record Your Financial Activity

One of the difficulties of being self-employed is that you have to account for all the money you spend. At tax time, you use your records, not those of an employer, to calculate how much income tax you owe. And because you can deduct certain expenses from your gross income on your income tax report, you have to record expenses as carefully as you record income.

Money, of course, makes recording income and expenses an easy task. But you have to stay on top of it. Don't let several weeks or months pass before you update your savings and checking account registers. Be sure to reconcile your account on a monthly basis, too. Falling behind is too easy.

Make Sure That All Tax-Related Expenses Are Marked As Such

Being self-employed, you can deduct certain expenses from your gross income when you file an income tax report. Office expenses, rent payments (if you rent an office), and any payment you make on behalf of your business are tax deductible.

To mark an expense as tax deductible, you assign it to a category or subcategory that has tax-related status. Chapter 14 explains how to give categories and subcategories tax-related status. Give all categories and subcategories that have anything whatsoever to do with taxes a tax-related status.

Print a Tax-Related Transactions Report for Your Accountant

Transactions that are assigned to a tax-related category appear on the Tax-Related Transactions report. Under the name of each tax-related category and subcategory, the report lists transactions and gives the total amount that was spent. For example, the report lists each transaction assigned to the Charitable Donations category. At the bottom of the list is the total amount you spent on charitable donations.

Charitable donations are tax deductible. An accountant who examines the Tax-Related Transactions report knows right away how much you can deduct for charitable donations. You don't have to pay the accountant to study your account registers and find charitable donations, because the numbers are right there on the Tax-Related Transactions report.

Chapter 15 explains how to generate reports. You can save a great deal of money on accounting fees by generating a Tax-Related Transactions report for your accountant.

Use the Memo Box Early and Often

As a self-employed individual, you have to track your own finances — your income, expenses, and so on. In account registers, you have to describe the money you spend and the money you take in. Usually, the Category boxes on transaction forms are adequate for describing your income and expenses, but consider using the Memo text box as well. When you record an odd expense, describe it in the Memo box in case you have to explain it to an accountant months from now, when you will have forgotten what it was.

Set Aside a Tenth of Your Income in a Savings Account

Being self-employed takes discipline. Employers deduct income taxes, Social Security payments, and Medicare payments from the paychecks of wage earners and salaried employees. Not so with self-employed individuals. The self-employed are responsible for paying their own taxes and Social Security.

You should make tax payments four times a year, on April 15, June 15, September 15, and January 15. More important, you have to be ready to make these payments, which means setting aside some of your income throughout the year to meet your tax obligations.

I suggest stashing a tenth of your income in a savings account. If you're making more money than the previous year, set aside more than a tenth because you'll owe extra when April rolls around.

Schedule Your Quarterly Tax Payments

Missing or being late with a quarterly tax payment is catastrophic. Heads roll. There is much sorrow and gnashing of teeth. To make sure that you make the quarterly payments on time, schedule them. Chapter 12 explains how to use Money to schedule a payment. Depending on how you set up your Home Page (see Chapter 2), you can make scheduled bills appear very prominently on the Home Page under Bills & Deposits.

Use Classifications to Track Business Expenses

One of the dilemmas of being self-employed is keeping your personal expenses separate from your business expenses. One way to keep them separate is to create a classification called Business and assign transactions that pertain to your business to the Business classification. See Chapter 5 for more about classifications.

Open a Checking Account for Business Transactions

Another way to keep business expenses and personal expenses separate is to open a checking account for business transactions. I got this idea from my accountant, who told me — mysteriously, I thought — that I had "some ambiguity" between my personal and business expenses, but I could "resolve these ambiguities" by opening a business checking account.

Now, I deposit all incoming checks in my business checking account. When I need money for my family's personal finances, I transfer it into the family checking account. Expenses for office supplies and such that fall in the business category are all paid out of my business checking account. I'm unambiguous. I'm as cut-and-dried as a salami sandwich.

Write a Check to Yourself Periodically

My accountant also told me that I need to spend more money on my business. "Why should I spend more money?" I asked. "I'm trying to save money." He said that my overhead was extremely low and that I should "beef it up." To do so, he suggested writing down all the piddley cash payments I make — for pencils, bus fare, and so on — in a book, and when the total expenses reach $100 or so, to write myself a check for that amount. By doing this, I can spend more money on my business and lower my tax bill.

I was surprised by how much the little expenses added up. Personally, I don't like having to write down payments in a book, but I do like saving money on taxes.

Keep Your Irons on the Fire

In the days before the electric iron, when people used irons that were made out of, well, iron to smooth the wrinkles from their clothes, the person whose job it was to iron clothes had to keep more than one iron on the fire. While one iron was in use, a second and third iron lay on the fire. That way, the person who ironed clothes never lacked a hot iron.

If you are self-employed, you also have to keep more than one iron on the fire. You need to devote an afternoon every other week to looking for work. Looking for work means sending out your résumé, making phone calls, and maybe going to lunch. Looking for work does not pay well. In fact, the hourly wage for looking for work is zip. But looking for work is something you have to do if you expect to stay self-employed.

Chapter 22

Ten Things Ex-Quicken Users Should Know about Money

About eight years ago, on the idea that "if you can't beat 'em, buy 'em," the mighty Microsoft Corporation made a bold attempt to purchase Intuit, the company that makes Quicken, Money's rival. Everyone shook hands, and the deal appeared completed until the Federal Trade Commission stepped in. The FTC insisted that the deal created a monopoly and constituted unfair business practices.

After being rebuffed by the federal government, Microsoft redoubled its efforts to make a financial management application as good as or better than Quicken. I believe Microsoft has succeeded in doing that. As one who has written books about Quicken and Money, I know both products very well, and Money is the better of the two by far. It offers more features, it is better integrated with the Internet, and it is much, much easier to customize. I think the interface is easier to use, too.

This brief chapter is for people who have made the switch from Quicken to Money. I describe the chief differences between the programs and tell ex-Quicken users what to watch out for as they use Money.

You Can Use Your Old Quicken File in Money

Money offers a wizard that you can use to convert a Quicken data file to a Money file. Actually, the wizard doesn't convert the file. It makes a copy of the Quicken data file, converts the copy, and leaves the original data file intact. So if you decide after all that you like Quicken better than Money, you can go back to Quicken and continue using the data file as if nothing happened. After you convert a Quicken file, a new file called Qdata.mny opens on the Money screen. The file extension of Money files is .mny.

Before you convert your Quicken file, open the Quicken file (in Quicken, of course) and do the following to make the conversion go smoothly:

- ✔ **Back up your Quicken file so that the backup copy is completely up-to-date.**

- ✔ **Validate the file.** To do so, choose File➪File Operations➪Validate.

- ✔ **If you formulated more than one budget, open the one you want to keep.** Sorry, only one budget can make the trip from Quicken to Money.

Follow these steps to convert a Quicken data file to Money:

1. **Close Quicken if the program is running and open the Money program.**

2. **Choose File➪Convert Quicken File.**

   You see the Convert Quicken File dialog box.

3. **Find and select your Quicken data file.**

   Unless you tinkered with Quicken's default settings, the Quicken data file is called Qdata.QDG, Qdata.QDF, Quicken.QDF, or Quicken.QDT, and it is located in the C:\Quickenw folder.

4. **Click the Convert button.**

5. **In the Back Up dialog boxes, click the Back Up button to back up whatever data file is currently open in Money.**

   You land in the Quicken File Conversion window.

6. **Click the Next button and follow the on-screen directions.**

   When Money asks where you want to store your new Qdata.mny file, be sure to choose a folder whose name and location you will remember.

After the conversion is complete, a Summary of the Conversion window appears. It lists account balances in Quicken and account balances in Money. Compare the two to make sure that the Quicken data was converted successfully. You can click the Save button, save the file, open it in your word processing program, and print it.

You Can Find the Modified Transactions

To look for transactions that were modified when you converted your Quicken file to Money, choose Tools⇨Find and Replace and, in the Find and Replace dialog box, select Regular Accounts or Investment Accounts in the Search Across drop-down list. Then type **modified** in the Find This Text box and click the Next button.

Some Things Are Lost in the Conversion

The following elements are not converted from Quicken files because Money does not offer similar features:

- ✔ Memorized charts
- ✔ Transaction passwords
- ✔ Category groups
- ✔ Savings goals

Some Quicken Features Have No Equivalent in Money

Besides savings goals, converts and forced converts to the Money 2005 Standard edition will not find equivalents to Quicken alerts and the financial planners. You have to own the Money 2005 Deluxe or Premium edition if you want to plan ahead.

In Money, Transactions Are Entered on Forms

In my opinion, the biggest difference between Quicken and Money is that, in Money, you enter transactions on forms at the bottom of the account register. In Quicken, you enter a transaction by typing it directly into the register. True, you can choose Enter Transactions Directly into the Register on the View menu in an account register window and enter transactions that way, but the people who designed Money make that hard to do. The drop-down lists in the account register are unwieldy and hard to use.

The transaction forms in Money take a bit of getting used to. Chapter 4 explains how forms work and how to record a transaction on a form.

Some Old Bank Transactions Are Not Shown as Reconciled

As Chapter 6 explains, you can reconcile, or balance, bank accounts in Money to make sure that your records jibe with the bank's. You can do that in Quicken too, as you probably know. When you convert a Quicken data file to Money, some transfers between accounts are shown as unreconciled, and this can cause a problem when the time comes for you to reconcile a bank account. Instead of seeing a month's worth of unreconciled transactions in the Balance Account window, you see some old transactions from years past.

You can find these unreconciled transfers very quickly and reconcile them by following these steps:

1. **Click the Banking tab to go to the Account List window.**

2. **Click the name of a bank account.**

   You see the Account Register window.

3. **Click the Balance This Account link.**

   The first Balance dialog box appears.

4. **Enter any number you want in the Ending Balance text box, and then click the Next button.**

   It doesn't matter what number you enter. Your purpose is to get to the Balance Account window and find unreconciled transactions.

5. **In the in the Balance Account window, look for transactions from years past and reconcile them by right-clicking each one and choosing Mark As⇨Reconciled on the shortcut menu.**

   Each time you reconcile a transaction this way, it is removed from the Balance Account window. These old transactions will not bother you next time you reconcile this account.

6. **Click the Postpone button to leave the Account Balance window.**

Your Quicken Checks Are Good in Money

Money puts Quicken check options in the Check Setup dialog box so that users who switch from Quicken to Money can use their Quicken checks. As long as you printed checks with Quicken, you can find the following options in the Check Setup dialog box:

> ✔ Laser Standard (Quicken)
>
> ✔ Laser Voucher (Quicken)
>
> ✔ Laser Wallet (Quicken)

Chapter 7 explains how to reach the Check Setup dialog box and select a check option.

If the Quicken check options do not appear in the Check Setup dialog box, choose Tools⇨Settings, and, on the Microsoft Money 2005 Settings page, click the Print Checks link to open the Print Checks tab of the Options dialog box. Under Printing Checks, select the Use My Existing Checks from Quicken check box.

Quicken's Online Banking Services Are No Good with Money

If you bank or pay bills online with Quicken, you can't pick up where you left off after you switch to Money. Sorry. You have to cancel the online services you use with Quicken, reapply for the services, tell your bank that you use Money now, and start all over again. Chapter 17 explains how to set up the online banking services in Money.

Your Payee List Is Way, Way Too Long

Quicken has a very nice feature whereby payees whose names haven't been entered in account registers for a certain amount of time are dropped from the Payees list. Unfortunately, Money has no such feature. When you import a large Quicken file, you may end up with a Payees list as long as a brontosaurus's tail.

The only way to delete payees is to do so on the Payees list. Chapter 11 explains how.

Money Offers Help for Quicken Users

So anxious is Microsoft to woo Quicken users to Money, the program offers special help instructions for converts from Quicken. Choose Help⇨Microsoft Money Help (or press F1). In the Help panel, click the Find button, enter **Quicken** in the Search for Help text box, and press Enter. You will see a list of help topics that help you leap the chasm to become a better user of Money 2005.

Glossary of Financial Terms

401(k) plan: A tax-deferred retirement plan by which a portion of an employee's pay is deducted from each paycheck and invested. Employees do not have to pay taxes on income from the plan until they start withdrawing it at retirement age.

403(b) plan: A 401(k) plan for public school teachers and employees. See *401(k) plan.*

adjustable-rate mortgage (ARM): A mortgage whose interest rate is changed periodically. Usually, ARMs are tied to a money index such as the prime lending rate.

amortized loan: A loan for which you make regular payments of equal size. With each payment, some money goes toward paying interest on the loan and some goes toward reducing the principal (the amount you borrowed). See *interest* and *principal.*

asset: Something of value that you own, such as a house, stocks, or jewelry. Money that is owed to you is also an asset, as is the money in savings and checking accounts. See also *liability* and *net worth.*

asset allocation: Refers to how investments are allocated among different investment classes such as bonds, stocks, mutual funds, and real estate. Asset allocation is an investment technique for minimizing risk.

balance: The amount of money in a bank account; also, the amount left to pay off on a debt. In the case of an asset account or investment account, the balance is the worth of the account. The balance on a liability is what you owe.

basis: See *cost basis.*

bond: A paper promise to pay back a debt with interest by a certain date. Governments issue bonds, as do companies. With a standard bond, regular interest payments are made to investors. With a discount bond, the buyer pays less than the face value (also known as the par value) of the bond. When the bond is redeemed, the owner receives the face value or more than the face value if the bond has increased in value. Discount bonds are also known as zero-coupon bonds.

CD (certificate of deposit): A bank deposit in which the depositor agrees to leave the money in the bank for a certain period of time. Banks guarantee a fixed rate of interest on CDs that is higher than the interest rate paid on savings accounts, for example.

closing costs: The appraisal fees, sales commissions, and other fees that are charged when you take out a loan or mortgage. The costs, sometimes called points, are expressed as a percentage of the loan.

cost basis: The total cost of purchasing a security, including commissions, fees, and mutual fund loads.

creditor: A person or institution that lends money.

dividend: From the word *divide,* a portion of a company's earnings that is distributed to the holders of stock in the company. Usually, dividends are paid quarterly.

equity: A house's market value less the amount that is owed on the house. For example, if $100,000 is owed on the house and its market value is $150,000, the owner has $50,000 equity in the house.

escrow account: An account that a mortgage lender takes out on behalf of a borrower to make sure that property taxes, property insurance, and other such fees are paid.

index fund: A mutual fund that invests in all the companies listed in an index such as the S&P 500. Index funds provide returns similar to that by which the index grows or declines.

interest: The cost, expressed as a percentage of the loan amount, for borrowing money. Also, money paid to a lender or bank patron for the use of his or her money. See also **principal.**

IRA (individual retirement account): A tax-deferred retirement plan for employees. The maximum contribution is $3,000 per year. You do not have to pay taxes on income from an IRA until you start withdrawing income from it at retirement age. See also **Roth IRA.**

Keogh plan: A tax-deferred retirement plan for self-employed individuals. Money invested in Keogh plans is tax deductible. Withdrawals are taxed.

liability: A debt that you owe. Credit card debt is an example of a liability, as are taxes owed to the IRS. See also **asset** and **net worth.**

lot: A group of securities purchased simultaneously at the same price. Also a nephew of Abraham whose wife got turned into a saltshaker.

money market fund: An interest-earning mutual fund that invests in Treasury bills and other short-term securities.

mutual fund: An investment company that raises money from shareholders and invests the money in a variety of places, including stocks, bonds, and money market securities.

net worth: What you are worth, not as a human being but as a financial entity. Assets add to net worth; liabilities count against it. See also *asset* and *liability.*

P/E ratio: The price of a stock divided by its per-share earnings. If the price-to-earnings ratio is high, the stock is being traded for its future value, not for its present value, which indicates that the investors are expecting high earnings on the stock.

points: The amount, expressed as a percentage of a loan, that you have to pay to a loan broker or bank to take out a loan. Also called *discount points.*

portfolio: The securities owned by an individual or investment firm.

principal: The actual amount of money borrowed on a loan. The principal is different from the interest, which is the price — expressed as a percentage of the loan amount — that you pay for borrowing the money. See also *interest.*

rollover: When you transfer funds from one investment or retirement account to another. Also, what Beethoven did in an old Chuck Berry song.

Roth IRA: An IRA to which investors can make after-tax contributions. Unlike an IRA, withdrawals from a Roth IRA are tax free because taxes on Roth IRA contributions are paid before the money is contributed. See also *IRA.*

securities: Bonds, stock certificates, and other financial instruments that can be traded and whose value fluctuates.

SEP (Simplified Employee Pension): A retirement plan, similar to an IRA, for the self-employed and small businesses. Money invested in SEPs is tax deductible. Earnings from SEPs are tax deferred.

stock: Shares of ownership in a company. Stocks pay dividends and can be bought and sold. See also *dividend.*

tax deductible: In income tax reporting, expenses that can be deducted from total income.

tax deferred: Refers to income for retirement on which you don't have to pay taxes until you begin withdrawing it at retirement age.

tax-deferred annuity: An annuity for employees of nonprofit and education organizations whereby a part of the employees' income is excluded from taxes and is invested in securities. Tax on income from the annuity is paid when employees withdraw money from the plan.

Index